DEDICATION

I have chosen to dedicate this book to three generations of love and light, my unwavering husband *"Big Mike,"* my sweet son *"Little Michael"* and the newest love of my life, our beautiful, bouncy and bubbly boy, *"Baby Seth."*

Mike's great love has healed me from my deepest pain and given me my greatest joy. I could never convey all he is as a husband and as a Father. Michael and I are everything we are because of his love. I am everything I am because he loved me.

Michael, I always struggle with just what to say about this amazing, accomplished and remarkable man. To summarize all he means to me may be the largest task of all. When my self-worth was as big as a mustard seed, he gave me hope and purpose. I gave my life to him and in return, he has filled my world with pride and my heart with love. He is the greatest thing that has ever happened to me!

Seth, our sweet Baby Seth has captivated our family. With the many mysteries that will unfold in the years ahead, Seth may or may not enter the wide world of Fatherhood. If he does, he has the benefit of two of the greatest men I know to guide and mentor him. He will surely continue the legacy of love, devotion and integrity that has been so firmly established by the solid men who have come before him.

It has been my great fortune to share my life with such awesomeness. Truly, this world owes me nothing. My life is full because of their love. My legacy is safe in their hands.

Let this dedication forever be a symbol of my complete adoration for each of them, regardless of where life may lead.

My love, forever and always, to the moon and back!

Forever Your Bride, Mom, Nanny Ace

TABLE OF CONTENTS

FOREWORD

In the early beginnings of writing this book, I was questioned as to why a Mom would feel worthy of writing a Dad book. My answer: I don't really feel worthy but I'm going to do it anyway.

Of course, I don't know what it's like to be a Dad, that's why I've recruited 100 Dads to help. I'm sure not an expert on Fatherhood. What I do have is an eagerness to help. What I also have is a respect for parents, parenting and the struggle. This book is built on those things, not on any professed expertise.

It is my intention that my personal reflections on my own childhood and the absence of a Father's love will serve to reinforce and validate the importance Dads play in the lives of their children. Regardless of the investment any Dad is able or willing to show, I can confidently say without a doubt that Dads are always loved by their children.

With minimal fraternal connection in my upbringing, I reflect as to how an engaged Father could have changed the course of my life. I see the immeasurable gift of a Father's love, a Father's touch, their kindness and teaching. I can only imagine what it brings to a child to have a Dad who is happy to see them. I would love that for every child.

Although a Father's love was not my experience, I am very aware, *maybe even more so aware*, of how special that love is. It has been a wonderful highlight in my adult life to witness such love in my son's life and in our own family. The cycle has been broken.

It is a fair starting point to begin with the story of a Father's love, the best of the best. I want to share a bit about the Father in our life and the hero in our story, "*Big Mike*."

Mike came to us when Michael was three. He started as kind of a buddy, then a brother, then a big brother. He intuitively knew how to conduct himself and how to build a relationship with *my* little boy. It was beautiful. Before long, Michael was *our* little boy.

The two quickly became fast friends. They played, built, laughed and learned. They grew together.

In two years, we made it official; we locked in and were married. Big Mike was every bit involved in all things. He attended parent-teacher meetings, coached soccer and even went to church although agnostic. He helped with homework, prepared meals, taught carpentry, mechanics and math. He hugged often and was reliable always.

Big Mike woke up, tucked in, read bedtime stories and even kneeled bedside for prayers. They raced remote control cars together, boxed together and drove dirt-bikes together. If Michael wanted to learn it, Mike was willing to teach, learn and play. They were the cutest duo. It was true love.

I definitely know the value of a Father's love, in both the aching for it and the witnessing of it. I watched a lucky little boy come to learn it first-hand.

In February 2008, our sixteen-year-old son, our Little Michael, acquired what was known as a *"catastrophic injury."* In a snowboarding accident, Michael was paralyzed and diagnosed with a condition called quadriplegia, a spinal cord injury.

In referencing synonyms for the word *"catastrophic,"* I found disastrous, devastating, ruinous and tragic. It felt inaccurate to use any of those words.

Although Michael now had minimal functioning in all four limbs, no longer had the ability to walk, run, jump, swim, or lift and would be likely spending his life in a wheelchair, this injury was not *"catastrophic."* It wasn't *"catastrophic"* to him and therefore, was not *"catastrophic"* to our family.

Admittedly, the news was catastrophic. It was catastrophic to me and to Big Mike. We held each other up and in doing so remained steadfast for Michael.

With everything Big Mike was, with all he did, it paled in comparison to what was to come. The strength of a Father was needed now more than ever.

Mike was a bit of a gritty brute, at times — most times. This gritty brute literally slid down the wall with grief upon learning of Michael's injury. It folded him.

I rested in shock in the hospital room that day, while Mike immediately understood the gravity of the situation. Fortunately, my denial allowed me to be there for him as we awaited Michael's return from x-rays.

Upon his return we had our armour on. We presented a strong front and the tightest unity. From that day onwards the strength of our family has been epic. Again, a Father's love was guiding the way, holding us up.

For the first two months Michael was unable to move at all from the neck down. During this time, my gritty brute of a husband became a gentle yet clumsy Florence Nightingale. He continued to amaze.

Mike again became a buddy, then a brother, then a big brother, then a Dad. He became a *'physio assistant,'* a *'crisis counsellor,'* and whatever else Michael and I needed him to be. He followed the same gentle path he did in our initial family adjustment. He was able to tap into a perfect, gentle and delicate approach.

Mike read to Michael, fed Michael and addressed his every need. He arranged poker games to keep Michael entertained, while prioritizing and protecting Michael's recovery. He participated in physiotherapy, occupational therapy and attended all meetings. He got informed, did research and modified anything he could to improve accessibility for Michael. He held us up both literally and figuratively. He was a rock, a sweet, loving, clumsy rock.

His clumsiness was a frustrating yet a comedic addition to that small hospital room. Every time he would accidentally bump into Michael's hospital bed it would cause alarm followed by an eye roll, followed by laughter. He was such a graceful, loving oaf. I can't imagine our world without him.

I am excited to dedicate my time and my appreciation to Dads everywhere, to all Dads. I want to share what not having a Father's love meant to me and also what finding a Father's love has meant.

Whether you are a clumsy and attentive "*Florence Nightingale*" or a licensed registered nurse, a new Dad just beginning or a WWII veteran, an accomplished Dad or a struggling Dad, an engaged Dad or an alienated Dad, a stay-at-home Dad or an incarcerated Dad, your voice matters and your love matters. We need you and your kids love you. If you are reading this, there is still time to learn, to grow and to love. There is always more to be done. Dads matter!

D. Coady

ACKNOWLEDGEMENTS

I thought I'd acknowledge a few special Dads in my past since I have an opportunity to do so.

1. My Dad, John —It's been a long journey for me and Dad. He was a flawed and broken man. Fortunately, through many years of therapy, I have come to love, accept and even understand him. One of my greatest therapeutic gifts was the ability to forgive my Dad. I realize he gave me all he could and more than he had. Dad did what he thought was right. He was a loyal husband and a provider. He could not hug if he had never been hugged. He could not give me things he did not have. Dad's loyalty and dedication to his wife and family did provide me with a strong foundation. Although disabled by a debilitating addiction, I love him in spite of it all and because of it all. I believe he did his best. I appreciate every blistering, dangerous moment he spent in Sydney's Steel Plant. I cherish our time together and all he did to love and provide for his family. I cherish him.

2. My Grandfather, Acey — Acey was also a flawed and damaged man. I learned he had a very dark past and a violent history; however, he changed. Luckily for me those days were far behind him by the time I arrived. Acey doted on me. He was the one person who was happy to see me. His love for me had a large and memorable impact. Acey loved me so much! He called me on the phone, he took me to the mall, and he bought me treats and hugged me often. He was amazing. Sadly, I lost Acey when I was only in grade 3. *See how influential love can be?* More than forty years after his death I still see his face and treasure his love. He made me feel special. My love for him will remain with me forever, so much so that I now carry his name in my

own grandparent journey, *"Nanny Ace."* Acey was the greatest man of my childhood.

3.   My uncle, *"Big Kenny"* — My time with Kenny holds special memories for me. He, too, was flawed and damaged. Big Kenny was my Dad's brother, so they shared some dark traits. He left this life far too soon, passing away at only forty years old. Kenny treated me like an equal. He respected me. He talked to me and didn't curl his lip when I entered the room. That was enough to get a permanent place in my heart. Being with him made me feel special and feeling special was a hard feeling to come by.

4.   100 Dads — Finally, a heartfelt acknowledgement to the upcoming 100 Dads. To entrust me with their words, their thoughts and their tips for the world, they have shown incredible faith in me. I am beyond thrilled to carry their messages, tips and a piece of their journey. Having their trust compelled me to continue when I was tired and gave me confidence when I was fading. I can never completely thank them. I cherish each word and every second they've given in making this dream come true.

Thank you all!

INTRODUCTION

It is a privilege to have been captivated by this work. I've been lost in the words of these men.

I'm going to go out on a limb and will speak for these Dads: I'm sure (*I hope*) all would agree no one is perfect. Some mistakes were big, some small and some even went unnoticed. As I noted in my acknowledgement, the most flawed of men can reach the heart of a child. In spite of prior failures, even grave failures, a positive impact is possible.

I wanted this compilation to be completely authentic. I encouraged Dads to submit what they could. Some provided just a few tips, others much more. Some Dads submitted short tips and some long.

Each Dad submitted independently. Some sought suggestions from their kids and some invited their own Dads to participate. Dads conveyed what they felt was important to them, on their time, in their words, according to their abilities and their schedules. Each and every keystroke was meaningful to me and I hope it will be meaningful to you.

I made minimal edits. I allowed the voices of Dads to hold each line in an uncensored way. They come from different backgrounds, hold diverse values and have had varying levels of success.

Having completed *"100 Moms"* I noted three significant distinctions when compiling *"100 Dads."* Firstly, on occasion Dads asked, *"Is it tips for my kids or for other parents?*" At times, Dads submitted tips with their children in mind. I opted to accept all submissions regardless of Dad's intended audience. I felt the messages were relevant to both growing children and to Fathers.

The messages we give our children generally represent the values we hold. What I want for Michael would likely translate into advice for other parents. It's my intention to capture what is important to Dads, in hopes it will reach other Dads and their children both.

I advised, "*What do you want your children to know about your values, your parenting? If you were to leave this earth, what messages would you want your children to most remember?*" In some cases, I can determine Dads are leaving a direct message for their children, which I feel are principles that guided their parenting as well.

The second distinction is Dads were more likely to mention, include and highlight the importance of Moms. I found this not only beautiful but insightful.

As Moms, we may sometimes forget or maybe take for granted the value of Dads. Maybe we think they already know. Maybe we don't consider. Maybe our minds are too busy, and we sometimes forget. Regardless, I felt the mention of Moms was heartwarming and cause for reflection.

Moms have a wonderful opportunity to ensure Dads are included, involved and most of all appreciated in the role of parenting. For those of us fortunate to be sharing this journey, we should be mindful that we **are** sharing it -the good, the bad and the ugly.

Finally, the third distinction is, Dads were a little more protective of their privacy. More often Dads did not want to disclose details about their race, background, children or occupation. I can speculate as to why that is; however, I did not delve into the why. I wanted Dads to share, depending on their comfort level.

As a result of personal disclosures, in some cases I did not get a great deal of backgrounds on individual Dads. Regardless, I appreciate their willingness to contribute in the way in which they were comfortable.

Each Dad provided much consideration in their words, actions, and hopes for the future. It is my honour to have been entrusted with such touching sentiments.

So, I'm ready to deliver *'the goods.'* I wondered how I should start, what the order should be. I thought maybe alphabetical, maybe in order received? Should it be priority? Preference? It was difficult to determine how to organize one hundred Dads.

In the end, order is somewhat random, and somewhat deliberate. But for the first Dad, I thought I might as well start with my own.

#1 Dad – He Tried

By now you may have some sense of my Dad. I don't see much benefit in sharing his upbringing, background or past. I will say he was raised in a chaotic, alcoholic home wafting with the scent of piss, cigarettes and stale beer. He hid under a bridge instead of attending school and I'm not sure he was missed at all.

By all accounts, he would likely score as remarkable considering what he saw and how he lived. He provided far better than he received, although falling terribly short on delivery. He did his best given his limitations and illnesses. Actually, given that, he did really great!

I once asked my Dad, *"What are your top three best decisions?"* (*A question suggested by Brendon Buchard's, The Charged Life.*) He replied, *"Marrying your Mother, giving up a life of crime and adopting Alexina."* I'm so happy I asked.

I asked Dad a lot of questions over the years. Usually his initial reply was, *"I don't fucking know."* Then he would gaze off, contemplate, and if my patience permitted, I would get a little more.

Here is what I got out of him in terms of best tips:

1. Every time you think of looking at another girl, think of your wife.
2. Love them. Sit and talk.
3. Don't beat or whack them.
4. Respect them but tell them they must respect you first.
5. Tell them how good things are when they do well. When they don't, threaten them.
6. You don't have to show the world that you love them; make sure they know you love them, even if they move away.
7. There is nothing a parent can do to make their kids hate them. My old man was a real prick and I still didn't hate him.
8. Marry a good woman and be nice to her.
9. Respect all women.
10. Help a boy to be a man.

11. Hope for the best.
12. Children are God's greatest miracle. Being able to make a child is everything.

There you have it. In his usual raw form, my Dad tried his best.

As I mentioned earlier, one significant distinction with Dads was their frequent references to Moms. It's fitting to start with my Dad as he mentioned Moms a great deal.

It was interesting and heartwarming to hear about Dad's respect for women. It was also heart breaking as alcoholism and unresolved trauma prevented him from demonstrating that respect; however, it was clear his respect for women ran deep and was a core value he held.

Through his tips I can absolutely confirm he did have respect for women, in his own way. He had a great love for my mother. In this conversation he said, "*I married a good woman. She had ripped leotards and all. We met putting books away. When our eyes met it was like in a movie.*"

As my Mom has now passed, one of Dads greatest heartaches, he said, "*You have to accept the fact that they're dead, but they are never gone. How I miss your mother. Mothers are the most powerful people in the world.*"

He went on to say exactly this, "*Mothers have all the control. They control the president, prime ministers, they control everyone. Mothers have more strength than any soldier. You can't imagine how much a mother can take.*"

From that comment I speculate he watched his own Mom handle a great deal. I could see a slide show of pain playing in his mind as he spoke. No question, he definitely loved my Mom and his own.

From my own perspective, I think he spent most of his time resting in tip #11, "*Hope for the best.*"

We did have a beautiful conversation around this topic. I asked him if he knew any "*good*" Dads. He mentioned, "*Deedoe.*" Deedoe was an uncle of his whom I had never met. I asked what made Deedoe a good Dad. My Dad thought and replied, "*He never cursed, screamed or hollered. He was a nice man, good guy all around.*" Dad spoke a little more about that family. He clearly held them in high regard.

In this recollection I also envisioned a slide show as he described them. A slideshow of a functioning, loving family being watched by a sad, little boy with curious and confused eyes. I wish I would have known them. They sound wonderful.

It was sad to see Dad's lack of understanding around parenting and love. Admittedly he had a great deal of physical and mental damage at the time of our discussion.

When he said tip #2, "*Love them.*" I asked, "*How do you demonstrate love?*" He replied, "*You sit and talk and don't beat them.*"

I can't confirm that we ever did "*sit and talk,*" although I'm sure we must have. Thankfully, Dad did not physically abuse us. I speculate it took some restraint as he was so very angry. Luckily, I did not have to recover from physical abuse, not to minimize the extreme psychological abuse in anyway. Maybe that's what he meant by "*talking*?"

Either way, Dad is an old, harmless senior now. He is no longer the domineering tyrant he once was. His alcoholism resulted in severe disability and the loss of all he had earned. He may not have been a great Dad, but he didn't deserve his fate.

In an effort to help him convey what *I* think his best parenting practices were, I would say:

1. Stay loyal.
2. Bring home your pay.
3. Don't blame your child if they're sick.

My last point brings me to my fondest memories of Dad; he didn't blame me when I was sick. I was a severe asthmatic as a child. When I needed to go to the emergency room, he brought me. He didn't scold me, blame me or berate me, at all. I recall those occasions as my most memorable father-daughter moments.

We spent many nights in the emergency room; although not a Hallmark Special, he was there when I needed him. Now I also know, he likely was "*hoping for the best.*"

While my years in his care were traumatic for me, I still love my Dad to the moon and back. Thanks Dad.

#2 John C. – Never Stop Teaching

"*Poppa John,*" as he is fondly known, is a wonderful member of our extended family. He is a strong, healthy, intelligent and well-informed patriarch. Not only does John possess all the qualities of a caring Grandfather, he also possesses the characteristics of an exceptional and youthful Dad, even over age seventy. He makes the Golden Years look golden.

John has all the things I could hope for in a role model for both Michael and Big Mike. His youthful demeanor, richness of life and appreciation for his family are just a few of his many admirable qualities.

John has put much thought into his top parenting tips. I'm so pleased to carry his wisdom forward and to share his thoughts on what continues to be important to him in the realm of parenting.

1. Never stop teaching, preferably by example. In my experience kids are always watching and learning from the behaviour of parents. We strove to be good role models but recognized our kids would periodically experience us under less than ideal conditions. Remember, they learn what not to do by observing parents.

2. Be adventurous with your kids. It does not hurt to let them know that you still have some of the spirit of youth even though you're a "*parent.*" I recall one time when my son challenged me to put the pedal to the metal when driving on a country road. It was a long, straight, stretch with no traffic. So I did just that. My son and daughter were amazed as our little Honda Accord zoomed above 120 km/h. No great speed, but a moment of excitement and adventure we all shared, a common flight of fancy. A bonding moment that would have been missed had I not taken the challenge.

3. Encouragement works. We always encouraged our children to believe they could do whatever they set their mind to and never settle for less than their best effort. Their school projects were their responsibility. Sure, we helped and offered suggestions, but we always insisted they do their own projects. This proved to be a challenge at times, especially when they procrastinated, but they always came through with excellent work.

4. Forgiveness, not punishment, is the key to building a positive relationships. Sometimes kids do stupid things, things we may be inclined to criticize them for. If their actions are potentially harmful to themselves or others then there should be consequences, they should be held accountable. This does not mean they should be ridiculed or belittled. Rather, parents should ensure their children understand how their actions were hurtful, then openly forgive and embrace them, to let them know your love is unconditional and move on.

5. Self-discipline inspires self-confidence. I recall a time when my son was required to read a rather complicated book and respond to several questions. These questions were targeted to university students, but the teacher assigned them to junior high students. My son, an avid reader, was severely challenged to analyze the story in a manner he had not experienced. He was totally frustrated with the assignment. I sat with him initially for an hour at a time helping him understand each question and learn to explore possible answers. After three or four of these sessions it was evident my son was developing the intellectual skills to complete much of the assignment with less and less assistance from me. He had disciplined himself to read for

understanding and apply his learning in the answers he developed. A lesson that would last a lifetime.

6. Be trusting, dependable and reliable. There may be times when trust is lacking, when it seems your child is lost or on a track to self-destruction. These are challenging moments for both parent and child. At times like this the most important thing a Father can do is offer support and encouragement. Let your child know he or she can depend on you to be there when they are ready to reach out. Be patient and vigilant without being overbearing. Always, always, always reach out and never stop trying. Trust me, this strategy works, but it only works if it is sincere and consistent. Trust that the values you have instilled will guide your child to take the right steps at a time that is appropriate. When this time comes, when he or she finally reaches out, do not hesitate to do whatever is necessary to get support.

7. Never compare to other siblings. I grew up the youngest of nine siblings. Experience has taught me we are all unique with our own skill sets, needs, desires and challenges. Thoughtful, caring and loving parents should never negatively compare one sibling to another. Encourage each child to live up to their potential and recognize each child has the capacity to achieve personal success.

8. Teach respect by being respectful. Children are constantly observing and absorbing what their parents do. By being respectful of one another parents pass this behaviour on to the next generation. Holding the door for others to enter before you; not interrupting while others are talking; offering assistance to someone in a predicament and openly encouraging others to offer opinions are all examples of respectful behaviour your kids will emulate.

9. Model responsibility and accountability. Sometimes parents make mistakes, errors that are their responsibility. When this happens (and believe me your kids will know it happens) take responsibility. Your kids will appreciate that you have held yourself accountable and they will respect you more for having done so.

10. Love your children unconditionally and let them know you love them at every possible opportunity.

In John's first tip he highlights, "*Never stop teaching, preferably by example.*" John holds for us a fine example of Fatherhood. Unknowingly, or knowingly, he continues to teach us all by example. To me, John represents everything I could have hoped for in my own Dad. He is the picture of health, is active in life and as a parent. His years are golden.

As I practice being a Mom to an adult child, I hope to follow John's lead. I love his frequent contact with his adult children and his non-intrusive interest in their lives. I hope to be, as John is, respected and eagerly anticipated by my family. I hope to share his enthusiasm for all life holds and to be always planning my next adventure. I hope to be the teacher, the example he is for us, and to also never stop teaching.

Through John I've come to appreciate what the senior years hold for those of us lucky to reach them. Through him I've learned how to be there for family even when you can't always there in person. John's enjoyed a life-long career in the teaching profession, and I've enjoyed his long life of teaching.

I, too, believe teaching by example is the key to effective parenting. While raising Michael, I monitored all actions and behaviours of myself and of others. I was intense when it came to role modelling.

Initially I knew only what not to do. I knew what I didn't want in my home or around my son. Through the years I sought literature, counsel, and therapy. Ultimately, I did learn some of what to do and how to it.

Unfortunately, time did not always permit me to find the sweet balance I sought. Through much work, helpful support, a little luck and John's example, I believe Michael will effectively balance life's challenges, as has Big Mike.

Thanks John, for all you bring to me and the special men in my world. You are as golden as the years you've given to us!

#3 Darren H. – Family Vacations

Darren is the third Granddad in our family. He's an extra special Dad whose parenting efforts have changed my life forever. His work and dedication to family have given us our favourite girl, Chelsea, our amazing daughter-in-law. Chelsea is loved and cherished by us all every single day.

Darren's example has provided his three children with a solid foundation and an excellent standard on the importance of family values. His work has become our reward and his as well, of course.

Having raised twin daughters and one son, Darren's contributions to their well-being and development have had far reaching and positive impacts to all those fortunate enough to know them. He is the quintessential Dad who loved everything from diapers to wedding day.

Darren is patient, kind and always smiling. His tips clearly outline all his parenting journey has meant to him and the wonderful childhood they all shared.

1. Patience! If you want your kids to look up to you never show frustration.
2. Give your kids your time. It doesn't matter how rich you are to a two-year-old, all they want is your time, hugs and kisses.
3. Always tell your kids you love them, every day. Draw a heart on their napkin and put it in their lunch bag.
4. Listen to your kids. Listen to what they have to say and then offer them your advice.
5. Take your kids fishing and play catch with them.
6. Go to your kids' school, sporting and music events. Go to whatever they are involved in. Kids love to hear their parents cheering them on.
7. Take your kids on vacation. It doesn't have to be Disney, but every kid deserves to go on vacation.
8. Build your kids a tree house, sandbox, swing set and slide. It gives them a place to dream, pretend and enjoy adventures.
9. Teach your kids manners, respect and love. Teach them by example. Your kids will follow your example, not your advice.
10. Read to your kids, tuck them in, say prayers and kiss them good night. Tell them you love them every night.
11. Skinned knees are a lot easier to fix than broken hearts. Sometimes I wish they were little kids again.

After reading Darren's tips I can clearly see it's no wonder our kids fell in love. Our family values were so similar. Our lives were practically parallel, right down to the bedtime routine. It's amazing to see the connections in how we parented and a comfort to know our shared beliefs will now be the foundation for our new, baby grandson.

I appreciate that Darren's seventh tip, "*It {vacation} doesn't have to be Disney, but every kid deserves to go on vacation*." I agree. The important thing is a break away, regardless of the destination.

Luckily for us, our kids continue to believe in family vacations. We have both been fortunate to have been gifted vacations in the sun with our now adult children. Not only have we taken them on vacations, they were inspired to do the same for us. It was unforgettable!

Although many of Darren's tips touched my heart, having enjoyed vacations with our children both in their childhood and their adult world has been a uniquely special privilege. It was an honour, and such fun!

He's right, it doesn't have to be a luxury vacation. Any vacation, any break from the day-to-day is considered special. It can be in a tent, a tree house or a resort.

Darren mentions fishing, camping, tree houses, sandboxes, dreaming and pretending — all vacations in their own way. At times, especially in the early years, and with large families, "*fancy*" vacations are not always possible. For some families, expensive vacations may never be an option. Regardless of resources, there are still vacations that are possible for everyone. I remember our first getaways were hikes, playgrounds, picnics and library trips. They were not what most would call a "*vacation*," but they were our mini getaways.

Later we enjoyed museum tours, theatres and afternoon movies. We advanced to weekend adventures, went camping and took road trips. Michael even attended some super fun summer camps, a vacation away from us. We never did get to Disney as a family, but we found togetherness in other ways.

It's important, especially in social media times, to not minimize vacations and getaways in any form. It's great to plan together and enjoy each other in different settings. It doesn't have to be difficult or expensive, but it does require time, energy and imagination.

Maybe it's a fort in the living room with a flashlight campfire or a winter hike with handmade walking sticks. Whatever, wherever or whenever you decide, as long as it's fun and focused on togetherness.

Some may get the advantage of frequent and luxurious trips; however, that may not necessarily be child-focused, fun or about togetherness. They might even be stressful times.

It's important not to compare vacations but to work together in sharing an adventure. Be creative. Imagination and thoughtfulness can provide a fun time —away from teaching, disciplining and the daily grind.

Doing *with* your child is a welcome break from doing *to* or squawking *at*. Be a kid with them. To me that's a vacation, a vacation for you both. I was not great in the area of imagination, creative play or being silly. But just because it wasn't a strength of mine doesn't mean I don't value it. I can see from Darren's tips that he did get the point early on and put it into practice. His fun and easy-going spirit still exists and will now reach into the next generation.

I see much of his influence already taking shape in the life of our shared grandson. I look forward to the fun times and vacations ahead, no matter where, no matter when.

Much love to you Pops!

#4 George – Teen Hangouts
George Edward Howard Hustins (January 23, 1936 – January 27, 2019)

George was Dad to Darren, Granddad to Chelsea and the Great Granddad to our little Seth. He was a wonderful man who will remain forever in our hearts.

George and his wife Tory (*100 Moms, Mom #96*) both shared their tips with the world. Together they represent beautiful and respected family leadership. They loved being parents and had old-fashioned and well-placed family values.

George was an excellent example of everything it means to be a Dad. He was a solid and gentle man with firm values and an enormous strength of character.

Most importantly George was a loyal, hardworking and proud husband and Father. He was even cool, very cool. George drove a motorcycle, was in the Air Force and was Chief of the Fire Department. He was both handsome and handy.

At George's memorial service, where there was standing room only, many spoke of his dedication to his family and his community. A beautiful tribute highlighted his contribution to the larger community and his remarkable leadership. There was frequent mention of the importance he placed on family and his hands-on parenting approach. Much of what was said on that day is reflected in the tips George himself shared.

I'm beyond proud that George provided his thoughts for this book. It is a privilege to share his wisdom.

1. Our children were not allowed to go to "*The Square.*" That was a breeding ground for trouble.
2. Make it home in time for Parent/Teacher meetings and other things at their schools.
3. When our children asked to go to a friend's house, we made sure that is where they would be. We met the parents and had a phone number.
4. We brought our children up to know there was nothing worse than telling us a lie. There would be a price to pay if they were to do that.
5. We tried to treat them fairly in everything we did.
6. Community work is important but should not come first.
7. Sometimes you have to say no.
8. Model a strong work ethic for your children.
9. Pay the bills.
10. Appreciate your wife.

George's tips were all noteworthy; it was difficult to choose one in particular to expand on. I landed on his first tip, "*Our children were not allowed to go to "The Square." That was a breeding ground for trouble.*" This proved to be a good choice when I heard it referenced during his celebration of life. George's son recalled his restrictions from the teenage hangout known as "*The Square,*" although he had not yet reviewed his Dad's tips.

I couldn't pass up the chance to write about the ever-so appealing teenage hangout. For me it was *"The Rez."* I think there is a *"square"* for most teens. They do like to congregate and as George mentioned, they are *"a breeding ground for trouble."*

"The Rez" was my first forbidden hangout. Growing up, our neighbourhood was surrounded by wooded trails and a reservoir. I was definitely not allowed in the woods, or near *"The Rez."* This was a real sticking point as *"all the fun"* was happening there.

Of course, as an adult I now realize it absolutely was a breeding ground for trouble; however, it did sound like fun when I received the next-day details. At the time I was certain my parents hated me and were attempting to ruin my life.

Surprisingly, and fortunately, I never made it into the woods. My parents did a great job of terrifying me about what could be found lurking behind the trees, or even more scary, what would await should I get caught. I have to say, the intention behind this rule is one of few things that I agree with them about.

I guess it may be somewhat universal that engaged parents are trying to identify and prevent pitfalls for easily influenced, vulnerable teens. Admittedly I was, at times, hard to contain. It's no question, their watchful eye and hard rules did prevent some mishaps.

It sounds as though George was also successful at preventing mishaps. He had a good handle on where his children should be and who they would be with.

Although my time with George was short, it was long enough to know that he lived each of his tips. His values and his love were known by all those in his life. George provided stability and security not only to his family, but to those who were fortunate enough to work alongside of him.

George added, *"I never made big money, so I had to work when work was available. This meant that Tory had to be Mom and Dad a lot of the time. I had to decide between my family and the community. To do that, I declined nominations and tried to work less whenever the children had something going on."*

His legacy now spans three generations and rests in the hearts of his many great-grandchildren. Luckily for me, it has reached the heart of his youngest great-grandson, my grandson, our little baby Seth.

Rest easy George, you did a wonderful job!

My Dad, John, Darren and George are a collection of Seth's Granddads; Big Mike is still to come. I'm grateful to include them and their wisdom in this book. I am forever thankful for their direct and indirect contributions to our

life and to Seth's future. They represent a solid patriarchal team that will remain forever in our hearts and an honoured part of our legacy.
Our love for them and their life's work will be with us always.

———————————

Sharing our strength, struggles, wisdom and wishes is at the essence of why I developed this book and 100 Moms 1000 Tips 1 Million Reasons. I wanted to capture the experiences of others and of myself before we left this world. I didn't want to take what I learned with me. I wanted it to matter and to benefit those parents who might be seeking advice.

I felt it was important to record my journey, the collective journey. It's my dream that in doing so new parents will have a resource, a "village." I hope that those left behind will value and cherish the sentiment as shared by their parents, grandparents, aunts, uncles or friends. It's a labour of love.

My next two Dads illustrated the intention and the purpose of our shared and precious history. Sadly, these Dads passed shortly after making their contribution to this book. I cherish the time they had taken to reflect on their parenting and their belief in my work and in this project.

Jerry Rose and Peter Sheenan are special Dads who have enjoyed a life full of love and adoration. It was a privilege to be in a position to share their messages with their families. I am grateful and proud to introduce these men and convey their practices to Dads everywhere.

I respectfully present the first of these two men.

———————————

#5 Jerry Rose – No Drinking
The Great Jerry Rose (December 1, 1944 ~ January 2, 2018)

Jerry is one of my all-time favourite Dads. He was one of the first I asked to participate and was the first to contribute.

I'm not even sure how to describe him because he was so great! Jerry was funny, witty, charming, charismatic and most of all, family focused. Big Mike and I are friends with his grown children and share his adoration for his sweet young granddaughters. Independent of our love for his family, we considered Jerry to be a favourite friend.

We met Jerry and his family only a few years ago but have come to love and appreciate all that his visits brought to our world. Jerry was loved by everyone. He was the kind of guy who always left you wanting more.

My favourite *"Jerry story"* begins on the day he said, *"Hey, why don't you invite me over to supper?"* Putting us on the spot for supper really gives a sense of his unique foolishness.

I said, *"Jerry, I don't like having people over for supper; it makes me nervous, but I'll make you supper and send it over."* And, I did. Jerry got his supper and quickly called asking for dessert. He followed up by providing me a map of where I might go to purchase dessert next time. That map hangs in my cupboard. I think of it as Jerry's special thank-you card.

Every encounter with Jerry was of a similar nature. It usually included a trick and a splash of humour. He was so fun!

My favourite thing about Jerry is his relationship with his grandchildren. I can't tell who shone brighter when they were together. Those girls were so lucky to have had a man like him in their lives and to know a love such as this.

I only had my Grandfather *"Acey"* until I was eight; yet, each and every memory with him is etched in my mind, as though surrounded by a fancy, gold frame. My Grandfather made me feel like the luckiest girl in the world. I love Grandfathers, and I loved Jerry too.

Jerry's top tips:

1. Listen.
2. Pay attention.
3. Tell your kids when they leave the door, *"Don't get in trouble."*
4. Tell your kids, *"Go to school and get an education."*
5. Tell your kids, *"Always listen to your elders, even if they aren't smart."*
6. Tell your kids, *"Be polite and kind to people."*
7. Tell your kids, *"Always keep yourself clean and healthy."*
8. Teach them not to touch, take, or destroy anybody's property.
9. No smoking.
10. No drinking.
11. Always tell your kids you love them and hug them.
12. Tell them, *"When you drink don't drive. Even if you have to wake me up in the winter at 3 AM like Amanda!"*

I love how Jerry's tips involve teaching, telling and showing. It's clear to me his methods gained the respect of his children and his larger community. He was a Dad to many. Jerry had gained the respect of all who knew him.

When I read Jerry's tenth tip, *"No drinking,"* it is as if a veil of sadness had been draped over me. I can't help but to imagine how different my childhood might have been had that been a parenting value in my home. Parallel to that thought is the joy I have for his children and the benefits they've enjoyed having grown up in that environment.

As for our parenting, Big Mike and I also upheld that value around alcohol. I have seen how different a childhood can be, and also how adjusted an adult can be having been raised in the absence of drugs and alcohol. I believe an alcohol-free home is the best gift we gave to Michael.

It wasn't easy. For me, it required intensive therapy and peer support. I needed to completely transform my life. Providing this life for Michael demanded my constant attention, deliberate action, frequent clinical interventions, undying love, an unwavering commitment to Michael's future, the full support of Big Mike and a great deal of personal energy.

I'm not sure what was required of Jerry to provide this environment, maybe not as much, maybe even more. What I do know, Jerry's values and practices resulted in a life full of love and respect. He and his wife enjoyed wide devotion from an extended family and the community. Their collective legacy continues to impact all those who know them. It's been my pleasure to reap the rewards of Jerry's hard work. He has a far and unforgettable reach.

Jerry's *"little"* girl describes him as, *"a neighbourhood Dad who was a teacher, a mentor, a friend, a designated driver, a fisherman, a camper, and a mechanic. He was whatever was needed to whoever needed him."* Such great love is bound to leave great loss. She said, *"Dad is missed every second of every day."*

It was a sad day for so many to say good-bye to the *"Great Jerry Rose."* Though gone, he will never be forgotten.

Rest in peace my friend.

#6 Peter Sheenan – Surprises
(May 21, 1944 – June 13, 2018)

This Dad is described by his daughter as, *"an advisor, voice of reason, confidante and friend."* Peter will be lovingly remembered as a selfless, wise and witty man who, if love could have kept alive, would have lived forever.

Peter loved all things about parenting, except the discipline. Watching his children grow and succeed was the joy of his life. He cherished memories and highlighted special moments as his most prized parenting gift. He loved all thoughts of the early years, as well as the scenes of recent times. Sharing his life with his grown children and their families was everything to him.

Peter's best tips:

1. Communication – We always communicated. To this day all the grown-up kids regularly *"report in."* Practically every day there's a phone call. Texting is optional and they get fewer points brownie points for that.
2. Quality time is important. It's nice having time together that is just spontaneous.
3. Celebrate events and family/relative connections.
4. Walk the talk.
5. Admit mistakes.
6. Give advice, even if it's critical.
7. Learn to mind your own business.
8. Surprises are good. Do the unexpected every now and then.
9. As long as you can, travel together or go to events together.
10. Encourage (and attend) what they like to do, be it sports, school events or anything they host.

Peter had lofty family dreams. Happily, he was able to see them come to fruition. He wanted all to have continued success, a strong financial plan, good health and much travel. Peter had the great fortune of knowing his dreams were firmly developed and continued to grow in the hands of his two children.

It is truly an honour to have Peter's contribution, along with the contribution of his wife Joan (*100 Moms, Mom #25*). Together they led a loving, engaged and cohesive family.

Peter and Joan nailed it! They have successfully imparted their values and have fulfilled their wishes and dreams for their family.

In Peter's eighth tip, *"Surprises are good. Do the unexpected every now and then,"* he brought a beautiful memory to my mind. It was a surprise reflection for sure. This surprise confirmed, and continues to confirm, my own Dad loves me. He had his moments.

One of these moments took place during my high school days. High school was my own personal hell. One day my Dad pulled up unexpectedly and everyone announced *"Your Dad! Your Dad is here."* Of course, I figured his arrival was certainly to kill me for some unknown infraction.

This visit may have been the largest and most lingering surprise of my life. Dad arrived with a Wendy's combo for my lunch.

My Dad never came to school before, or after that day. I've wondered what warranted such a valiant gesture from him. I was elated.

I met him at the school door, he handed me that brown bag as if I was a homeless stranger. He turned without a word or a hug and drove away. This lifelong memory took under ten dollars, and less than 30 minutes. So, I couldn't agree more with Peter's encouragement to surprise your children.

No matter how much or how little, for kids to know you care is everything. I can speak for myself in knowing a little bit goes a long way. It's been thirty years since high school and that memory remains one of my most precious thoughts of my Dad.

Peter's children never questioned their value. Their Dad's love was expressed, unwavering and reciprocated. His far-reaching efforts continue to carry a positive impact, and message, many years beyond his parenting journey. Peter enjoyed a life to be proud of, and he was proud of it.

Rest easy Mr. Sheehan. Your legacy is safe and sound.

The natural flow and order of things led me to the placement of my next three Dads, the elders in the group. The following three men represent the most senior Dads. Their content was collected by way of interview, in each case, to ensure their intended message and sentiment was captured.

Men of this era were known to work hard, and they typically kept quiet. This time was known as the "Silent Generation."

The "Silent Generation" refers to people who were born between 1925 and 1945. The children who grew up during this time worked very hard and kept quiet. They were characterized by determination, strong willpower and work ethic. They are said to have had an appreciation for the simplicities of life.

Commonly referred to as traditionalists, this group remains well respected with a sense of endearment and struggle. Although it is argued the older generation is set in their ways, there is so much to learn from their life lessons and experiences. They did not have the many privileges that most of us know today.

As far as parenting goes, these Dads were raising children in a time when it was commonly understood children were to be seen and not heard. As they discussed their views it was clear to see, they did see and hear the children in their lives.

I'm so thankful to share their personal reflections and their professed love of family. I had unforgettable moments in speaking with and learning about these men. They have forever touched my heart and I hope they will touch yours as well.

#7 Charlie – No Regrets

Charlie is the oldest of the three and the oldest in the book. At the time of our meeting, he was ninety-four and fabulous! It was an absolute pleasure to meet Charlie and share memories of his parenting journey.

Through our discussion it was apparent: Charlie's life was based on the principles of honesty and hard work. He had five children and he beamed with pride as he told me about each of them. An 8x10, seventies style picture was framed in gold and sat prominently on his top shelf. He identified the position of each child as he spoke of them.

Sadly, two of Charlie's children had passed away. The depth of his sadness was something that will never leave my heart and clearly has never left his.

While raising his family, Charlie enjoyed a career as an elevator repairman. He attributes that career as having been a major positive influence in his life. Charlie previously had several labour-intensive jobs; the lumber industry was one example. He felt that having secured employment in the field of elevator repair was a *"big boost."* Charlie was very humble in expressing what made him a good Dad. He paused often. His moments of quiet reflection evoked emotion in us both.

I can only imagine the comfort, stability and guiding force Charlie was as a Dad. Even at ninety-four, he had strength and a presence that emanated protection and love. I'm honoured to have spent time with him. Together we uncovered his thoughts on Fatherhood.

1. Do the best you can for all the children.
2. Make sure not to put your children in a bad position.
3. Be a hard worker.
4. Be as good as you can for all your days.
5. Set an example wherever you can, a good, honest example.
6. Teach respect.
7. Get your children involved in sports.
8. Always do things with your family. I wish I had vacationed more.
9. Be a reasonable Father.

10. Keep smoking and drinking to a limited amount. Don't do anything so much that you influence the children.

When Charlie stated his fourth tip, it ended up serving as a fine summary to his overall message. "*Be as good as you can for all your days*."

In my parenting, I tried as Charlie stated, to "*be as good as I could for all my days*." Of course, some days were better than others. I did always try, and I continue to do so.

Charlie mentioned in his final tip, "*Don't do anything so much that you influence the children*." Again, his humility rose to the surface as he explained he was not a perfect Father. No specific indulgence was highlighted by Charlie, which I believe only added to the wisdom of his advice.

Although Charlie and I parented in a different time and under completely different circumstances, we were more alike than different. Our methods may have varied; however, our intentions couldn't have been more aligned. I was proud to see our similarities, both then and now. His pride in his family sparkled from his eyes.

In closing our meeting, we reviewed his section and I asked Charlie if he knew of the internet. He explained that he didn't. I did my best to inform him saying, "*Kind of like the news on TV. The whole world can see your business*."

I asked if he would be OK with me sharing his "*business*" with the world. He said, "*Sure, I have nothing to hide*." Then I asked for a picture.

I'm not sure if this was Charlie's first selfie, but he was fascinated! It was really fun taking the shot and watching his intrigue. I shared some family pictures and of course he couldn't believe I had an adult child. He was sure to add that it was obvious Michael got his good looks from me!

Charlie's closing remarks were most beautiful. His final words to me, words we should all be so lucky to repeat, "*I have done nothing in my life to be ashamed of. You can share whatever you like.*"

Thanks, Charlie, for sharing a small piece of your journey with me, and the world. You'll be forever in my heart.

#8 Joe W. – Education and Immigration

Joe's submission also comes by way of team effort. His daughter Janet is a special friend of mine who was featured in the final five of *100 Moms 1000 Tips 1 Million Reasons (Mom #97)*. She was eager to collect her Dad's contribution and describes him as, "*truly one of the good ones.*"

Sadly Joe, ninety-two at the time of his comments, was diagnosed with rapid onset Alzheimer's. Janet's help was needed to assist him in gathering his thoughts and in formulating his responses. She highlighted the discussion around Joe's parenting advice as one she will "*cherish always.*"

Joe began life in 1925 in a Romanian village where he remembers a carefree and barefoot childhood. At age nine, he and his sister embarked on a three-week journey to Canada. They voyaged overseas on a trip Joe recalls as fun and largely unsupervised. He remembers eating his first orange and tossing large grocery carts overboard. It sure does sound fun.

At the time of his settling, Joe had no English skills when he began his education at a solely English-speaking school. During those days, additional support for newcomers was not even a consideration. Joe was left to fend for himself.

With no understanding of the language, he recalls his first day and not knowing how to find a washroom. He left school and went home for that reason. He described it was a difficult transition. Joe pushed on; at age sixteen he began working at General Motors. Shortly after he joined the Navy and fought in WWII. Joe is the only WWII veteran in the book. I'm so proud to include his thoughts on parenting.

Janet indicated he was "*entirely engaged*" in the conversation and happy to revisit his parenting. She speculated he had likely never considered what kind of Dad he wanted to be, as with most men in his generation.

Joe's top parenting tips:

1. Spend more time with your children. Work less.
2. Show a good work ethic.
3. Provide financially.
4. Be involved in community.
5. Value education.
6. Love your partner: happy spouse, happy house.
7. Be strict, but no spanking.
8. Respect women.
9. Be kind, reasonable and approachable.
10. Value friendships and social engagement.
11. Remember, family is most important.

In knowing Joe's daughter, I have the privilege and advantage in seeing how his values and parenting practices have played out in who she is. I can attest to his beliefs having been firmly planted in the core of his next generation. Joe's children hold a deep respect for him. Janet describes him as *"hardworking, loyal, kind, dependable and unshakeable."* Traits he and his children share.

As Joe was a newcomer to Canada, he had a heightened appreciation for many things that some Canadian-born citizens might take for granted. With English as his second language, and non-existing educational support, obtaining an education had its challenges. This experience elevated the importance of education and Joe's dedication to assure the resources would be available to his children, as identified in his fifth tip, *"Value education."*

Joe and I shared a dream of providing more for our children in the area of education. In my parenting, I started explaining the value of education to Michael at an early age.

As soon as Michael started school, we had conversations about long term and short-term academic planning. We established goals and expectations. I encouraged Michael to consider the type of lifestyle he wanted and educated him on what was required to achieve that. We also talked about alternatives and what requirements were involved in those.

I quickly introduced vocabulary such as average, above average and below average in lifestyle and in GPA. We talked about university, trades and scholarships. We talked about labour and what that looked like. We spoke about employment versus career. Then when he turned seven, *smile*, we talked about the tough stuff.

We talked about failure and success, work ethic and commitment. We talked about networking and reputation, pitfalls and struggles. With early conversations, as was the case with Joe's children, Michael immediately saw the advantages available through education. From the beginning, his grades were important to him. Homework was automatic and not something I had to enforce or even monitor. Michael maintained honors throughout his academic career. He was internally driven to do so based on his proclamations as to how he wanted his life to go.

He achieved a high degree of education and an even greater interest in learning. Michael wanted to learn everything and understood learning was power. He also knew learning would provide independence and opportunity. Michael wanted it all.

Joe and I share many philosophies when it comes to parenting. It's no surprise how I have come to love his daughter given our common beliefs. I am thankful Joe came to our country, learned the language, built our cars and fought for our freedom. I'm also thankful he gave me Janet.

It's wonderful to have captured his thoughts, despite the disease of Alzheimer's at work. I'm honoured this contribution led to a deeper conversation between a Dad and his daughter as time continued to race. The scene of their shared memories is the essence of why I do this work.

Much love to this Father-Daughter Duo!

#9 John P. – Foster Children

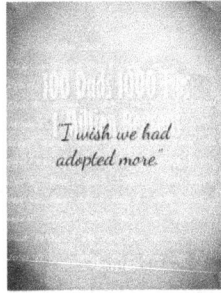

I wish we had adopted more."

John concludes this special trio. I had the pleasure of meeting him, along with his wife Olive, one cold winter morning the day following his most recent hunting trip. He loves hunting. John fondly reflected on his life-long career in the fishing industry which began at age fifteen. Since those early days, John keeps busy and still enjoys the outdoors.

Together, he and Olive have shared their home with what they estimate to be more than fifty foster children, while raising their own three boys. John lit up when he recalled how the children would run to him. *"They all called me Dad,"* he stated.

John had a very calm demeanor, a calmness that can be seen throughout his tips. He identified many practices some might feel common sense; however, what he offered to children are gifts not granted to all. When I asked, *"What is a dream you have for your family?"* he emphatically responded, with a smile on his face and downcast eyes, *"To have everyone together."*

Immediately, in my mind's eye, I saw a country-styled kitchen filled with the many lives he has impacted over the years. What a family portrait that would make.

It was difficult for John to recognize his greatness, although, it was not at all difficult to see. Despite sharing his life with more than fifty foster children, he said, *"I wish we had adopted more."*

John's top tips:

1. Be good to them.
2. Look after food, clothing, shelter, and hugs.
3. Give hugs. Hugs are very important.
4. Attend church.
5. Talk to them.
6. Don't get mad and no hitting.
7. Do what you can to help your family.
8. Agree together and stick to the point.
9. Hold a good job.

10. Do everything for your kids, but not too much.
11. Teach them not to steal or take drugs.
12. Love them.

When John mentioned his sixth tip, *"Don't get mad and no hitting,"* it really struck me that his philosophy was present and likely influential in the lives of more than fifty children. It's no question many of these children had previously seen *"mad"* and had certainly been *"hit."* What a comfort to have shared space with a man who held the value and mannerism of calmness.

In my case, I sought much support in terms of professional help and education around appropriate parenting practices. What was obvious to him had to be learned by me. I held the principle, however, I needed a lot of help to do so.

At times, I lacked the capacity to keep calm. Raising a child based on respect rather than fear was an effort for me, yet a belief I shared with John. It's clear, each of John's tips held an abundance of respect, even though the word itself was not used.

Through research and personal development, I came to learn much of what John discussed with me that wintery day. What seemed to come natural to John had to be explained and re-explained to me. Getting help and guidance with parenting was key in learning the things John seemed to inherently know.

John's Dad was his greatest influence. He stated, *"Dad never hit me."* My guess, a man in those days who did not believe in *"hitting"* was equipped to give John all he needed to provide a loving home to so many children.

John and his wife Olive spoke so warmly of their years raising children. Sadly, it was through deep hardship they found the life they so fondly spoke of. Through their many years of giving, they carried the loss of two young sons. It was in losing those lives that numerous children found a home, a Mom, a Dad and a guaranteed hug.

I will forever treasure my time with John and Olive. Their lives have had a far reach in this world. I can attest that they continue to have a powerful impact on those fortunate enough to meet them.

Our time together was a treasure.

Learning about these men and sharing time with them was a gift.
I will forever cherish their wisdom and great influence in my life and in this world.

#10 Rodney – Demonstrate Love

Rodney, a kind man and a trusted colleague, was one of the first to contribute his thoughts on parenting. Sharing his life with two young boys, he's an eager Dad and a solid role model. No question he's raising a couple of great partners for some lucky people, as is his dream. He states, "*I want them to meet a good spouse and be happy.*"

Having been parented by a single Mom, and having lost his Dad at only age four, Rodney has a great appreciation for all it means to be an engaged and loving parent. He loves everything about being a Dad.

Rodney takes the job very seriously and only has one complaint: random and unexpected wake ups. I'm pretty sure even when he is grumpy, it is the sweetest grumpy ever.

1. Have patience.
2. Talk to them about whatever is on their minds as much as you can.
3. Remember what it was like when you were their age.
4. Make sure they are rewarded when they do good things.
5. Always hold them accountable. Remember ages one to five are key.
6. Show them how to be, don't tell them. They watch everything you do.
7. Display love to them and your wife openly. Boys need to see affection.
8. Wrestle with them, boys need roughhousing.
9. When they are young, read to them every night at bedtime.
10. Eat supper at least five times a week as a family.

I just love how Rodney highlighted the need to, and how to, demonstrate love and affection in a number of his tips. As he states, "*They watch everything.*" In my upbringing love was professed, but not often demonstrated. I knew I wanted that to be different for Michael.

Throughout my parenting there were times I wasn't feeling very present or expressive. Times I wasn't thrilled with having to be a parent. In those moments I employed what I referred to as a "*Meryl-Streep-Mother-Mode.*"

I reached to put my feelings aside, act mature, responsible and even thrilled. I put on a happy face and "*acted as if.*" We can all do this. It does require focus, skill, selflessness and most of all maturity. It kind of follows the premise, "*fake it until you make it*." Parents must be convincing. Action and expression are prerequisites.

As a child, the phrase "*I love you*" was bounced off the wall every day; however, authenticity was missing, actions were missing. It's hard to believe you are loved if the person telling you has their lip curled, if they don't reach out to touch you or if you don't see it in their eyes.

As a child, I felt the words were empty when I heard them and when I said them. I was not convinced, and my parents were not convincing. There was little expression and no demonstration of happiness when I entered a room.

I wanted to ensure Michael felt love without any question. I wanted to convey it in words, actions and feelings. I wasn't always in a loving mood, but when I wasn't, I did launch into "*Meryl-Streep-Mother-Mode*." Even when I wasn't feeling so loving, I was sure to include expression, epic-award-winning expression.

I remember when Michael would return from a sleep over, I would await his arrival sitting on the front step. When I saw him I said (*with a big smile*), "*I haven't moved from this place since you left. Life is so boring without you.*" Michael would smile back, knowing I was kidding, but maybe wondering if this could be true. For certain, love was conveyed. I was present and expressive even if, at times, not entirely genuine.

As a single Mom, of course, I was happy to get an overnight break. Sometimes, I was stressed when Michael was returning. I had many things to do. Sometimes I didn't want to be a Mom! I would never let him see it. Never!

I think at times, parents give themselves too much credit for just '*being there.*' Those parents love to belly ache about how they are "*always 'there.*'" Sometimes just being '*there*' can do more harm than good. I can say from experience, the magic lies in being *present*, not just '*there.*'

Thanks, Rodney, for sharing your thoughts. What a strong foundation your sons will have with a present Dad and the benefit of witnessing a loving husband. I'm sure with all your love, your dreams for them will certainly come true.

#11 Bradley – A Happy Dad

Bradley is a new Dad and one of the youngest in the book. Not yet 30, he loves Fatherhood and all the joy his baby girl has brought to his life.

Having known Bradley as a young boy, it is beautiful to see him as a family man. His new wife and daughter have expanded his heart and his goals. Bradley is dedicated to ensuring his little girl has everything she needs to follow her dreams.

Influenced by his own parents and his Granddad Ches, he has a solid understanding of the importance of family and has an even deeper regard for the role of a Mom.

Although a new Dad, he has already developed great insight and wisdom. His tips can not only serve as a guide for other Dads, but also make for great parental advice as his little girl begins her journey into the world.

1. Life is complicated, and never easy. Enjoy the challenge and love the journey.
2. Always challenge yourself to be a better person, set the example.
3. Time is the most valuable thing in the world.
4. Make yourself proud and strive to continuously learn from your experiences.
5. Be a leader and learn from those who inspire you.
6. Always put family first.
7. Understand everyone makes mistakes.
8. Challenge the norm, think outside the box and consistently embrace change.
9. Study and seek to understand.
10. Follow your dreams and listen to your heart.

Bradley encourages internal drive in his second tip, *"Always challenge yourself to be a better person, set the example."* Any Dad seeking to be a better person and follow his own dreams can bring a great deal to the life of a child.

To me, Bradley's tips highlight the importance of self-care and personal development. I also tried to practice both, while simultaneously attempting to instill those traits in Michael.

I didn't have to tell Michael that education was important, he knew because he saw me value and pursue education. As I began to develop personally, I could share things I learned with him, in an age-appropriate way. As I modelled self-care, Michael learned I was important and so was he. These things became ingrained in him. Lectures were not required.

For the first few years of Michael's life I was attending secretarial school and later university. I was involved in counselling and was identifying goals and dreams for myself. I believe setting this example gave Michael an inherent understanding that learning and development were valued parts of life.

I didn't realize to what extend rebuilding myself would impact Michael. In reading Bradley's tips, I could clearly see many of these things were present in my own parenting. In reflection, I realize my transformation became Michael's foundation.

I guess it goes back to the age-old adage, *"If Momma ain't happy, ain't nobody happy."* Bradley's tip can remind us all that just maybe, Dad's happiness is pretty important, too. *"If Daddy ain't happy, ain't nobody happy."* I hope all Dads don't lose focus of their dreams, as they are guiding their family and children to theirs.

Thanks Bradley! I'm looking forward to watching your little family grow.

#12 Greg R. – Music

Greg is one of our *"boys in blue."* His commendable career in the police force is second only to the adoration of his family. This Dad shares a home with three strong women and is up for the task.

Currently enjoying the growth and achievements of his two young daughters, Greg works diligently to instill high morals and a drive to succeed. He's a hands-on Dad in all areas: academics, sports, community and personal development. He is on deck.

Greg loves everything about being a parent. His goal for his girls is that they will be independent, self-respecting and will always respect others. He emphasizes strong physical and mental health and does all he can to ensure positive growth with himself and his family.

Greg's top tips:

1. Always explain the consequences of their actions or consequences of not taking action.
2. Teach them to be confident, not arrogant, be self-assured taking gauged risks.
3. Encourage and support them to get outside of their comfort zone, it allows for self-development.
4. Model contributing to your community, giving back, volunteering and helping others who may be struggling.

5. Involve them in a team sport so they can learn about teamwork.
6. Identify a hobby or sport that will help them to learn more about themselves.
7. Introduce music and a musical instrument. Exposure to music will help them to identify talents and will also provide relaxation and confidence.
8. Share your own talents and ideas with them. Share in family discussions; offer your opinion and experiences.
9. Talk to them about the opinions of others and teach critical thinking.
10. Teach them to learn from their mistakes as well as the mistakes of others.
11. Guide them in rebuilding when they don't initially succeed. Lift them to become even stronger and more driven.
12. Help them to never surrender and to be the best. Ensure they are proud of themselves and remind them of their power.

The mention of music always reminds me it's an area I forgot to cover. Greg's seventh tip, "*Introduce music and a musical instrument. Exposure to music will help them to identify talents and will also provide relaxation and confidence,*" is a consideration I never had. I'm happy to remind others who may also be forgetting all that a musical interlude can offer.

Knowing a little bit about Greg and his family, I can't help but appreciate the solid foundation he has built for his girls. This Father's love is so apparent, as are his effort and his pride. Having not had a Father's love, imagining this level of support seems like a story that starts with, "*Once upon a time...*" I'm thrilled for his girls. What solid ground they are launching from.

Music and instruments weren't in my parenting reel. I was not exposed to music as a child. I didn't really consider incorporating it into our lives. I do wish we had danced more. I think integrating music and the arts is a great idea. Those teachings would brighten any home, expand possibilities and as Greg states, provide "*relaxation and confidence.*" There's so much to be learned, so little time.

Although a musical interest was not developed in our case, Michael did end up with an appreciation for Frank Sinatra and a love of dancing. I'm happy to report, now that things have calmed down music has become more prevalent for our family, although no one has grabbed an instrument just yet.

One of the many values Greg and I share is our belief in providing an abundance of opportunities. We also share our valiant efforts in ensuring attention, love and adoration were, and continue to be, ever present.

Sometimes, parents can get so caught up in day-to-day survival, as I at times was. We can forget the fun of music, art and play. There are a great deal of topics to cover in ensuring the development of well-rounded adults. Greg is certainly doing all he can to facilitate experiences in a wide variety of areas.

Thanks for sharing your thoughts on parenting and for working to raise strong, independent and accomplished women. I know these girls can step out on any ledge with a Dad like you waiting at home.

Onward and upward.

#13 Craig – The Extras

Craig and I go back to my early parenting days, the very first days. Immediately I came to know him as a kind and understanding man. He was always easy to talk to and had the sweetest of smiles.

Knowing Craig is now a Father to two grown girls, I'm sure they have had a full life given the unwavering love of this devoted Dad. He's worked diligently to ensure a fine example of health, happiness and love. Craig enjoyed all Daddy duties except the really tough stuff like illness and discipline. Craig, like myself, learned much about parenting through his own personal development, education and consult with the experts.

Craig was happy to share his top tips:

1. Love and security are key. Providing that foundation allows them to explore the world, their surroundings from a safe place.
2. At all costs avoid controlling or manipulative tactics. You will destroy your credibility and foster shame in kids.
3. Every once in a while, give them a no-reason stress day from school. Spend it together in pj's watching movies. They will love it.
4. The five most important words to remember throughout your journey, from beginning to end – How important is it anyway?
5. Make silly memories. I remember one time we were staying in a hotel in Halifax, before leaving for Florida the next morning. I initiated nicky-nicky-nine-door while walking back to our room and then we ran like the dickens. We laughed our asses off. I love crazy Dad memories.

6. If at all possible do not miss any of the extracurricular activities. They will always look for you, in the stands, theatre etc., and you should be looking back.
7. Educate yourself on how to parent. Although there is no cookie cutter recipe it is important to know the basics.
8. Never say I told you so. Why would you say that? It will only make you feel superior and them angry. They already know what they did.
9. As they enter the twelve to fifteen range, strict values and rules supervision should be increased not decreased. You are the parent not their friends.
10. When they say something like, *"But Becky's parents let her stay out all night. They never get mad,"* it's an opportunity for you to sit down with them, tell them how Becky is probably really feeling about this freedom.

Craig was aware his children were watching and looking for him in the stands. As he advises in his sixth tip, *"If at all possible do not miss any of the extracurricular activities. They will always look for you, in the stands, theatre etc., and you should be looking back."*

Craig's point around parenting in sports and extracurricular activities is well taken – *"they will always be looking for you."* I also believe attention is a key piece, the most important piece, of supporting extracurricular activities. It is not enough just to pay the fee.

Mike was an active coach and I was a complaining yet ever-present Mom. Michael was fortunate to have both parents involved and I'm super fortunate cell phones were not yet popular. I'm confident I would have missed many special moments with my head pointed in the completely wrong direction. Not only is it important to show interest, I also believe processing all of the plays and practices is a great opportunity to learn from the many teachable moments that arise.

Support and communication are keys in parenting. It's up to us to provide the narrative, not just hand over cash. I remember Trina (*100 Moms, Mom #98*) advised sports parents, *"Keep all emotions other than pride and happiness undercover."* I think that should be the guiding principle from the sidelines and on the drive home.

Parents should be on deck. Teaching, learning and imparting knowledge should coincide with all aspects of sports — the drives, the fee, teamwork, individual commitment and attending the games. Sports can be crushing for some. We, as parents, should maintain perspective, given we are needed to provide it.

I'm sure with a smile such as Craig's on the sidelines, his girls were well-positioned to excel and give it their all. This Dad is one who shares successes and builds on setbacks.

Thanks Craig, for your example to your girls and to me!

#14 Matt – Self Awareness

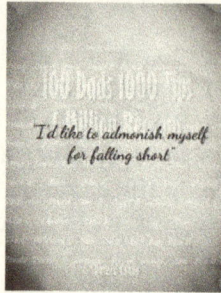

"I'd like to admonish myself
for falling short"

Matt is a proud Dad to two sweet babies. As a writer, Matt submitted his tips in the form of narrative. Within his writing he identifies real life situations and practical tips on how to navigate the parenting terrain.

In Matt's narrative he highlights:

1. Be patient.
2. Be self-aware.
3. You're role modelling.
4. Take action.
5. Try your best.
6. Be better.
7. Stay honest.
8. Learn and grow.
9. They notice.
10. Fight against your worse self.

Matt's narrative focuses on the importance of self-awareness, which is especially significant in effective parenting. He mentions "*a fight against my worst self*" which, I know first-hand, is more of an epic battle than just a 'fight.' For me it was more of a war, a war of the worlds.

In his reflective entry, Matt describes the best and the worst of what self-awareness can bring to parenting. He writes:

"Daddy, what happened?"

My four-year-old is reacting to a reaction of mine. I've just sighed or sworn under my breath or made an angry groaning sound, which has prompted him to look up from whatever he's doing. There's a note of concern in his voice, like he's wondering if he needs to be worried or if he's in trouble. And it breaks a little piece of my heart to hear it.

Because the truth is, nothing happened. Not really. I've spilled a cup of milk or dropped my phone and gotten audibly angry with myself. It's a pretty common thing for me; I have a fair amount of patience for people but a short fuse when it comes to these minor irritations, these random things that happen and momentarily disrupt my day. Especially when I'm the cause or when it's my fault.

I like to admonish myself for falling short of some unattainable and meaningless perfection, for occasionally failing at tasks that don't really matter. It's not a character trait I'm proud of. I've learned to be a bit more aware of it and to tame it as best I can, but it's probably a lifetime battle.

This fight against my worst self is all the more important now that I have a son and daughter. They notice. They notice when Daddy is suddenly and inexplicably frustrated. They wonder if they should be worried, or if they're in trouble. Even worse, they may one day stop wondering and start imitating me, beating themselves up over things that don't matter, not really. That would break my heart in pieces.

These days, people tend to talk about "*parenting*" the same way one would talk about "*kayaking*" or "*basket-weaving*" –a verb, a thing we do.

We talk about, and read books about, parenting "*styles*," as though raising children was like choosing clothes or martial arts disciplines. We talk about it as a series of conscious and strategic choices through which we shape happy, successful children into happy, successful adults. Like pretty much everybody, I try my best at "*parenting*."

But sometimes I knock over a glass, and I groan, and my son looks up and says, "*Daddy, what happened?*"

In these moments, it occurs to me that all the doing and all the conscious choices that parenting involves are only part of the job. The other part – maybe the bigger part – is not about doing, but about being, being my best self in the presence of my children. Being a better person when they're looking and listening, and being a better person when they're not around, so that the person I am with them feels honest.

The stuff they take from just observing me, as a model of a human being, is going to have the largest influence on the human beings they become. I feel like being a Dad is less about what I explicitly do for my children and more about my own growth and learning. It's less about parenting and more about being a parent.

Matt's narrative is beautifully illustrative.

In my early parenting days, well actually all of my parenting days, I may have been a little too hard on myself while simultaneously not requiring enough. As with Matt, I wanted to be the best example, the best parent, all around the best. It was, of course, impossible to achieve yet also non-negotiable. I was relentless, unforgiving and had an abundance of self-imposed requirements.

I love Matt's description, "*audibly angry.*" I was audibly angry, a lot.

Matt's mention of spilled milk reminded me of a conversation with my therapist, likely after a very audibly angry and unwarranted outburst. Those days it was much harder for me to contain my upset. Luckily, therapy helped minimize the damage in many ways.

To guide me to forgiveness or understanding, my therapist attempted to provide some context. She explained why spilled milk can at times cause upset, anger and even rage. Surprisingly, it isn't always about the milk but it can be.

She highlighted the added pressures on a single parent living in poverty, *as in my case*. She said, how you react to *"spilled milk"* may depend on how much milk you have left or by how many children are waiting for milk. It may also be compounded by not having access to another carton of milk, nothing else for breakfast.

I vividly remember that discussion, and the relief she provided to me in the face of my typical over-reaction. From that day, one of my life goals was a dream to be able to purchase milk when I needed milk. To this day, when I'm reaching to find gratitude, I appreciate my ability to buy milk.

I no longer cry over spilled milk, regardless of who spills it. That said, I have had tons of therapy and an estimated 10,000 hours of personal development – not sure if it takes all that but it did for me.

Thanks Matt. I hope we always have extra milk!

#15 Brad F. – Cherish Them

Brad is a Dad who's spent his career helping others while ensuring his two children had all the love and opportunity they needed to thrive. In his professional life, working in the field of Corrections and Justice, Brad has learned the value of care and compassion. He knows love makes a difference.

An adoring Dad and family man, Brad's ability to care extends beyond those he loves in his immediate family. All of Brad's interactions come from a place of respect and compassion. He is confident and hopeful his children will continue his legacy of kindness.

Brad is proud of their contributions and the effort they have given to their lives, and in the larger community. Watching them build their future is one of his greatest joys.

Now his children are in their twenties, Brad still finds time to worry. Some say small kids' small worries. Brad continues to watch with bated breath hoping his children will always be safe. His dream for them is good health, prosperity, continued compassion for others.

Brad's tips:

1. Be consistent, firm and fair.
2. Treat both children equally.
3. Be involved. Coaching was my opportunity to be involved.
4. Take an interest in school and extracurricular activities.
5. Be supportive.
6. Allow your children to be independent but let them know you are there when they need you.
7. Give autonomy. Allow them to be part of decisions and to make some decisions independently.
8. Don't be afraid to communicate no matter what the topic. I always felt talking openly was a huge opportunity to build strong communication.
9. Care about them! Cherish them. It goes by extremely fast.

Brad's closing tip, "*Care about them! Cherish them. It goes by extremely fast,*" is a common and well-placed reminder from many parents. It comes more frequently from those of us with adult children. The most fortunate parents recognize it in the early stages.

Over the years, Brad and I have enjoyed some meaningful conversations, about the importance of family and his love for his children. It's as though I can see his heart fill when he speaks of being a Dad and all Fatherhood means to him. Brad's practiced caring and cherishing from the very beginning.

Intact families and engaged Dads might believe, "*All Dads care for and cherish their kids.*" I assert, all Dads do not care for and cherish their children. Sadly, some Dads do not feel caring and cherishing is a part of "*the job.*" Some Dads may not know how to care for or cherish. Other Dads may assign that as a maternal role.

There may be cases whereby Dads are not permitted to care for and cherish for any number of reasons. Family breakdown, geographical separation, mental illness, addiction, or a general and complete inability to do so may impede a Dad from this level of involvement. When I read the word *cherish* it stopped me instantly. The gravity of the word *cherish* is not lost on me.

I hope *care* for and *cherish*, is a '*given*' to all Dads. I hope if it isn't a '*given*' that Dads will pause and consider what it means to cherish and be cherished.

Cherish is defined as "to protect lovingly, hold dear and keep in one's mind." Defining this word brought tears to my eyes. I can't imagine what it would have meant to have felt cherished by my Dad. How would my life have been different? How would I have been different?

On behalf of those of us who did not feel cared for and cherished, please reflect on the meaning and the action required to convey and convince a child they are cherished. If your children feel cherished by you, they will expect to be cherished by others.

Brad's additional tips provide ideas as to how you can demonstrate to your children they are loved and cherished. It doesn't seem too complicated to achieve but it does not happen without deliberate and loving effort.

I cherish Brad's involvement in this book and his service to his community and his family. In cherishing his children, Brad has given himself and them a gift that is not available to everyone.

Much love to you and your cherished families.

#16 Scott – Quality Time

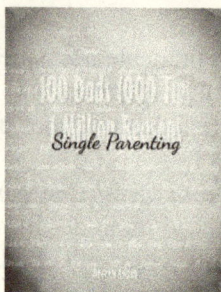

Scott is an extra special Dad who worked extra special hard in his journey to become a Father. As a bachelor, Scott decided to become a Dad and knew he was up for the job of single parenting. His little boy is the light of his life. Parenting was everything Scott expected it to be, with smatterings of things he never expected.

I have the utmost admiration for Scott and his journey to Fatherhood. I, having only spent a few years in the world of single-parenting, had just a taste of what it takes. Scott has all it takes. His young son is in a love-filled world full of opportunity. He has an attentive and engaged Dad who loves every second of the changes and challenges.

So far, this parenting journey is all Scott has dreamed. His hope for the future is more of the same, health and happiness.

Scott's top tips:

1.   Do as you say, follow through.

2. Be present.
3. Make time to be free from technology.
4. Take time to listen before you act.
5. Enjoy the moments.

Scott's tips are short, sweet and thorough. His third suggestion to, "*Make time to be free from technology*," is sure to provide high quality parenting in a variety of ways. I really appreciate his overarching theme of quality time, particularly his dedication to techno-free time.

As I mentioned before, I am extremely grateful that I didn't have to worry about cell phones in my parenting days. I hope I would have ensured techno-free time as well.

As our children get older, one-on-one time grows increasingly challenging to find. I think techno-free time can often be best found during drives and dinners. For me, those were some of our most special moments, and best parenting opportunities.

My sister-in-law Angela (*100 Moms, Mom #27*) first introduced me to the concept of "*technology-free-drives*" when announcing it to her kids. I immediately loved this idea! The kids were instructed to leave their devices home. I thought that was very cool, and also brave. Although I'd never had the luxury of handheld devices and never had to implement "*technology-free-drives*," doing so still sounded a bit onerous.

I haven't forgotten the incessant chatter or the ache for silence when entrapped in a car with my sweet little boy. In my day, I packed a bag full of potential distractions. If I had the option of "*i-technology*," I certainly would have approved it. It is the harder choice to opt for a "*techno-free drive*." As in most cases, the harder choice has the highest reward. The moments when you can secure a captive audience can be enchanting.

I think the phrase "*techno-free time*" can interchange with the old-fashion notion of "*quality-time*." Much can be covered, and uncovered, on a family drive. You don't even have to be eye-to-eye, and is sometimes richer for it.

This can be some of the most undervalued, underutilized and unpredictable time. The car is a great stage for communication and conflict resolution. Drives are great, even when they aren't.

I hope all families find a way to ensure there is a high level of eye contact, and communication with their children. I hope Dads will make a deliberate attempt to encourage children to put devices down. Of course, the best way to teach is to model, which might be the toughest part of all. No question this duo finds plenty of "*techno-free*" time.

Finding true love and quality time changes everyone in every way. I'm sure this team will continue to enjoy many more years of happiness, wilderness and wonderment.

Thanks Scott!

#17 Zachary – Alone Time

Zachary is a self-proclaimed "*Awesome Dad*" who is doing his part to break down stereotypes about men and Fathers. He operates a comprehensive website highlighting all things thought to be "*Dadly*" and all things thought not-to-be "*Dadly*."

Zachary's site is insightful, enjoyable, informative and enlightening. He recognizes the need for togetherness and support when working to build a strong family.

Still in the early stages of parenting, Zachary shares about caring for infants to carrying infants. His website covers all topics from grilling to guns.

With all of the above going on, Zachary still made time to contribute to my project, even though his own project is highly advanced and gaining in popularity every day. This Dad's parenting beliefs are generously shared with his own audience and now with mine.

Zachary's top tips:

1. Honesty – Be honest and open as much as possible with your kids. Refrain from answering questions with, "*Because I said so*." Provide a real reason.
2. Trust – Trust your spouse with raising your child with you. While you may not see eye to eye, being demeaning to each other is very bad in front of your child.
3. Communicate – Talk to your child constantly, and your spouse too.
4. Hang tight to your faith – Your faith is perhaps the greatest influence of how you will raise your kids. Question your faith, and know why you choose to raise your kids in a certain way, but don't force your beliefs on your kids.
5. Be in the moment – This goes along with the communication piece. Put the phone away and be with your kids. Enjoy the time and the experiences that you can share together.
6. Don't get offended – People are entitled to their opinions and yours will differ from other parents and people. Do not get offended at other

people's thoughts and ideas. Instead, understand each person is different and celebrate diversity.

7. Take time for you – Sometimes you need some alone time, everyone does. Be sure to include some self-healing time whether at the gym or a date out with the spouse.

8. Set goals – Set goals for you and your family; both short and long-term goals to help govern your family and keep you moving forward to where you want to be.

9. Focus – Focus on building your family, quality. Work hard to enhance your family's lives and experiences.

10. Gratitude – Above all, be thankful for what you have.

Zachary's seventh tip to take time for yourself states, *"You need some alone time, everyone does. Be sure to include some self-healing time whether at the gym or a date out with the spouse."* With all he has on the go I was surprised and pleased to see that he hasn't forgotten the importance of self-care.

I love the reminder and have come to be a fan of self-care. It's true we need it. It's often recommended, yet continually needs repeating.

Self-care may be a more common concept among women; however, I hope the word is spreading for all parents. Dads also require time to re-energize and refocus. As Zachary said, we all need some *"alone time."*

When Michael was a baby, my therapist suggested I start simple. She encouraged an ice-cream at the end of the month. I remember the guilt, and the haste with which I would finish that cone. It felt more like punishment than a reward. I will say, it's worth the effort, and anxiety. Parents are worth the effort! We need to find some *"alone time"* for the children, our families and for our own well-being.

I know for sure it is important, it gets easier with practice and it will absolutely make you a stronger parent. We should keep reminding each other of self-care. It would be great if we can encourage self-care to others, maybe we can even facilitate it when we see it is lacking especially with new parents.

As a more *"senior"* parent I'm now able to find a little time to support a new parent with an offer of time or assistance, maybe even a surprise meal. It's fun for everyone to help in large, small or unexpected ways. Shared understanding is sometimes the best gift of all.

As parents *"through the woods,"* Zachary and I both hope you'll find some energy and resources to help a new family, or an overwhelmed parent. Maybe help can be providing a few minutes for a much-needed breather, encouraging words, a pizza delivery, a gift card or an anonymous basket. Sharing a little personal time will add to your own development and help out another parent. Making time for your own self-development will add the bonus of further development in your family. It will model your importance to your children and serve to remind you that you matter.

A little bit of time to yourself will even make you better, in every way. I don't think there will be any disappointment in the practice of providing time to a parent or finding some for yourself, whatever the reason.

To learn more about Zachary and his journey to awesomeness check out his site at *www.awesomeDadgear.com.*In the meantime, I hope we parents can all find a few minutes to enjoy a double scoop!

Thanks Zachary!

#18 Lewis – Go Last

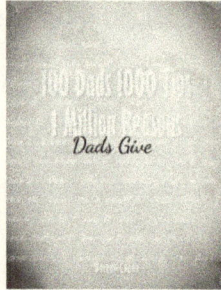

Lewis is the proud Dad to two bouncing little boys. He and his wife Lisa (*100 Moms, Mom #18*), work to provide all the love and opportunity they can muster. They share in the joys of teaching skills and watching each child develop in their own unique ways.

Lewis works with youth by day and in his spare time he's an avid football fan, having both played and coached the game. With this solid foundation, this Dad is prepared for the parenting journey.

The earlier years were a little rough, summarized by Lewis as "*constant whining.*" He reports now that his boys are older and able to communicate, things are going smoother. Lewis wants only two things for his sons: health and a life of laughter. I'm sure they're on their way.

1. Put your needs last.
2. Keep your wife happy, then the children.
3. Show the children, through actions, how a man leads a family and respects his wife.
4. Never disrespect their mother.
5. Always remember, children see and hear everything.
6. Get out of bed for your children.
7. Change the diapers, especially late at night.
8. No matter how tired you are, or how upset things may be, make time to play each day.

In reading Lewis' tips, his respect for his wife leapt off the page. Knowing Lewis professionally, I knew Lisa's happiness was a top priority for him. His love for his wife is his most endearing quality, I'm sure Lisa would agree.

I couldn't help but highlight Lewis' first tip, *"Put your needs last."* That was something I didn't realize initially, but fortunately learned in record time. I remember being surprised that babies had no patience or understanding. I was actually shocked with how demanding a baby could be. *I guess that's why they don't recommend that teenagers have babies.*

I now know in the infancy stage babies don't stop crying until you address their needs. Babies are no help with communication; they seem to add to any frustration which was also news to me. Obviously, I had little understanding of child development. When a parent lacks understanding, it makes sense addressing a baby's needs might take some extra time. Babies will scream that entire time, and never realize how hard you are trying.

I learned hard and fast. Thankfully I learned.

Sleeping-in was no longer an option. Drinking and carrying on had to stop. Life was groceries not parties, laundry and not beaches. It was a grind, but it was beautiful. The good ole days.

Happily, Lewis values self-care, recognizing the importance of it, and the impact his personal self-care will have on his family. With this awareness he makes time to rejuvenate himself, while ensuring his wife and his children have what is needed to do the same. What a gift to not only his family, but the next generation.

I hope it gives Lewis comfort to know, twenty years does fly by. At just about the time you start tasting freedom, one of your boys might be arriving with a new *"constantly whining baby"* and before you know it, you'll all be back at the end of the line again.

Thanks to you both for your great teamwork and for participating!

#19 Greg J. – Enjoy It

Greg is the husband to Christina (*100 Moms, Mom #19*). This solid parenting team has tackled the teenage years and is now on the downward slope of parenting, with barely a scratch.

Greg is an encouraging and ever-present Dad, which of course is the type no teenager wants around. I can speak for those of us who didn't have this type of Dad, we ached for one. To have had a Dad like Greg would have saved me years of therapeutic repair without question. My heart heals a little just knowing this kind of Dad exists for others.

Greg's love for his girls is the first thing you learn about him. He delights in their successes and quietly aches in their struggles. He is engaged and adoring, the last two things a teenager wants, but the first two things a teenager needs.

The largest parenting challenge for Greg was knowing when to move in and when to backup. That is a delicate dance, I'm sure most would agree. I think any Dad who is even, if only, aware of that struggle is on the road to amazing.

Greg's dream for his girls is that they have positive family relationships. He hopes they will grow into confident and successful young women, which is a dream he has already started to realize.

Greg's top tips:

1. Try to enjoy something about every stage of their lives. For example, at 4 AM when they are crying and you are trying to rock them back to sleep and you need to get up for work in a couple of hours, just remember some day they will be too big for you to rock them back to sleep. Everything is temporary so find something positive.
2. No matter how well prepared you think you are to deal with the challenges your children will present, particularly when they enter the teenage years, don't be surprised when they throw you a curveball that you are not prepared for.
3. Our world is changing fast and the challenges we caused for our parents are obsolete. The world they are growing up in is more complex and some of the challenges they will cause you will be things that you have never even thought of.
4. Protect their environment as best you can not just their physical safety but emotional safety as well. Provide them with an environment that will give them the best chance to succeed.
5. With the internet they will be exposed to so much more information than we were. Some of it will be appropriate and some not appropriate at all. Try to protect what they are putting into their minds.
6. When they stumble and fall, they know they have made a mistake. They already know they should have followed your advice; they don't need you to remind them how smart you are and how dumb they are. Don't say, "*I told you so.*"
7. I have always loved my children but there will be times when they seem to hate your guts. It's going to hurt. It's only temporary.

8. Always keep the lines of communication open, either with you or with their mother. A co-worker of mine, with older children, once told me that someday it will seem like aliens have taken over your kids' bodies and you no longer know who they are. He said, one day the aliens will leave, and you can have your children back. They will eventually come around.

9. I have made lots of mistakes along the way and said things I should not have said. Tell your children you are not perfect but because you love them, you are doing the very best you can. I am still trying to get better and be the best Dad I can.

10. Being a Dad is the most important job you'll ever have.

Greg states in his first message to Dads, "*Try to enjoy something about every stage of their lives.*" He also advises, "*Everything is temporary,*" both important points to remember in every stage, from shitty diapers to the shitty teens. I think a great deal about the wisdom in Greg's first tip. I vividly remember this advice, especially in the early years. It is likely the most common piece of advice I've ever received, and the most ignored.

Everyone seemed to say it. I hated it!

Today I'm a little wiser and I see how quickly the stages pass. I've become a little more skilled at enjoying moments. In my early years, I do wish I had taken that caution more seriously. It has gone by in a "*blink.*"

Whenever I heard, "*Enjoy it. It flies by,*" I felt the words were condescending, and complete bullshit. Regrettably, I wished time away. I thought, I can't wait until he talks, walks, wipes his own butt, sleeps in, goes to school, finds a job, drives and graduates. I wanted freedom! It felt as if each stage was a lifetime. I was dramatic, immature and so short-sighted.

Maybe my distorted perception had something to do with my age, my development, and my fears. I thought the diapers would never end and soccer games would last forever. Whether it was one factor or a combination of many, my egocentric attitude prevented me from seeing things clearly.

I did cherish some moments, just in case there was any truth to the phrase. I recall pulling myself into special times I suspected might be fleeting. I slowed down during birthday parties, Christmas mornings, school concerts, evening snuggles and oddly parades — when I had the mind to do so. I don't know what my hurry was, I had nowhere to be. I certainly had nothing more important to do.

In a flash, my son was twenty-five. I have nothing more important to do. I have no toys to clean up, no little socks to match, no bums to wipe, no concerts to complain about and no soccer games to slice oranges for. I no longer need juice boxes, milk money or student fees. I never could have known I'd miss the lengthy bedtime routine, reading time, parent-teacher meetings, and even the relentless obligation of mealtime.

In what now seems to be a blink of an eye, all the expectations of Motherhood have vanished. Nobody is looking for me, needing me or asking me to peel or sign anything. It's quiet, deafening.

Back then, things seemed in slow motion. In reflection, it feels as though days, not years, have passed. How I wish I believed the wisdom in the sage advice. I didn't know the depth of the truth. I was quick to disregard many cautions.

I'm glad Greg is giving this message. I'm hoping others can better heed the warning. There is much to be gained by slowing down. In the moment the chaos, and seeming inconveniences of parenting, might just be the noise your heart aches for when the quiet settles in. I'm guessing things are a little calmer and quieter for Greg and Christina these days. The silence does get loud sometimes.

I have come to learn, as the silence becomes comfortable the rustle of another stage fills the air like crispy fall leaves. Whether it's a family celebration, a graduation, wedding or celebrating babies, the walls will vibrate again with all the hustle and bustle a beautiful family brings.

Best wishes for all that and more. Thanks to you both for sharing your thoughts and a piece of your journey.

#20 Said – Let Them Teach

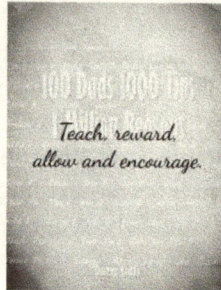

100 Dads 1000 Tips

Teach, reward, allow and encourage.

Said is enjoying a career in research for the faculty of medicine while caring for his three growing children, two girls approaching their teens while his young son is still a toddler. Said loves all things about parenting and enjoys working hard to take care of his family.

Like most Dads, Said hopes his children will be happy and healthy, with a special emphasis on education. He wants them to reach high and be the best they can be in all aspects of their lives.

He humbly submitted his tips to Dads, wishing them all the best in raising children and providing for their families.

1.   Saying "*no*." At times it will be tough. Children need to realize that there are some things we cannot do and the reasons why.

2. Find a time each day to gather as family. Let your children tell you about their day, tell them about what you did during your day.
3. Reward them for the good things and size the reward according to the progress they made.
4. All the time I tell my children how proud I am of them.
5. I ask my children to show me something. I pretend they are teaching me a new thing to help increase their self-confidence.
6. Allow them to do some things their own way to make them more independent.
7. Teach them indirectly, practice in front of them so they can watch you learn. This will help them.
8. Share your success stories with them.
9. Let them play more than one sport so they can find what's right for them.
10. Encourage them to read and reduce the electronic time.

When I was learning to parent, I always found it helpful when people provided examples as Said did in many of his tips. With limited role models in my life I needed highly specific information so I could develop skills for myself and with Michael.

Of course, I wanted to teach things like independence and self-confidence, but I wasn't sure how. I knew those qualities were important but I hadn't quite learned them myself; it was going to be difficult to teach them.

Said mentions in his fifth tip, "*I ask my children to show me something. I pretend they are teaching me a new thing to help increase their self-confidence.*" That sounds fun and effective.

Frank Oppenheimer was a renowned physicist, cattle rancher, and a pilot. Among other things, he was known to have coined the phrase, "*The best way to learn is to teach.*" Through Said's fifth tip I'm reminded of how allowing your children to teach you can have a multitude of positive outcomes.

Said elaborates further in a subsequent tip, "*Practice in front of them so they can watch you learn.*" Envisioning teaching, learning and practicing between Dads and their children conjures up such heartwarming scenes. How loving it would have been to have shared this time with my own Dad. I'm sure I would have worked extra hard and have felt very important to be imparting my "*wisdom*" on him.

I'd like to think I may have given Michael the opportunity to teach over the years. I am confident he taught me; he continues to teach me twenty-eight years later. I think I learned more from him than he's ever learned from me; however, deliberate practice sessions intending to develop and reinforce his skill set brings things to an entirely different level.

I'm glad Said brought forward examples to guide Dads in both teaching and learning. I'm also glad that I can put these tips into practice with my next generation. I look forward to the education and the opportunities that await.

Thanks, Said, for sharing your thoughts and direction on guidance and making memories.

#21 Jeff – Fear

Jeff is the proud Dad to two sweet babies who are moving full speed through the early years. He and Georgina, (*100 Moms, Mom #21*), are enjoying their new world and all the love it brings.

Jeff holds many aspirations for his children; however, it's most important to him that they live their lives how they want, not how others dictate. Having worked with children and teens throughout his career, Jeff has a solid understanding of childhood development and future pitfalls.

With the love and support of his parents he has an unshakable awareness as to the value of parental influence. Their guidance, and with Georgina's support, there is no question the parental influence will be positive, progressive and love filled.

1. Don't be afraid to be afraid. It is scary thinking that you are responsible for another human being's needs. Embrace the anxiety, the nervousness and the am-I-doing-this-right feelings. Talk about your feelings with your spouse and other parents if you can.
2. Make sure you are ready to have children. If you do not think you are it is OK. I know myself; I was not ready when I was in my twenties. It wasn't until I had found a partner I could love and trust. I knew when I was mature enough to raise a child.
3. Be ready emotionally and financially.
4. Know you need to be ready to always put someone else's wants and needs first, this may be the most difficult thing to do.
5. Go on family vacations and trips. One of the things I'm looking most forward to is family vacations with my children. Some of my fondest childhood memories are of family trips, short drives to the beach, long drives or even flights to another province or country. It doesn't matter if you sleep in your car, eat hotdogs at a campfire twenty minutes

from home or stay in fancy hotels in foreign countries, your children will remember each adventure.

6. Show your kids a world outside their home; expose them to other people and experiences.
7. Self-care. If you aren't healthy and happy, your ability to parent will probably suffer. It can be difficult when you must spend most of the time you have with your kids. Getting an hour or two to yourself is very important.
8. Exercise, keep up an old hobby or find a new one, read or nap. Do anything but kid stuff! You won't be able to do it every day and some days you will have more time than others, but it is important for yourself and your kids.
9. If you want your kids to do something like eat healthy, play outside, go to bed you need to do to these things yourself. Be consistent and model the behaviour you want. If you eat ice cream every night for supper, then guess what, your kids will want it every night for supper.
10. Bonding: there seems to be this idea that the moment you see your child you will immediately fall in love and everything will be perfect. This is often not the case. Relationships and bonding take time and you may feel guilty for not instantly feeling that, especially since most parents won't talk about this part of raising a child. It will come, but like any relationship it needs time and work, especially with children. Be patient. The fact that your child may cling to their mother by screaming and crying when you look at them is not an indication of your parenting. Be patient and make time to ensure they also bond with you.

Even with a concrete and unshakable foundation, Jeff still had some insecurities and fears. That's a comfort to me as I enter into the world of grand parenting. I can relate to much of what he said in my new role as a grandma. It is scary too.

As Jeff reassures in his first tip, "*Don't be afraid to be afraid. It is scary thinking that you are responsible for another human being's needs. Embrace the anxiety, the nervousness and the am-I-doing-this-right feelings you will have. Talk about your feelings with your spouse and other parents if you can.*"

Upon reading Jeff's first tip, "*Don't be afraid to be afraid,*" I knew I would be expanding further. As far as the fear of parenting, it's about the only thing I had going for me. I wasn't afraid to be afraid. I was terrified and I talked about it. As Jeff states, "*It is scary.*"

I've recently identified my life's five largest fears, being a parent was number two *(preceded by talking about abuse, also scary)*. Luckily, I didn't know how much I needed to learn or how much there really was to fear.

In my case, I had no prior success, nothing significant I can think of. I did graduate, a gift from some generous teachers rather than a personal success.

I had no critical thinking skills, no understanding of child development, or my own. I made bad choices and trusted all the wrong people. I had no job, no education, no home, no supports and generally no clue. I had every reason to be afraid. Although I was terrified, what I didn't know was even scarier.

As Jeff advised, *"talk."* I did talk and I talked a lot. I talked to other parents, my Mom and a therapist. I accessed supports and all available resources. I returned to school, cut ties with the darkness and grabbed up any piece of training I could find.

My anchoring thought during this time, a word of advice from my Mom, and I think the best tip of all time: *"As long you make decisions with Michael's best interest in mind you won't go wrong."* I lived by that!

I appreciate Jeff's fear and his willingness to share it. I look forward to watching their little family blossom. I'm completely confident the days have grown less scary and will continue to do so as he and Georgina move united through the stages and phases of parenting.

Thanks Jeff!

#22 Tyler – Be Mom's Rock

Tyler is the partner to a special girl, I mean young lady, who I will always fondly remember and adore. I'm so pleased she was able to convince him to share his parenting tips, so I could carry a piece of her with me in this book, forever. *"Hi Holly!"*

Together these young parents share their lives with a sweet baby girl who is the apple of their eye. Tyler has hearts in his eyes when he sees *"her tiny smile light up the room."*

This self-described *"Super Dad"* loves his happy home and intends on ensuring it is forever full of laughter and love. He has a deep appreciation for his Mom and Dad and hopes to share their teaching and values with his little girl. Tyler's goal is to make sure she'll never be afraid to follow her dreams and he'll be sure to support her in doing whatever she sets her mind to do.

1. Laugher is the best medicine. It doesn't matter how shitty a day you had, your child's laugh will always fix it.

2. Live in the moment, not through a screen. You may miss the perfect picture, but you can always remember the moment.
3. Let your kids fall. Falling is part of life, but always be there to pick them back up.
4. You only get to see your kids grow up once, don't miss it. No amount of money or any job is worth missing your children grow up.
5. You still need your "*man time.*" Don't forget to hang with the guys now and then.
6. Take care of their Mom. She has been through a lot. She will go through even more. Be her rock.
7. Kids are sponges. The more you show them the more they will absorb and learn. It's scary and amazingly cool at the same time.
8. Be a part of the routine. Find at least one thing that is special to you, something that's yours. I always put our daughter to bed. It's our time and we both enjoy it every night.
9. Diapers are not that bad, so man-up and do it.
10. Above all else, in a changing world, raise your child to be a good, decent human being, and be one yourself.

Of course, with love in my heart for Tyler's leading lady, I was happy to see him highlight her importance in his sixth tip. Tyler states, "*Take care of their Mom. Be her rock.*" I love when Dads remind other Dads about the women in their lives. It's great when there is an understanding that Moms need support and help along the way. Sometimes we Moms forget to mention that and sometimes it's hard to ask for help.

My Mom didn't have "*a rock.*" She carried the entire burden and my Dad as well. She was so heavy from this weight that she didn't have much left over for herself or her kids. No one was looking out for her.

In my world, Big Mike was my rock and still is. Because I was able to share my life and my worries with him, I had a true partner. He helped me with things and looked out for me. He carried weight, a lot of weight. Whenever I found something to be difficult to manage, he would offer to take it on. He never made me feel like a bother or a burden. His support allowed me to be a better Mom and a better person. I felt stronger. I was not heavy, as my Mom was. I had more room to think, to be and to become. I had space to do and to dream.

I am everything I am, have everything I have and achieved everything I have achieved because he loved me and, as Tyler suggests, was my "*rock.*" I'm thrilled Holly has a "*rock*" too.

Tyler also encourages Dads to take on a special piece of the day-to-day routine. For him, he and his daughter share the bedtime routine. That's a beautiful idea providing a win for everyone. Holly, Tyler and his little girl will enjoy that soft addition to their day. This sounds like something a "*rock*" would do.

I know Tyler's little girl will benefit on so many levels knowing she is treasured by her Father. I can imagine the sweetness this memory will bring. Sometimes if things become routine, we can take these times for granted. I hope Tyler never forgets all he is building by making time to be at his daughter's bedside.

I recall Michael's bedtime routine and can appreciate bed time isn't always a Hallmark moment or a Rockwell painting, but what peace for Mom to know, even if there's clanging and banging it's being handled with love and attention.

This idea gives Mom a moment to catch her breath. She may finish something otherwise undone or consider something that might have escaped her. Perhaps she will just sit. Whatever happens for her in these few short moments, it's no question this time will build a foundation for trust, security and self-worth in the heart of their little girl.

Tyler, on behalf of all Moms, thanks for the mention and on behalf of Holly, thanks for the moments. From my little girl's heart to my tired Mother eyes, I know that your time is well spent and far reaching.

Hugs to you all.

#23 Greg S. – Positivity

Greg is Dad to two teens, a boy and a girl. As we know, the teen years are tough on most of us. It's important to remember and to remind each other, chances are the kids *will* like you again.

In the meantime, Greg has the beautiful memories of the early years to warm his heart and remind him of their cuteness. Christmas, Halloween and special family moments are his dearest memories and what he's loved most about his parenting journey.

Greg was happy to share his tips and his journey. He's thrilled about parenting and the years ahead.

1. Kids are like baby ducks. They imprint behaviour of their parenting. This imprinting starts at an early age and can last forever.
2. You must have fun and a sense of humour with the kids. They learn this as well.

3. Instill confidence in them. Praise them, support them, do not get angry or yell. Talk things out.
4. Encourage them to do sports or activities that they want.
5. Have expectations for them. Assign chores.
6. Expose them to the dark side of life such as funerals, volunteer at soup kitchens. They need to learn to be grateful and thankful.
7. Be a good role model; work every day, treat people with respect. Treat service providers respectfully. Allow them to see you do this.
8. Be responsible in front of them. No smoking, no drugs or intoxication around them.
9. Respect elders and partners. If you have conflict be mature about it. Don't yell or name-call.
10. Tell them frequently how beautiful they are and how beautiful the world is. Focus on the positive.

Greg is sure to focus on the bright side in life and in parenting. "*Tell them frequently how beautiful they are and how beautiful the world is. Focus on the positive.*" His closing note is a great summary of his practices. I love the opportunity to highlight positivity. It was a pillar in my parenting, my most deeply held value and likely my most successful technique.

That said, maintaining positivity was the hardest perspective to uphold and encourage, particularly when raised in negativity. I did my very best to role model positivity, security and confidence, while simultaneously working to make gains in all areas myself.

I was careful to not discuss my overall generally grim perspective. I wanted only positivity in Michael's environment. To me, role modelling was my most significant responsibility as a parent. I took it seriously.

I didn't want to darken Michael's world in any way. I didn't call attention to my dissatisfaction, fears and angst. I refused to put my lens of life, or of the world, over Michael's eyes.

I only knew the world to be a hurtful and a hateful place; however, in spite of that I believed differently. I sought to find different views, different ways. I was intentional in ensuring a better outlook for Michael. Parenting in spite of this negative perspective may have been my greatest feat.

It was important to me that Michael see the world as a positive place, full of opportunity and happiness. I wanted him to be considering all possibilities, always knowing he had the personal power to do anything. I was painfully aware of how negative messages could defeat a spirit. I was determined this cycle would not continue. Kids should only see the bright and colourful side of life for as long as possible.

As Greg mentions in an earlier tip, kids do have to be exposed to the darker side. I, too, have come to learn that darkness does appear. In my experience, a light can be found even in the deepest sadness. Admittedly, sometimes it's hard to find but it's up to parents to dig for that light.

I can report, positive parenting methods have been highly successful. So successful in fact, these days, the student has become the teacher. Michael has become *my* positive role model. With no time for gossip and depressive anecdotes, Michael is happy in and happy out. He's the real deal.

Of course, he's is not immune to negative feelings and has not been protected from life's hardships. Michael chooses to give the 'dark-side' little to no time. He is progressive in all he thinks, all he does, and in what he says.

Michael demonstrates the value of 'clear-coloured glasses' with every interaction we have. He does not have the burden of 'shit-coloured glasses,' nor will he have to contend with the issues found in 'rose-coloured glasses.' He gets reality and knows his personal power is unstoppable.

Imposing my own sour views on Michael may have kept in line with my thinking, on my side of any argument, and may have even been easier; however, that would have been selfish and immature. It would have definitely resulted in great consequences and high expense to us both.

I didn't want Michael to think like me, even if it meant he'd agree with me. I wanted Michael to form his own thoughts and opinions. I didn't want his heart to be heavy.

I've found kids with negative role models to be greatly burdened. I've observed their sunken shoulders, downcast eyes and have been told about their "*belly full of anxiety.*" Contentment and happiness seem to escape them. They seemingly know nothing of their personal power.

Today, Michael is a secure, confident and forward-focused positive thinker who has found contentment and happiness. Keeping my shitty thinking to myself "*paid off in spades!*"

Given Greg's wish for his children is they, too, have happiness and confidence, focusing on the positive will lead to exactly those outcomes. I don't want to ruin the surprise, but the view is spectacular.

Thanks Greg! Keep your chin up.

#24 John H. – Freedom

John is Dad to two growing little babies, just two and five. He loves their bright and shiny faces and while envisioning them says, "*their smiling faces can turn any bad day.*"

Surprised by the busy land of parenting, this young Dad is adjusting to a new life and shifting priorities. Now focused on health and happiness for his family, John admits losing touch with other interests can lead to tough decisions.

John shares fresh insight on the early "*daze*" of parenting.

1. Your life is going to change significantly, the faster you realize it the better. Going out with your buddies may not happen for months.
2. You are pretty much going to hit a new low for sleeping. Sleep is now a luxury, enjoy it when you can.
3. Every baby/child is different. Don't compare to others, it will drive you crazy. Social medial doesn't always help. Careful not to brag and don't read too much into things. Comparisons will stress you out.
4. Take help whenever you can get it. Don't be proud or try to be brave. It literally takes a village to raise children.
5. Don't be afraid to try new things. Everyone is going to tell you how they did it but don't be afraid to try something different. Find what works for you.
6. Your wife is a saint and needs your help. Don't be *that* Dad who thinks it's a woman's job to raise the kids. It's a joint responsibility. You both make them; you both need to raise them. The kids will learn different things from each parent, embrace it.
7. You will struggle mentally and emotionally. It's tough, but you're not alone. Build a team, tag in and out accordingly.
8. Have realistic expectations; keep your new life in perspective. Dining out or family vacations are things that may not be doable. Be comfortable staying home.
9. Kids are expensive. Be careful not to overspend needlessly. There are many gimmicks on the market for new parents. You may not need to buy things; chances are your friends have some stuff to sell or share.
10. It's a marathon not a sprint. Don't burn yourself out. It's a long road but will get better once you hit your stride. It does get easier.

John's reminder regarding life changes is an important tip to mention, although rarely realized until it's learned firsthand. As he so accurately states, "*Your life is going to change significantly, the faster you realize it the better. Going out with your buddies may not happen for months.*" Although he's clear in the message, the level of what he means by "*significantly*" is hard to fathom.

This "*significant*" loss of freedom was my biggest surprise. Not knowing the impact having a child would have on my freedom truly illustrates my lack of maturity. I am comforted to know this surprise is not unique to me. There are many of us. I am not alone in the stark awakening.

Preparation is not really possible, we can't practice. John's right, "*the faster you realize it the bettter*". In hindsight, three decades later, I see the lack of freedom is the very thing I needed to improve the quality of my life and the possibilities for my son. I'm glad I understood "*sooner.*"

It is a good reminder. Freedom is limited and it should be. Acceptance is, however, a process; it can come and go. It's important to remember, especially during the exhaustion that freedom will return. In my case, I thought things would never change, even though they changed every day. I thought my freedom was gone forever. It may have been a disadvantage of teen parenting, or a lack of perspective, likely a combination of many things.

I want parents to be prepared for the lifestyle. It is quite a commitment.

I didn't know, before long, weeks and even months would pass without my son bursting through the door. I didn't know someday he wouldn't need me. I didn't realize someday my home would have a deafening silence. I never would have guessed the freedom I longed for would quickly return in no time, and I would be missing the busyness that once filled my days. I didn't know doing a great job would mean I'd be lonely. I didn't know my returning freedom would leave me feeling empty.

Had I known these things, there may have been more time for love and play. There would have been less focus on hurrying, urgency and moving to the next stage. Maybe I could have given more attention to slowing down, which was advised, but not a practice. Although this advice was provided, I never understood. I am hopeful John's tip will provide parents with a clearer sense of this reality and a more accurate understanding of the timeline.

Parenting is the most wonderful, most important, most valuable, most rewarding, and most precious "*blip*" of your life. It will be the most meaningful and most memorable source of wonderment anyone can be fortunate enough to experience.

Freedom, meh, it happens before you know it.

#25 Bob – Choose Your Words

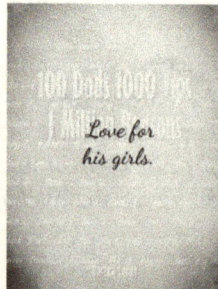

Bob is the Father of two girls, both now with families of their own. While the teen years are far behind him the memories remain fresh. He is thrilled to announce everyone made it out successfully!

This proud Dad now has four grandchildren ranging in age from ten to twenty-six. His family and his legacy have recently expanded to include a great-grandson who is, of course, enjoyed by all.

With a deep respect and appreciation for his own parents, Bob's only wish is that his children could have known them. He reflects often on how they would have enjoyed the growth and joy his girls have brought to his life.

His favourite reflection on parenting is the time he's spent watching his girls grow. He loves the uniqueness of their personalities and how they have developed in different ways. It is his greatest joy to know his girls are on the right path.

Bob's best tips for Dads:

1. Respect the values, religion, culture and opinions of others and encourage your children to formulate their own.
2. Keep kids involved. Encourage them, not force them, to volunteer or actively participate in school and in the community.
3. Keep communication open and ongoing without interfering.
4. Teach them the value of money.
5. Involve them as much as possible in family budgets and planning.
6. Encourage education but only as far as they want to take it.
7. Kids are interesting. Let them teach you, they will be proud of it.
8. Teach them how to cook.
9. Set goals, responsibilities and limitations. Don't call them rules.
10. You need to know when to get involved and when to back off. Find the balance.

Bob's ninth tip is a great example of how the words we choose are so important. He advises, "*Set goals, responsibilities and limitations. Don't call them rules.*" I appreciate the underlying message of empowerment. It gives a sense everyone is walking in the same direction, rather than a Dad dictating what is to be done. Together they set "*goals*" and "*limitations,*" rather than enforce pre-determined consequences.

Bob's repeated mention of encouragement conjured visions of soft discussions and careful guidance. Giving children room to spread their wings in their own way is a wonderful gift to them and to the world.

I believe Bob's framework and language would establish trust and security from the early stages. The words we use are powerful.

When a Dad uses words such as encourage, respect, teach, involve and balance, children are surrounded by possibilities. I hope I also conveyed each of these concepts in my own parenting, even if not so clearly articulated.

Providing safe, age-appropriate opportunities to participate in family, school and community will certainly develop self-esteem and leadership in the years to come. Bob's wording invites involvement. In further consideration, Bob's tip also highlights clarity. Support with goal setting, action items and expectations can, at times, be burdensome. I, too, worked to ensure success when helping Michael establish goals.

There is a lot of conversation required in this area and conversation was something we definitely had a lot of. Getting your children to think ahead and to identify how they want their lives to be will go a long way in determining their ability to critically think and behave responsibly.

I recall in the very early days, elementary school, asking Michael, "*What kind of life do you hope to have?*" I explained to him the differences in an average lifestyle versus an above average lifestyle. I told him my version of what was required to attain each. From those conversations Michael began to imagine the direction of his life. He started setting personal, educational and financial goals as well as dreams. He lived deliberately, strategically.

Any missteps were tied back to his established goals. Michael was encouraged to consider how any given behaviour might impact his targets, his long-term plan. He quickly began to self-correct, not because of what *I* wanted or imposed on him but because of what *he* wanted for himself. My job became much easier.

I'm so happy for Bob's girls and for Michael. I know life is easier to navigate with this foundation. I know Michael feels comfortable participating, expressing himself, accepting opportunities, identifying goals and accomplishing them — all of which happened because I did *with* Michael and not *to* or *for* him.

Thanks Bob, for the reminders and the memories. I'm sure you will continue to enjoy and teach, as the rewards of your work reach your third generation.

Enjoy!

#26 Dave S. – Honesty

Dave is the Dad of two teen girls and fortunately he's strong enough to handle the job. With a solid career in motivating and supporting others, Dave has an arsenal of tools both personally and professionally. In addition to his mad skills, he also comes from a beautiful foundation built on generations of love. What a great combo!

With the influence of both parents and grandparents, Dave values his role as a Dad as well as the role of extended family members. His dream is that his girls will continue to enjoy each other in love and happiness, valuing their relationship well into the senior years.

It's clear from Dave's tips that he holds honesty and truth in high regard. As much as we may want to cradle our kids forever, to shelter them from real life, it's our job to prepare them for it, rather than to protect them from it. A Zen Proverb states, "*Obstacles do not block the path, they are the path.*" It is up to us to teach careful navigation. I think Dave's tips illustrate a desire to prepare his daughters for that path.

1. Always be open-minded to their ideas.
2. Never lie, honesty is the best policy.
3. Have unconditional love no matter what.
4. Sometimes the best thing to do is walk away and cool off.
5. It's nice to be their friend but it is more important to be a Dad.
6. Rules are made for a reason. You are trying to raise nice human beings.
7. Manners are a must for children and adults.
8. What you do or act like is what your children will be or do. Be careful with your actions.
9. Never encourage violence but do encourage defending yourself.
10. Your kids can do anything. Make sure they know that and give praise for a job well done.

Dave's respect for honesty, rules and manners are sure to result in his goal of raising good people and as he says, "*nice human beings.*" In his second tip he states, "*Never lie, honesty is the best policy.*" Complete honesty is tough but an important standard to hold and uphold. Of course, for the first few years "*sheltering*" may be doable. In fairness to the kids however, we should work diligently to expose them to and facilitate real life things in age-appropriate ways, in honest ways.

I attempted to always bring a grounded and honest perspective, as well as explanations wherever possible. We should not just let them listen to the news, explore the internet or mindlessly watch TV, without providing an appropriate narrative. High level monitoring is especially important in instances relating to death, illness and even war, the heaviest stuff.

I believe if we are honest with our children, they will come to us for answers. I wanted Michael to know he could count on me, even if the truth was ugly. It's important to start these conversations early.

Heartbreak, disappointment, betrayal, sadness, disease, death, violence and other not-so-fun, even unthinkable, experiences may be racing toward them.

It's our job to plan for the darkness ahead. Prepare them to be resilient. It's up to parents to teach children how to handle liars, cowards and cheaters. We need to help them to recognize risk and risky people. They should know many people do not have their best interests at heart.

We need to train them for disappointment, so they can handle devastation. There's a lot of ground to cover. They should expect things will not always go well. Things do not always go well. Teaching life's pain is a parenting-ballet. It is a carefully choreographed dance for engaged parents. Conversely, it's a non-issue for disengaged parents, more like a mosh pit.

Teaching about death and life simultaneously is definitely not easy, but it is necessary; if we are focused on doing what's best for our children. Of course, it isn't always appropriate to be one hundred percent honest. After a few stumbles I, too, have come to learn that. I guess the distinction for me was to hold a general truth about life overall, but not necessarily the truth about adult issues, or my own issues.

I am a huge fan of parenting truthfully; however, sometimes the truth is a bit much for developing brains. One of my most common philosophies is, get as close to the truth as you can. At times, complete honesty may not be the best approach. Michael's environment was tailored to him, for him, free of fear and doubt. A childhood is no place for complete adult-level honesty. Honesty can be scary, especially when we, as parents, have no idea what we're doing or where we're going. Sometimes we have to choose between providing honesty or a sense of security.

For example, I didn't want Michael to know I was terrified, broke or betrayed. I didn't want him to know I failed, had poor judgment or no idea what to do. Instead I would tell Michael I was tired, or maybe cranky, "*still learning*." Those words were close to the truth but were not scary. Michael deserved an explanation for my sour moods; however, he didn't deserve to be fearful and to feel unprotected. He didn't deserve to believe the world was a scary place because his Mother couldn't handle it.

I tried to always provide love, security and a lot of room for fun. I'd like to believe Michael moved through life a little easier, and a bit more quickly, not having been forced to carry the extra baggage that can come from parents who over share. I agree with Dave in that honesty is the best policy, adding at times it may require adjustments and fine tuning when in discussion with children.

As parents, we have to discern what information to disclose to our kids. Right or wrong, we try to do our best. I think in weighing information, not acting irrationally and with maturity, we can find our answers. It is the consideration that will make the difference.

Thanks Dave, for all of your consideration and for the solid focus on parenting two special young ladies. Their lives will be a lot smoother because of your efforts.

#27 Kevin – Let Them Help

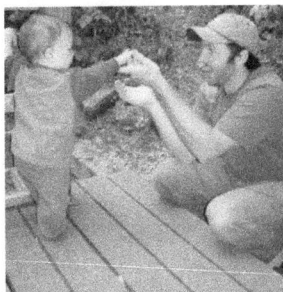

Kevin enjoyed a career as an advanced care paramedic prior to a significant spinal cord injury. At the time of his injury he had a toddler who is now quickly approaching his teen years. Kevin said, "*He {my son} makes me realize what's important. Being a Dad is what keeps me going.*"

We were brought together at Toronto's Lyndhurst Rehabilitation Centre. I guess it's fair to say we both have a deep respect for the importance of family. When meeting folks at a rehabilitation centre a lot is understood, even if not much is spoken.

Kevin had an amazing, hardworking and ambitious spirit and an equally amazing, hardworking and ambitious family. He was surrounded by love and hope. Kevin and his family are a sweet collection of people, a group I wish I had never had to meet. Everything was a paradox.

This time was built on tears, yet full of victory; times of feeling helpless, yet hopeful; meeting great people while wishing you were never there. It was messy, yet beautiful. Our journey with spinal cord injury was one which led us to wonderful people, and forged a bond through deep sadness. We were catapulted into the world of disability. A new vocabulary, a new world, new people, lots of new people; yesterday's priorities had quickly disappeared! We knew nothing about each other, yet somehow knew each other intimately.

Ramps looked steeper (once unnoticed), doors heavier (never considered before), bathrooms and booths too small, and stairs, I can't even stand stairs. Members in this club live differently and notice more. Membership was pricey!

Kevin's family exuded strength, togetherness and love. I am thrilled he shared a piece of his parenting journey.

1. Be your child's Father first. It's okay to be their friend, but it's more important to be their Dad.
2. Listen to your child. Put down your phone/tablet and turn off the TV. Really listen to what they are saying.
3. Get interested in what your child is interested in.
4. Make sure your child learns how to swim and ride a bike.

5. If you can, have your child grow up with a dog. If you can't, teach them to interact with dogs.
6. Teach and give your child responsibilities. Let them help you. You'd be surprised what they can accomplish when they really need to.
7. Children hear everything!
8. Let your child explore. Don't cover them in bubble wrap.
9. Teach your child humour. Let them laugh at you and teach them to be able to laugh at themselves.
10. Encourage them to have a job they love.

Reading Kevin's tips made me think a great deal about Big Mike's influence in Michael's life. What a gift to have had a Dad who is a Dad, who wants to be a Dad, and who enjoys being a Dad.

Michael was so fortunate, is so fortunate, to have a Father who listened and who showed interest, as Kevin suggests. They did swim and ride bikes. They laughed together. They loved a dog together, boxed together, built together, worked together and played together. They shared video games, soccer games, card games, actually all games. They joined soccer together, wrestled together, they did it all! Mike was able to hold the role of Dad and best buddy most effectively. He earned and enjoyed unwavering respect and still had fun.

Kevin's advice brought the fondest of memories to my mind. Dads matter so much. Without Big Mike, Michael would have missed much of what Kevin encourages. I did want to wrap Michael in "*bubble wrap.*" I didn't know much about laughter or fun. I'm not sure I was a great listener.

Kevin is reminding me in every line of all that Big Mike was busy doing. At the time it seemed effortless. Through Kevin I'm able to see the effort a little clearer.

In Kevin's sixth tip, "*Teach and give your child responsibilities. Let them help you. You'd be surprised what they can accomplish when they really need to,*" I vividly recall Big Mike suggesting he take Michael to work with him. He worked in construction and wanted Michael to learn more about the trade.

Michael was six when he began. Every Saturday they marched off together with their tool belts and all the love two guys could share. Big Mike gave Michael age-appropriate learning and opportunities, with not-so-age-appropriate exposure to bad language, which I must admit was also adorable. He loved teaching Michael. Michael learned not only about construction but also that cursing was allowed on the job site.

As promised by Kevin, I *was* surprised with what he could do, they could do. I am still surprised. Giving them room to grow and not succumbing to my own fears did a great deal for their relationship. They did, and still do, enjoy each other. Mike has always let Michael help and they both had a great time doing it.

In addition, Michael learned about the workplace, social norms and a little about being a *"carpenter's assistant."* Big Mike loved these special times and always looked forward to Saturdays with his *"little buddy."*

I love both the simplicity and the complexities in Kevin's tips. In reflection, I see a great report card for my cute, little duo. I'm sure Kevin is enjoying high scores as well.

Thanks Kevin! Much love to you and your special family.

#28 Aron – Reading

Aron is the husband to Meghan (*100 Moms, Mom #28*), and Dad to two very cute, bright-eyed little girls. He and I share a mutual niece and nephew, so I happen to have some inside information that he is absolutely great!

This fun-loving guy lights up every room he enters, a trait inherited by his girls. He loves everything about being a Dad, especially having an audience that can truly appreciate his comedic charm. He does confess he has found a whole new set of worries now that he's firmly planted in parenthood, but is up for the challenge.

It isn't surprising that Aron states his parents are his biggest influence. It's clear he was surrounded by love. Family and friends are of the utmost importance to him, and he holds the same hope that they will be important to his girls. His dream for them is health, happiness and a continued circle of love. I'd say they are well on their way.

Aron's top tips:

1. Let your child be their own person. Create as many opportunities as you can for your child to express themselves.
2. Smile and laugh, don't be afraid to be goofy around your kids.
3. Play and make playtime with your kids memorable.
4. Venture outside your comfort zone from time to time. Take some trips with them by yourself. Take them grocery shopping, by yourself. Take them to a restaurant, by yourself.
5. Talk to your children the same way that you would like someone to speak to you.

6. As difficult as it may be, let your kids be adventurous!
7. Make sure each parent gets some *"me time."* This is vital for sanity.
8. Read to your kids. Bedtime reading is a great time to connect with your kids. Be animated.
9. Bake with your kids. Let them experience how fun it can actually be.
10. Play them some good ole fashion soul music whenever you get the chance, especially when you're cooking supper.

Aron, Meghan and their girls have a really great time. Their lives are full of adventure, family, fun and everything they both hoped for. In reading his tips I could almost see through his living room window. I envisioned baking flour lightly dusted on those rosy little cheeks, as the girls dance off to read another colourful rendition of *"Good Night Moon."* There's no doubt stories told by this Dad are a source of delight for everyone.

As highlighted in Aron's eighth tip, a bedtime reading routine is a great way to connect. In our home, we also had an evening reading ritual. Michael loved reading time and eventually independent reading. I do believe he became a better student and life learner because of it.

Reading also brought stability, routine, tradition and tenderness. Michael gained a thirst for knowledge, adventure and creativity. He had admiration for good writing and an appreciation of reading. It made bedtime easier. All of that for only fifteen minutes a night. It was a non-negotiable commitment in our home. I believe our dedication to reading may have been the biggest contributing factor to raising a happy, well-adjusted, secure and intelligent child.

Ironically, I hated reading and reading time. Now, in reflection, that time represents some of my fondest parenting memories. Our commitment to reading was a commitment to Michael's future. This is such a strong piece of advice. I was never read to as a child and struggle with reading to this day. I knew before I was even pregnant that I would raise a reader. It was my number one goal. I was certain my kid would be able to read and would read well. I started reading to Michael as soon as I found out I was pregnant.

I remember going to the library and picking out books on all topics, English, math, science and French. Yes, I even read math books. I wanted him to have a sample of all subjects. I was not exceptionally strong in any subject, so I had no bias.

The consistency of bedtime reading was a pillar of togetherness. No matter what event was planned, Michael would have his reading time. He insisted! Every night, without fail, reading time was before bedtime. Big Mike and I would secretly, at times painfully, banter about whose turn it was. When we were tired and dared to attempt a shortcut, Michael was on to us.

As Michael got older he would eventually do his own reading. For a transitional period, he would read to us. Soon he was enjoying a solo reading journey and the adventures of *"chapter books."*

To add another layer to this wonderful tip and *it is gold, so grab your highlighter*: When your child is looking to extend their bedtime, they feel they should stay up later – extend reading time, not TV/computer time. I thought this was brilliant, even if I do say so myself. This gradually added an hour or more to Michael's reading routine. What skill building!

In the early years, continuing to this day, Michael has been an exceptional reader. He is able to understand and retain large amounts of information, which has served him well throughout his education. These days, it is more important than ever to raise a reader. With the vast amounts of information on the internet, there is a lot to sift through. In internet searching and in earning his law degree, Michael's reading skills have been key components of his success.

I think if a parent gets it "wrong" all day long, a great deal can be undone with a commitment to a daily reading routine, even fifteen minutes. To me, consistency is more important than duration. As painful as reading may sometimes be, the pay-off is immeasurable. Raising a reader is one of my proudest accomplishments!

Thanks to this great team for sharing their tips. I wish them all the very best with their adorable, and dynamic duo.

#29 Andre – Communication

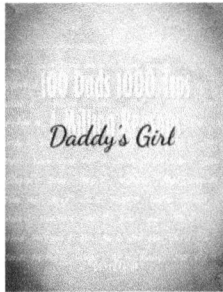

Andre is enjoying his parenting journey with his wife and teen daughter. He reports his daughter has all his good qualities and his bad ones as well. Having known Andre for a few years, I'm confident the good far outweigh the bad. Andre has given a great deal of thought to parenting, and beams when he speaks of his *'little girl.'* His one wish for his little girl is that she *"set no limits."*

1. Compliments are good but make sure they are not only focused on her appearance. Compliment intelligence, resourcefulness, imagination, hard work and strength.
2. Model respect for and equality for women every chance you get, if you want her to believe she deserves respect from her male counter parts.

3. Stay engaged with your little girl when she gets older and is talking about boys, emotions and how bodies start to change. Don't run and hide.
4. Make memories with your daughter. Take trips, vacations, movie nights and play sports together.
5. Make sure you tell her when you are wrong, made a mistake or could have dealt with a situation more appropriately. Nobody is perfect but make sure your apology is sincere.
6. Time flies so take advantage of every moment you can spend with her. Don't sweat the small stuff.
7. Make time to talk, play, laugh, cry and support your children no matter how tired you might be. Before you know it, they will be graduating from high school.
8. Keep open the lines of communication. The car ride has really been the best time to find out what she likes, who her friends are and how she's doing.
9. Celebrate her accomplishments and the opportunity to learn from her failures or life setbacks.
10. Do your very best as often as possible, through your words and your actions, to make sure she knows how much you love and appreciate her inside out.

Seeing a Dad value communication with his daughter is a heart-warming concept, especially to a girl who didn't have the benefit of a Father's communication. In Andre's eighth tip he states, "*Keep open the lines of communication with your daughter.*" Not only does Andre value communication, he even suggests where to do it and what to ask: "*Find out what she likes, who her friends are, how she's doing.*" Being specific with your questions can be a great help in guiding you both with a deeper discussion.

In learning just a little of Andre's parenting practices, I began to imagine that his '*little girl*' is as proud of him as he is of her. What an amazing bond they must have developed using his principles.

Like Andre, I felt communication was a parenting priority. I loved the car rides with my little boy and felt it was a great time to generate good conversation.

In my childhood, we weren't allowed to speak, generally. I can only imagine what it would have meant to have had my Dad's interest. My Dad never asked about me, my life or my friends. He taught me little and talked to me even less. I would have loved to learn more about him, to have had him ask questions about my life. With certainty I know such interest would have made me stronger, better, smarter and more confident. I would have stood up straighter. I would have felt loved.

Now, if I had felt love, one can speculate I would have made completely different choices; maybe, maybe not. Regardless, I'm not attempting to blame him, just to explain and to understand. I know he did his best. He was from a hard-knock school and a hard-knock life. He didn't know better. He didn't have it to give. I accept that, and I love him.

It's great that Andre specifically provides clear examples. Some Dads may not know where to begin or what to say. For any Dads looking for an icebreaker Andre's pointers provide a nice starting place. As our children get older, one-on-one time is increasingly challenging to find. We need to be deliberate about our communication, deliberate and consistent. If you can chat when there isn't much going on, it will be easier to chat when there is.

Technology isn't helping. We may be able to superficially connect quickly, but connection on a deeper level is not at our fingertips. We now know, talking to children helps improve their understanding of language and increases their vocabulary. So, if you really don't like your kids, or feel love and connection is over-rated, maybe communicate anyway, if only to help them out with vocabulary.

Thanks Andre! I'm sure you'll forever enjoy your beautiful family and all the drives, small and large.

#30 Wayne M. – Advice

Wayne is a high school teacher and the owner of a martial arts school. He's the proud Stepdad to three grown children and now a Grandfather to four. It's great to see and hear a Stepdad love and gush about his children and his parenting years. He deeply values their influence in his life, as well as the opportunity to provide a positive influence in theirs.

The connection he has with each child and the fun they've shared is highlighted by him as his life's biggest joy. There wasn't anything he didn't like about his parenting journey. Wayne was actively involved from the early days and remains involved in all their lives. His participation has always promoted happiness and life fulfillment, which I think is very apparent in his advice to Dads everywhere.

1. Don't be too hard on yourselves, none of us are perfect. We do the best we can with what we have got. Sometimes our children are not going to do everything just like we think they should.
2. Don't be too easy on yourselves. Your children can do awesome things and need your support. Be loving but tough at times.
3. Be careful of whose advice you listen to. Many times, people who don't have children tend to give the most advice. There are also those parents with young children who feel they have it all figured out and want to pass judgment. We're all evolving. What works with one may not work with the next one.
4. Children do not come with rule books. It is important to be fair, but it is also important to recognize what each one needs. Some will need more structure, discipline, etc. The next may need more freedom. Recognize individual differences.
5. Don't be afraid to let your children fail, sometimes. I am not suggesting to constantly let them crash and burn, but failure is a part of life. Some parents want to try to protect their children from every little bump in life, they aren't doing them any favours. Life is full of bumps and setbacks and we need to learn how to deal with things starting as children.
6. Learn to control your negative emotions. Not that you should ignore them or pretend not to have them, but it's important to learn to manage them. It is easy to be friendly, likable and fun to be around when the people agree with you; but that is not what defines you. What really counts is how you react when things are not going your way, when something or someone pushes all your buttons or someone is not being agreeable. Remember that your children are watching you, imitating you and learning from you. So, don't get all upset when they throw a big tantrum if you are the one that taught them how.
7. Don't wait to spend time with your children, do it now. When my kids were little, I spent a lot of time working, in school and trying to develop my own identity. I kept saying I would buy a video camera to preserve the wonderful memories. Eventually I did get a video camera, but they had already grown up. They grow up so much faster than you think they will. Twenty years passes in the blink of an eye. Be careful about waiting for the "*right time.*" I have found that with many things, the "*right time*" is when you get off your ass and take it.
8. Don't let them spend all of their time playing video games. I see so many children if given the choice to do something they enjoy or do nothing, they'll choose nothing. It blows my mind. I find that happens even more when they can play video games unrestrictedly.
9. Don't be afraid to make your children do things. My Mom was the main pianist for the church. She was determined I would also play piano. As child, it was difficult at times. I wanted to play Beethoven

70

but was stuck on *"Twinkle Little Star."* I had not put in the time needed to play more complex songs that required a lot of practice. I fought my Mom hard on practicing. I wanted to quit, and I would have if she had let me. Because she was firm and didn't let me quit, I learned when things are tough to keep going. Although my Mom passed away in 1998, I am still there, at that church, playing piano and singing. I also see a lot of this happening at my school. Many parents aren't strong enough to disagree with, or push their children. As soon as something gets tough, they allow their children to quit. From my perspective, we need to be teaching our children to push through things that are difficult so they can grow. For my grandchildren, they participate in activities and attend my Jiu-Jitsu classes a couple of times each week. Fortunately, my daughter and son-in-law support and encourage their participation.

10. Be involved with your children's lives. I love it when I have children in my martial arts classes and their parents join the classes as well. If your child is participating in a school sport or activity, you may not be able to be a part of the preparation but show up for as many events as possible. It shows them that you care. Not showing up (never showing up), says just as much. It says that you don't care and that they aren't important to you. What you don't communicate to them and others means just as much as what you do!

Wayne and I share many parenting philosophies and perspectives. His tips had a way of bringing me into his world. What a gift to recognize your influence on not only your own children but also the next generation, and the many other children in all areas of his life. A life well spent.

In Wayne's third tips he cautions parents to be careful as to who they are listening to and seeking advice from. It's true, as he states, *"we're all evolving."* Today's tips might be tomorrow's regrets. I always appreciate a caution to consider the source. It is important to "be *careful of whose advice you listen to*," the childless, the new parents, seasoned parents, the experts and even your Mom.

In my parenting years there was no Google. My knowledge and ability were limited, and my circle of information was small. At that time, whatever your Mom said was gospel, unquestioned. I now know, my Mom said a lot of wrong things. She believed her information to be true. Her Mom told her, so how could it not be true? Her intention was pure, albeit misguided.

For example, as a child I suffered from severe earaches. Oh, I remember the terror. They were awful. Mom's home remedy was to blow cigarette smoke in my ear, *"to loosen the wax"* which was diagnosed by her as the issue. Research now shows cigarette smoke is linked to ear infections. Yikes!

So, not only was her smoking likely the cause of my ear infections and not-to-mention, (but-to-mention) my asthma, it was being used as a remedy to a problem which it only further aggravated. Sad, but true.

There were many occurrences of myths, home remedies and uneducated guesses on cause and effect. Luckily today, information and education are more easily accessible. I often find myself leery to even provide any opinion, as a lot of what I learned or think to be true may be completely inaccurate.

Although information is more available, some still resist research. There are parents who will trust an unreliable source because it's easy, fits their narrative or they trust the wrong person. I strongly believe in parents consulting parents. I love it, Michael was raised on the advice of others; however, do cross check. Consulting others should just be one source, not the only source. We really don't know what we don't know.

Often, as with my Mom, parents are well-intended. My Mom certainly wasn't trying to aggravate my earache or impair my breathing. It's possible even a doctor suggested she try that method. Sometimes they are wrong, too. Sometimes teachers are wrong. Sometimes trained professionals are wrong.

I encourage all parents to consider and collect opinions but do research. Consult professionals. There are many issues that arise in parenting that require a professional opinion. We don't know it all. I am not a parent who thinks we should trust our judgment, guts or even a Mother's intuition. I collected a lot of information and in the end the decision did rest with me. I did what I could to make informed decisions. I gave it my best effort. I was still wrong sometimes.

Exhausting I know.

Thanks, Wayne, for your thoughts, opinions and for working to exhaustion as well.

#31 Colin – Start Small

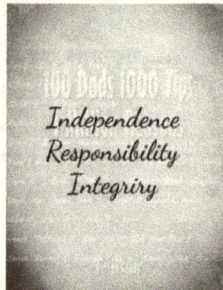

Colin is Dad to one son who has just become an official adult at age eighteen. Now that the tough part is over, he fondly reflects on the joys of parenting. Having loved everything about being a Dad, Colin particularly valued sharing his learning and his memories of little leagues.

Having had a solid parental influence, Colin worked to provide the same for his son. He wanted to be the kind of Dad he was thankful to have had. He hoped to be all of what his Dad was for him. With family values and work ethic firmly instilled, Colin was an actively engaged Dad and coach. Through his parenting, his most treasured qualities have now reached his son.

Colin looks forward to watching his son tackle the adult world. He wants him healthy, happy, and educated, hoping he too will enjoy a parenting journey. Colin is thrilled about the chance to influence and likely spoil (but just a little) the next generation.

1. Reward good behaviour not bad. In the early days, when my son was a toddler, on shopping trips he kicked up a fuss to get things he wanted. I never gave him those things. Often when he behaved and I knew he wanted something I would get it for him and ask, *"Do you know why I got you this?"* He would say *"Because I didn't ask."* I'd reply, *"Yes and because you were good."*

2. You only have one set of eyes and they are not in the back of your head. You are going to miss some of the things they get into. Do your best to pay attention. As long as they aren't doing something that will hurt them they will be OK. Hopefully they'll learn from their mistakes, I know I did.

3. Let them be kids but set boundaries so they know when they have gone too far. They will test these boundaries. Normally as long as they know where the limits are they will stay inside them, hopefully.

4. Kids imitate everything, especially their parents. The best way for you to raise a child to be kind hearted and hardworking is to be that yourself; set the example. That's what my parents did for me, until the day my mother passed away of cancer. They were inseparable, it seemed even more so as they grew older.

5. Give your child some responsibility, a little at first to see how they handle it. Expand and decrease according to the result and their ability. We started at a very early age, about age four. My son's first job was to help clear the table, something he still does to this day. Every time we gave him more responsibility he met the challenge. I think this shaped him/set him up for future success. He's been highly motivated and responsible. He got his Private Pilot License at just sixteen. He's obtained many licenses over the years.

6. Along the same thought process as giving them responsibility, also let them make their own decisions. Again, little things at first and gradually move to more important things. You may be surprised at the decisions they make and their rationales. I was always impressed at the reasoning my son used to make decisions but most of the time he simply said, *"Because it's the right thing to do."*

7. Remember they are a part of you but they are not you. Let them be individuals. You may not like something or even be afraid of something, don't let that stop them from doing or liking things that you don't. As long as it's not going to hurt them, let them do it. Encourage them to be who *they* are.
8. Teaching my son how to use tools seems to have worked out so far.
9. Teach them to respect other people and their belongings. I thought I failed in this one. I asked my son when he was about five, *"What are girls?"* He answered, *"Collectibles."* I was pretty sure at the time he did not really know the meaning of what he said, *hopefully*. It's important to teach them to respect girls and collectibles, but in different ways of course.
10. Don't eat dirt, or at least not too much.

Colin and I shared many values and practices in our parenting. We focused on independence, responsibility and integrity. I'm excited for Colin and what is ahead. With a ten-year advantage, I know what joy and pride will await from such teachings.

Many memories came to my mind when reviewing Colin's tips. From his first tip on not giving in to a three-year-old tantrum to his later focus on developing their uniqueness. We've both had the privilege of watching our young teens accomplish unimagined things. In Colin's case his son achieving his piloting licenses, in my case Michael rappelling down a 22-storey building for charity. The rewards of diligent parenting are plentiful and amazing.

In Colin's fifth and sixth tips he highlights building on the small steps. I love that approach. We started teaching responsibility and decision making early on as well, likely age four. Beginning with clothing choices and chores we consistently built on success and ability. I told Michael more would be expected always, not less. He knew we were preparing him to become a man and he was very interested in learning how to become a man.

As Colin's son based decisions on *"the right thing to do,"* we had hoped the same for Michael. When we learned of his reasons for any given decision we were always impressed. Michael trusted himself and had a strong internal compass. Supportive and attentive parenting will provide our kids a gumption that will serve them well.

Always with the long game in mind, we worked in a united way to the end goal. As with Colin, our collective goals were health, happiness, education and family love. We attempted to achieve them with family values and a demonstrated work ethic, as did Colin. With my ten-year advantage I can report, they stuck!

Thanks for your thoughts and advice. I predict you're in for a lot of fun!

#32 Jim C. – Listen

Jim is Dad to Susan, (*100 Moms, Mom #32*), the proud Grandfather to seven biological grandchildren and to countless honorary grandchildren. Jim loves all things about family life and hanging out with the next generation.

Along with his wife Marilyn, they've raised two boys and one girl. Both ensure they remain a strong presence in all their lives. Well into his retirement, Jim is a hands-on Grandfather and a Dad anyone can count on.

1. Listen.
2. Be firm and fair.
3. Express your love.
4. Be kind.
5. Be honest.
6. Be upfront in all your dealings.
7. Be truthful.
8. Take time for your family. Play with your kids.
9. Remember people and families are always changing.
10. As you age your abilities will change.

I always appreciate the reminder to *"listen,"* as Jim advises in his first tip. I still need that reminder often and in all areas. Beginning my journey with the mind of a teen, my listening skills were under construction. I was under construction. For some, listening may sound easy, like common sense; however, it was not so easy for me. I wish I had listened more. I shamefully remember far too often thinking, *just stop!* I was so tired, preoccupied and unprepared.

Over the years, I've shared a lot about parenting struggles, insecurities and inadequacies. There were times I didn't love parenting so much, I didn't listen so well. I ache to consider the moments that escaped me, as I hurried to do something far less important. Overwhelmed with life, frantic with myself, consumed by bullshit, I could barely hear through the racket in my own head. At times, Michael's little voice felt as if it were booming.

How I wish I had listened more to the soft sounds, the toddler tones. I wish I had stopped and slowed down when I heard the word, "*Mommy*" instead of thinking, "*What now!*" My skills were so limited.

I love this tip. I hope others can hear it and embrace its essence. Do listen! It's a simple word tip but it requires deliberate action. As said by a special Mom, (*100 Moms, Mom #42*) "*They are talking to you for a reason.*"

Thanks for always being such a great listener Jim!

#33 Julian – Get Outdoors

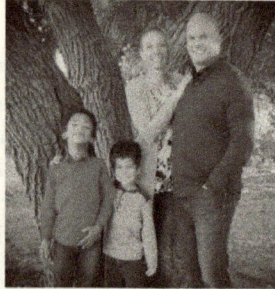

Julian is a self-described "*Chief Idiot Husband, Good Dad & Founder, GetConnectDad.com.*" He enjoys life with his children and their various ages and stages. There's a lot happening in the lives of his children, with his oldest being twenty-two followed by two growing toddlers at four and five. Julian loves the unconditional gift of love that comes with parenting.

With great love comes great sadness in this case. As a Dad who holds a deep appreciation for the love of his children, he shares that he has sadly been a victim of parent alienation. As a result, he and his daughter have lost their connection. This has been the darkest pain in Julian's parenting journey.

In moving forward, Julian's dream is that his children enjoy good health, a kind heart and will always pursue their passions. He hopes their love of God will fuel their direction, decisions and their lives.

1. Live your faith.
2. Read to your kids each day.
3. Take a walk every day outside.
4. Spend fifteen minutes focused on 'kid directed' activities daily.
5. Hug your kids daily.
6. When your child is upset (losing temper / frustrated), ask them to find something '*green*' or something comparable. It changes the way their brain is engaged and allows them to focus on something other than reacting.

7. When you have kids who are struggling with interrupting, require them to place their hand on your arm, you follow up by placing your hand on their hand. They wait patiently until you are ready to respond.
8. Eat dinner together more often than you don't each week. It becomes more important as the kids get older.
9. Let kids cook with you, regardless of the mess they make.
10. Limit your kids' outside activities to one per year. More than that changes the focus of your family. Family first, activities second.

I like the idea of a walk every day, as Julian mentions in his third tip. It falls in line with his highlight child-centred approach and is very doable. I think that's great advice for promoting togetherness, self-care and health, physical and mental. This tip provides a large return on investment; the simplicity of a daily walk doesn't cost a thing but has great rewards.

Breaking up the day with some fresh air is always going to be a good idea. Enjoying the outdoors or physical fitness doesn't come natural for me. I wasn't exposed to those options in a meaningful way. "*Enjoying*" the outdoors was not a familiar concept. A daily commitment to upholding a healthy lifestyle adds an additional layer of growth and positivity to family. I always appreciate a reminder on the benefits of fresh air and the outdoors.

As a child I was a severe asthmatic and had an overprotective Mom. I can appreciate why encouraging outdoor play was restricted. Sadly, I couldn't do much physically without a trip to the emergency room. When I became a Mom, I wanted things to be different.

I remember hearing an adage, when a child has climbed a tree, he will draw a different tree than a child who has never climbed a tree. I don't know if there's any truth to that, but I had never climbed a tree. I decided my son would climb a tree! I grabbed up my baby and off we went. I took a two-year-old Michael in my arms for a planned hike, picnic and tree climbing. I smile as I recall my lack of understanding in every facet of this plan, Michael was only two! He hadn't even mastered walking, but I was taking him on a hike.

Many years later, at about age seven Michael was a 'country-kid.' I'm happy he was able to play and climb. Sheila's (*100 Moms, Mom #7*) family really enriched his outdoor experiences. Around that time, I did implement a daily walk in our routine. Those walks bring back the fondest memories. I allowed Michael only fifty cents, which would purchase ten candies.

One day he asked, "*How come you just give me fifty cents?*" Before I could answer he said, "*I know! You don't want it to be about the candy, right?*"

"*Yes*," I smiled, "*That's right.*"

Michael had a wonderful childhood and a lot of exposure to nature and child-centred activities as Julian also suggests. I think time spent playing outdoors can help us all to feel like kids again.

Thanks, Julian, for reminding us parenting really is in the simple things.

#34 Ryan – Pre and Post Baby

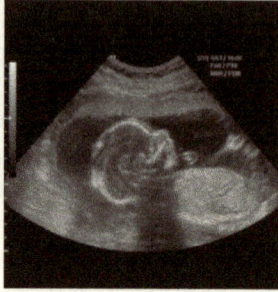

Ryan is one of only two Dads to submit his tips pre-baby. I was happy to have his involvement and to learn of his eagerness to step into this new role. Although Ryan's little bundle had not yet been born, it was clear the baby-to-be and the baby's Mom would be great hands. Ryan was able to provide a unique perspective to budding Dads everywhere. As the "*nest*" was being prepared. Great attention was being given to the large and small details.

It was beautiful to read Ryan's tips and to recognize his respect and consideration for his wife. Having identified his own Mom as being his most valuable influence, I suspect he will continue to prioritize his wife in the most loving way.

1. Guys, if your wife isn't sleeping, neither are you.
2. Remind her it's OK to eat more often than you. Just because you're not hungry doesn't mean she or the baby isn't. I used to have to eat so she'd eat. I was gaining weight quicker than her.
3. Be more affectionate. Their body is changing and not in ways they like. It's important you are understanding and loving.
4. My wife was incredibly flat in affect for the first two months. Her mood was different. She was sick, stopped going to the gym and wasn't herself. We went on a trip; it was the best thing ever. She got to have fun and snap out of her funk.
5. Encourage an evening stroll. It's a nice thing to do together while she's pregnant and after the baby arrives.
6. Attend the baby's appointments! It's so cool hearing that little heartbeat!
7. Don't leave the crib, dresser or required work too late. Get that stuff setup early and do it together.
8. Strengthen those hands. She's going to be sore from carrying the extra weight so remember a back rub while watching TV means the world!
9. If she's off work early, encourage her to connect with family, friends, pamper herself. Your reminders and support will help with positivity and happiness.

10. Prepare your hospital bag early; remember it's for all three of you.

Ryan noticed his wife's mood during her pregnancy, which is a great sign. He said, "*My wife was incredibly "flat" for the first two months. Her mood was different. She was sick, stopped going to the gym and wasn't herself. We went on a trip; it was the best thing ever. She got to have fun and snap out of her funk.*" There are a lot of good pieces in that one tip. His pre-baby tips were so touching.

Seventy percent of Dads encouraged care and concern for your partner. From the perspective of an expecting Dad, his words can serve to remind all Dads about the specialness of this stage. The pre-baby planning is such a cherished and exciting time. For me, pre-planning was so fun. Ryan's messages brought me right back to those early days, those exact scenes. I loved every minute of my pregnancy. People were so kind. It was unforgettably warm and loving.

Ryan's fourth tip, noticing she was in a "*funk*," amazing! He not only noticed, but worked to resolve it, such consideration. I think noticing our partner's "*funk*" is a golden skill. Suggesting a break in routine, large or small, can help to ensure cracks in communication don't end up being canyons. This is a tip not only valuable in the early stages, but a great check point and strategy for all the stages. Time for each other is not always easy to find. Remember, your relationship is the trunk in your family tree. It deserves planning, purpose and priority.

Although I haven't written marriage tips yet, I'll be sure to consult Ryan when I do. While it's on my mind, however, a tip for Ryan: *If you keep doing what you're doing, with the love and thoughtfulness you're doing it with, your marriage and family can only continue to grow in the most beautiful ways.*

Oh, the places you'll go!

Ryan – Part 2 – Post Baby

Ryan's enthusiasm about parenting has gotten even brighter. His excitement about the book, sharing his thoughts and about learning more is sweet, admirable and what great leaders are made of.

Mornings have gotten happier and brighter with the smiles of his little boy. Ryan's only challenge is identifying what all the crying is about, which he and his wife are handling with a valiant team effort. Envisioning the future and planning to live out dreams has already begun. Ryan hopes they'll travel the world and enjoy a lifetime of health and happiness. I'm confident together they'll be reaching any established goals they dream up.

Ryan's tips after three months of dedicated training and experience:

1. If you get paternity time, a leave, take it. It was so great to be able to help. After the C-section much support was needed. It was an amazing experience to help in so many ways and to watch my son become brighter every day.
2. Keep supporting your wife. She went through something we'll never understand. She's going to be emotional, deal with it. Be supportive, help her, order her favourite meals and tell her you love her.
3. Work as a team. There's no need in two of you being up every time the baby cries in the night. She'd get up one time; I'd get up the next.
4. Don't compare to other kids, just be there for your own and remind your wife not to compare with her friends or mom groups. Every child does things at their own pace.
5. Enjoy your family time. I work Monday to Friday, so I love waking up Saturday morning, feeding my boy and cuddling on the couch watching TV.
6. Go for family drives, even if just to get a coffee. Get out of the house, get the baby used to the car. It's nice to do something together.
7. Always come in smiling, put your crappy workday aside. Remember, she just spent the day trying to please an infant that either smiles or cries. Give her a kiss, kiss your baby and get to Dad duty.
8. Encourage your wife to ask for help and to accept help from family members so she can go to the gym, have visitors or do whatever keeps her from being alone day in and day out waiting for you to get home.
9. Don't be scared to tell people to put sanitizer on or to not touch your baby, some people just don't know and aren't educated. Don't take offence to it.
10. Have fun! They're so sweet and entertaining. Enjoy every minute.

Well, there you have it, a speedy and heart-felt evolution from partner to family man. It's just great to see Ryan hasn't lost focus of his wife. His love and attention must be the coziest of coverings in an otherwise hectic stage. I appreciate Ryan's mention of enforcing hand sanitizer in his ninth tip, as well as reminding folks, some aren't educated and not to take offence.

With the recent addition of our grandson, I had to be educated. It is sometimes hard to realize, or accept, that you don't know it all. There is always new research and even life saving measures discovered. It is important to keep an open mind, get educated and as Ryan states, *"not to take offence."*

In this new phase of life, I learned it's not OK to kiss babies on the face. I thought that was weird and I heard great protest from Moms and Grandmothers everywhere when I shared the news. So many dismissed what is truly a vital piece of information.

I'll just say, look it up, *"Google it."* If you do search some details, you will not kiss a baby's face ever again. I know, it's hard not to kiss their sweet little faces, but it's very important we don't. I hope to never stop learning. I sure don't want to miss details that can help to keep our baby or any baby healthy and safe.

Thanks Ryan! It's a long and lovely road, yet short. As you advised others in your final tip, *"Have fun! They're so sweet and entertaining. Enjoy every single minute."*

#35 Keegan – Laundry

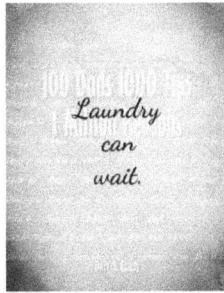

Keegan came to me by way of respected reference. When a friend of mine heard I was working on this book he said, *"Oh you have to talk to my buddy Keegan."* Keegan was happy to contribute his thoughts on parenting and speaks from the thick of it all with three young children, two girls and a boy.

He loves everything about being a Dad. In his words, *"I love it all. I love observing milestones and achievements. I love being their caregiver and their 'go to.' I love the hugs, smiles and the love."*

Although actively involved in his career in the Canadian Armed Forces, Keegan finds time to build and share in a fun childhood for his children. His only real complaints are laundry and mucus and I don't think he'll get any disagreement on that.

1. You're never as ready as you want to be, but you're more ready than you think you are.
2. Busy-ness is relative. Having three kids doesn't necessarily mean you're busier than someone who has one or two, it depends on what you put in to it. It does mean you have more laundry.

3. Your kids are going to grow up fast. Pick them up when you have the chance. You're both going to miss it when you can't.
4. Children are way smarter than we think. They observe, analyze and learn from us all the time. If you want them to be nice, be nice.
5. Don't coddle or be a helicopter parent. Kids need to get back up after they fall and are tougher than we think, too.
6. Let kids be kids, but don't let them be jerks.

It was fun to read Keegan's tips; they are so succinct. I wanted to expand on several of them but given his only complaint was laundry and mucus; I thought I'd give a little attention to the commonly expressed burden of laundry. It really never ends!

I cannot imagine the laundry in a family of five. These days I only am responsible for the laundry of two adults and I can't keep up. I dare not complain, especially to Keegan. I do want to share with the world, laundry is a challenge and unified cry for almost all parents. Mucus comes and goes; laundry only comes.

There are a few laundry enthusiasts I've heard about but have never met. Apparently, occasionally, there are individuals who find laundry to be rewarding and soothing. I have no knowledge of said person. It may be just a myth.

For those struggling with laundry, let me share with you what my Mom, a coal miner's daughter, shared with me: "*Mommy scrubbed her clothes on a washboard every day and I saw her fingers bleed.*" I did see a washboard but never used one and I never saw anyone's fingers bleed. I did see and own a 'washer spin-dryer.' For those who didn't, it's a two-part electric machine more like a large aluminum box, one side for washing the other a spinner. It accepted two pairs of jeans, was rarely balanced and shook the house with unforgettable force. It leaked, overflowed and really didn't spin dry. It was better than a washboard but not much better than hand washing.

I guess with these reference points I hope to spark gratitude for anyone who doesn't have to resort to such methods and to extend empathy for those who do. I remember the laundromat, air drying, hanging racks and board-stiff towels. It was dreadful.

These days I have a washer, a dryer and laundry detergent with a back-up supply. I even have fabric softening sheets and coat hangers which were once thought to be unnecessary luxuries. I am in no way meaning to brag, only to appreciate. I still hate laundry and still don't get it done.

With all the advancements in facilities and the abundance of supplies, why does laundry remain so labour intensive? It's a mystery to me, maybe to most, as to how laundry could have ever been managed with a washboard; and yet it is a seemingly impossible task even with the greatest advancements in technology. As I readily admit, I don't have all the answers and I don't have any under the heading of laundry. I only offer understanding and hope.

I guess I'll offer one piece of advice: Get those kids moving. In my parenting days, I only offered Michael a beginner's lesson in laundry. It seemed easier to do myself; however, maybe I gave up too quickly. Teach them, train them and put them to work. I don't know if the war can ever be won. Maybe parents can create some laundry minions with a little effort and preplanning. Maybe there are technological advancements underway. In the meantime, for those who also hate mucus, it may be some consolation to consider that laundry will remedy any mucus remnants.

Keegan, with your team you might have some hope. Helpers may be on the way. Thanks for showing highlighting the dark side shared by parents everywhere and good luck with the missing socks.

#36 Ron – Role Modelling

Ron also came by way of respected referral. My son Michael suggested I connect with Ron as he held him in high esteem from his high school days. Michael didn't suggest many Dads; Ron topped his list.

Ron is a retired teacher, proud Father and a very excited Grandfather. He has three grown daughters and a life full of love. He cherishes everything about family life, except disciplining. Ron did not like the discipline.

He modelled relationships based on love and respect and hopes his daughters will carry on with expectations of the same. Ron's tips focus on providing a strong foundation, strong enough for two generations of mutual love to stand firmly on.

1. Teach mutual respect in a loving and caring environment.
2. Say what you mean and mean what you say. Kids can spot fraud!
3. Set reasonable boundaries – fairness and consistency are the most important elements in discipline.
4. Establish a line of communication early – if your kids eventually become a closed door, at least you won't have any regrets. Teach them that listening is much more important than speaking.
5. Identify issues that need to be addressed as early as they become apparent. I would tell my children individually, that '*we are going for*

an ice cream'. They knew this meant that there's an issue that needs to be addressed.

6. Be the role model for your children, keeping in mind your example will help them choose a partner. Treat their mom like you want them to be treated in their relationship.
7. Teach them the value of a balanced life. Play is just as important as work.
8. Expose your children to many physical and cultural activities so that they will have an opportunity to adopt lifelong hobbies.
9. Teach them how to manage money – it's a gift that will keep on giving throughout their lives.
10. There is an old saying, *"Attitude is the mind's paintbrush – it colours every situation!"* Model for your children the simplicity and the reality of this truism.

As a parent and a teacher, Ron understood the value of role modelling, highlighting it throughout his tips. I agree the model you provide for your children will inform their choices for a life partner, as stated in Ron's sixth tip. I was so aware that my behaviour would be determining Michael's future.

Not only did I realize I was modelling relationships with my husband and with the friends in my life, I also considered I was informing standards through their money management, communication skills, boundaries setting and overall attitude as well as their environment. I knew the influence my parents had over my behaviour and I was very intentional as to what I wanted to model for Michael and the influence I had hoped to have. Positive role modelling was a guiding principle in my parenting and in everything I did.

How we treat others and are treated by others will largely impact and likely determine who our children will choose to share their lives with. How parents act toward each other will be the template for what our children will and will not accept in their own relationships. Modelling respect and loving relationships in a peaceful environment was one of the greatest gifts I gave to Michael as well as to myself.

Michael was surrounded by positivity, security, confidence and unconditional love, although lacking much of those feelings within myself. Despite my internal struggles I modelled effectively. I took the job seriously, albeit too seriously at times. I was uptight. I still am uptight. Being uptight is what it took for me to be effective.

I remember learning, *"Your kids will do what they see, not what you say."* That was a scary concept to me. I was a smoker until Michael was age ten. What I said was much healthier than what I did.

Example is everything.

We teach our children what is *"normal"* by the example we set and the standards we uphold. Our example establishes their normal; as is the case with door slamming, eye rolling, gossiping and bitterness. I would not have it.

Mutual respect was of the utmost importance to me; I ensured I gave it, so I was also in a position to expect it. If I slammed doors, Michael would grow to believe slamming doors was acceptable. If I did drugs at the kitchen table or had the language of a foul sailor, Michael would believe those things also to be normal. These patterns I was intent on breaking.

Example is deep.

From the simple things such as how we snack, to the not-so simple things such as how we act, what we show our kids becomes how they live and what to expect out of life. How we treat our children, or our partner, is how we can expect our children to treat others. If my standards were low in the home, I knew Michael's standards for life would be low as well. It is a great deal of pressure to hold high standards, particularly when you were raised with a lower set yourself.

I wanted better for Michael.

Increasing standards is worth the effort. Even if you can't quite reach the finer things, or find the ideal relationship, at a minimum talk to your children about what's available. Teach them about loving relationships and the meaning of respect. Teach them about fine dining, world travel and extra-large, fluffy bath towels, even if you can't afford to demonstrate it. Talk to them about what you value in a relationship, what makes them healthy or toxic. If you haven't found all you hope to convey, tell them it exists. Encourage your kids to work toward their own ideal and to think big. Teach them about love, respect and kindness and most importantly, show them.

I did my best to set a flawless example despite the absence of positive role models and respectful relationships for the first part of my life. In Michael's presence I didn't curse, scream, argue, gossip, gamble or use substances. It took great restraint as I wanted to do many of those things, a lot. I didn't even shake the salt and certainly didn't slam doors. Big Mike and I respected each other. We demonstrated love, displayed affection and modelled healthy communication.

It may seem like a lot, a little over the top. It was a very tall order; some might refer to it as over correcting. I would. If I wanted Michael to have peaceful and healthy relationships, I had to first establish them. This worked!

Today Michael's relationships have surpassed anything I could have imagined. He enjoys a loving partnership and dozens of healthy friendships. His life is full of love, open communication, mutual respect and peace. I broke my patterns and in doing so I broke the cycle.

Thanks, Ron, for your thoughts, attention to parenting, your students and your relationships. Based on Michael's opinion of you, your efforts have been far-reaching and have not gone unnoticed. He always knows good people when he sees them, and he never forgets them.

#37 Stephen O. – The Day-to-Day

Stephen is Dad to my second favourite teen, second only to Michael, a sweet boy named Lucas (*June 26, 1991 – April 8, 2012*). Lucas was a best friend to my son Michael. He had a twinkle in his eye, a spring in his step and always a minute or two for "*Michael's Mom*," and I enjoyed each minute we shared.

I was very happy Stephen was willing to participate in this project. I knew his doing so would allow me to think and write about his wonderful and unforgettable son. In some small way Lucas's memory can live in my writing along with the space I hold for him in my heart.

Stephen acknowledged both sides of parenting. He identified the uniqueness in each family as he mentioned the struggles in his own. In navigating life through separation, divorce, co-parenting and single parenting, Stephen recalls the magic in the day-to-day. He summarizes, "*Getting meals, making lunches, day cares, homework and going to work myself, it wasn't easy, but they were the best years of my life.*"

It was great learning more about Stephen's parenting philosophies and practices. It was clear to see he and his son Lucas shared values of hard work and enjoyed building skills. It's understandable he and Michael were friends, as Stephen and I held a lot of similar parenting values.

1. Compliment work rather than give negative comments. Let them know you're proud of them when appropriate.
2. Get them involved in activities. Interacting with other kids makes them want, encourages them to be better on their own level and creates a sense of pride.
3. Teach the value of money. Give some allowance for delegated chores. Only when they earn their first paycheque will they see the value of a dollar. It's also important not to give your kids everything or they'll lack ambition. Keep them needy so they must make things happen for themselves.
4. Get them involved in their own lives. Help them to handle the day-to-day. If the dentist calls with a reminder, get the child to call back to

verify. Doing these things will help to get rid of shyness and create confidence. Let them know they are in control of their lives.

5. Best way to teach is by example. Practice what you preach. Parents need to agree on kids' issues. This can be difficult at times. The last thing parents want to do is argue in front of the kids. Rules are rules.

6. Try to not get into arguments with the kids. When I asked my Dad for something if he said, "*No,*" I would ask why. He wouldn't respond. He knew if he gave me a reason, I would just shoot a hole in it, leading to a heated argument, the answer would have still been no.

7. Have fun with your kids while they're young. You only get one shot. They're a blank piece of paper and you get a chance to teach and shape them. Have family activities, games inside and outside, (card games, board games). Unfortunately, cell phones, TV, computers, video games are limiting family time. It's important to build in family activities and outings.

8. Being a parent can be the most difficult but rewarding experience in your life.

9. Parenting in a split family is hard. The kids see the way the parents treat each other and that can be the biggest factor in how they will treat their partner.

10. Don't place too much value on material things and money. You can't buy respect or a good relationship — that's earned. With families getting smaller, it maybe a little easier to spoil children, don't! If they have everything they want they'll have no desire to earn and achieve.

Stephen encourages working as team when parenting. In his fourth tip he states, "*Get them involved in their own lives. Help them to handle the day-to-day. If the dentist calls to remind of an appointment, get the child to call back to verify. Doing these things will help to get rid of shyness and creates confidence. Let them know they are in control of their lives.*"

Reading this tip brought to mind a number of scenes in own my parenting. I also worked to ensure Michael was involved in his own life. I knew it was important he learn the skills required to manage his own affairs. Independence was always the goal.

The first scene I recall, I was assisting Michael in ordering from the Sears Catalogue (such a dated reference). He was about five. I vividly remember this little boy holding the receiver (also a dated reference); it was bigger than his head. I coached him through the script, feeding him each sentence line by line. He ended that call and said, "*Mom I was too young to do all that.*" He was right. I started some of these things a little too early.

The second scene, I remember sending Michael to the register to pay for an item. I knew I didn't factor in tax. I allowed him to check-out although he was short on cash. My Mom was pissed! She happened to be there and was not pleased witnessing this teachable moment. She felt he was too young. She was right. I again started too early.

Next scene, I remember bringing a concern to Michael and asking his opinion. He was six years old. He said, *"Mom, that's too big a decision for a kid."* He was right. I replied, *"You're right, but it's too big for me to make without your opinion."* He agreed, gave it a great deal of thought and then gave me his response.

Admittedly, I was too early with much of my teachings. I was in an unnecessary rush with a false sense of urgency. That said, I still think it's important to start early, really early.

Parents need to balance the likelihood of success with ensuring that they are not setting their kids up for failure. Children still need to be prepared for challenges. The guidance, planning, scripting, coaching, line-feeding, support and debrief should all be a part of the process. We should be working to build skills and develop them further at every opportunity. Our window of influence is small, tiny.

Making and confirming appointments is a great place to start. Michael gained confidence with each call and every decision. He witnessed his own comfort level grow as his abilities improved. He was always so proud to handle his own business. By age ten, Michael was meeting with the bank and the doctor independently. He managed his homework, responsibilities and his chores. Michael had his life in order in his early teens. He rarely needed any interruptions from us.

Maybe I started a little early or, maybe not. Fortunately, we both found independence in the nick of time, albeit a little ahead of schedule, even considering my tight timelines.

Thanks, Stephen, for your participation. Know Lucas will always be lovingly remembered in our family, and by all who knew him.

Much love.

#38 Billy – Read the Signs

Billy is a much loved and soft-hearted Dad. He adores everything about being a Father and has a special appreciation for all the women in his life.

Four of the Moms in Billy's life participated in the development of *100 Moms 1000 Tips 1 Million Reasons.* In 100 Moms Billy's wife, two sisters-in-law and his mother-in-law shared their parenting tips (*Moms #37, 38, 39, sand 40*). I'm happy Billy's agreed to join them and generations to come will benefit from their shared wisdom.

This Dad comes from a large and connected family, the most adored of which is his own Mom. Billy said his Mom is the most influential person in his life, forever adored.

1. Always listen to your mother.
2. It won't get done unless you do it yourself.
3. Teachers are like mothers doing their best to teach you everything.
4. Never take without giving back.
5. Always have a smile on your face.
6. Anything you want in life can easily be earned.
7. Never look down on anyone.
8. Treat everyone the way you want them to treat you.
9. Never pass a sign without reading it.
10. It's really hard when you can't help your kids.

Billy shares the wisdom with Dads that he has also ingrained in his children. Now that he's a proud Grandpa, there's no doubt he will be modelling and teaching his grandchildren each tip he's shared.

When I read Billy's ninth tip "*never pass a sign without reading it,*" it really struck me that I rarely read signs. It's so important to read signs, now that I think about it.

With a career as a trucker, it makes good sense that Billy learned the importance of signs. I think that's an important point for me to learn, but even more important to teach it to our children. It may sound funny but my life is a little easier after learning this tip, navigating through airports is a lot easier. Signs come in many forms when related to parenting. Not only is it important to read road signs and airport signs, reading signs is worth considering in all areas of life.

If your baby has a red cheek, pulls on his ear, rips at his diaper — all signs. If your partner is cranky, if you smell smoke, if the roof leaks, more signs.

Having worked in the trucking industry I assume Billy meant it literally, "*Never pass a sign without reading it.*" Initially, I took it literally. I recognized how many things I complicated by not reading sings. I became more aware of how many signs there are to read and the great information on them. I know it sounds funny.

In a more careful review of Billy's tips I considered interpersonal signs, the signs we consciously or sub-consciously give about our wellbeing, our health or even our happiness. All signs are worth a moment, a read.

At home it's a good practice to not only read signs but to also question them. Is your ear sore? Are you upset? Can I help? You seem off? With deeper consideration I loved Billy's tip even more. In fact, the Moms in his life also suggested reading signs and questioning signs.

I'm going to pay closer attention to the signs I may have been overlooking, both at home and in the airport. I'm also going to make sure I teach our little grandson to read signs, too.

Thanks Billy! I appreciate the '*sign*.'

#39 Dunovan – The Forgotten Lunch

Dunovan is the Dad to one teen boy. He loves watching him grow into a man and all the specialness of what that means. He carries all the weight of his responsibilities, knowing that his decisions will impact his son in both positive and negative ways. He values the opportunity to influence his future and is aware that every choice he makes will be doing exactly that.

His wish for his son is health, wealth and happiness. Dunovan hopes his boy will enjoy a lifetime of good challenges and continued personal growth.

He wants the best people and the most positive influences in his son's life. In his case, he found those folks in his best friend's family. He realizes how great people become unforgettable. This family made a strong imprint in his life and who he is today. He is hopeful his son will also share his world with unforgettable and encouraging people.

Dunovan's best advice:

1. Let them fail, ask them to try again and tell them you are proud of them for every try.
2. Make certain they see by example how to treat people respectfully, during happy times and in the heat of the moment.
3. Get a rescue animal and teach your kids how to properly care for living things.
4. Make them carry their own bag for sports, books, groceries or whatever.

5. Give them responsibility, with greater responsibility comes greater privilege.
6. Pay close attention to their favourite people. That is who they want to become.
7. Make sure they know how to ask for help when they need it, but only when they need.
8. Make no excuses for their actions, let them own what they do, and suffer the consequences or reap the benefits.
9. Left their lunch or book bag at home? Leave it there, they won't forget it too often afterward.
10. Teach them how to make a budget, no matter how small.
11. Hug them for as long as they like, you will miss it when they stop.
12. Teach them to do their own laundry.
13. Help them get ready for job applications and interviews.
14. Teach them how to drive "*stick*," change a tire and fix a wiper.
15. Always ask what they did during the day and make sure you are listening.
16. Teach them that privacy and trust at home is earned, especially on their social media devices.
17. Have traditions they love more than you do, one day it will be the other way around.
18. Constructive criticism is necessary but never after praise.
19. A Father cannot be a friend to his children. Save that for adulthood.
20. Teach them to be on time and do it by example.

What a man these tips would make!

I've practiced much of Dunovan's advice and I can attest to the fact that a beautiful man did result. We have a lot in common regarding the pressure we felt and the pressure we applied.

Many of Dunovan's tips stood out for me. I see a predominant theme of responsibility, which was also our predominant theme. I appreciate the practical skills that he's promoting, and I encourage the same. Increasing privileges with responsibility, accountability, financial management, laundry, car maintenance and his thoughts on privacy, trust, criticisms and even job searching — all topics I worked to cover and did cover before Michael's sixteenth birthday. I started early, very early.

Dunovan's ninth tip, "*Left their lunch or book bag at home? Leave it there, they won't forget it too often afterward,*" reminded me of a specific incident from Michael's elementary school days. It was a very hard parenting decision. I was judged harshly for my decision leaving me full of self-doubt. To this day, I feel a little shame to relive it.

Michael called from school having forgotten his lunch. My boss was in the office, I worked close to home and close to school. I decided to leave my little boy hungry at school and she questioned my ability as a Mom, directly. My boss stated she couldn't believe I would do that. She highlighted it would take me five minutes and she felt I was making a terrible decision. I was confident it was the right decision, but I felt terrible about making it. Michael was quite surprised, too.

I can't believe I did it. I can see how someone would argue otherwise when witnessing it in real time.

What I can say is I always made decisions based on the long run. I was on a fast track to Michael's independence and my own. I wanted him to learn a lot and quickly. Selfishly speaking, I knew the more he learned, the more responsible he was, the less work I would have to do.

Truly still, twenty years later, it gives me butterflies to think of Michael sitting in school with no money and no lunch. Although my outcomes indicated he survived, still loves me and did achieve responsibility and unmatched independence, I acknowledge it wasn't at all easy, but it was right. I think. I knew I was raising an adult, not just parenting a child. It's clear Dunovan is playing the long game as well.

I must say, I never received another call about a forgotten lunch. Maybe there were others; however, I didn't hear about them. I will also add, my boss, years later, recalled that day. She approached me at a book signing for *100 Moms 1000 Tips 1 Million Reasons* and confessed she was wrong. She recognized it was a tough decision and confided she wished she had made more of them in her own parenting.

Thanks for your contributions Dunovan. Thanks for raising a man and for making the tough decisions. I know from my experience, he will make a fine life partner and will become a strong, responsible and independent man. Your '*thank yous*' might not come from a hungry child but I promise they will come in abundance as you watch your son's transition into the big, bad world.

All the best!

#40 Marco – Give Details

Marco is an extra cool Dad with an extra cool family. We met this family at a biker rally and the first thing you learn about them is that they're cool.

His two great kids are currently launching into the adult world, with the smiles and the confidence of two much loved children. Marco has given them all the experience, knowledge and love they'll need to build a solid foundation. It's no question they'll carry his legacy of family, fun and fulfillment into the next generation.

As a motorcycle mechanic and a business owner, Marco and his wife have emphasized and modelled the importance of chasing and catching dreams. Together they have sought advice, identified passion, followed their hearts, worked hard and supported each other. Marco is hopeful his children will follow a similar path in life and they, too, will enjoy the love and happiness he and his wife share.

Marco has always valued the advice of others, especially his parents. He's hopeful his parenting tips will help others who are seeking some input.

1. Give your kids respect and time to explain, they will do the same for you.
2. View them as ten percent children and ninety percent friend.
3. If you don't want your kids to do something, explain to them in detail why.
4. Take one day out of your weekend to spend time, do activities, make memories with your kids and start doing so at a young age.
5. When your children are young avoid using babysitters unless necessary. Bring them along, that creates stronger bonds between all family members.
6. Put yourself in their place before giving out a judgment.
7. It is best that parents work as a team and agree on decisions, so the kids know exactly where they stand.
8. Always enjoy time spent with your kids, playing outside, game nights, movie night, joyrides, etc.
9. Try to always be positive in life and your children will be, too.
10. It's hard to choose between what your children want and what they need. It's important to know the difference.

Having seen Marco with his kids I'm confident his tips will serve any Dad well. You can see the mutual love and respect shared in his family; you can almost feel it. I love when a parent believes in explaining things to their children, as Marco clearly suggests in his third tip, "*If you don't want your kids to do something, explain to them in detail why.*" I think that's the best parenting style.

The passive parent will often avoid the conversation. An aggressive parent will insist a conversation isn't required. An effective parent will make time to explain the "*details.*" I love that approach. In my upbringing I did not get any explanations. As an adult I didn't feel deserving of an explanation. I was even afraid to ask for one. It took a long time to realize I was entitled to an explanation.

Fortunately for Marco's kids, they'll never have that battle. Explaining to children will save a lot of confusion and self-doubt in their childhood and as adults. I'm so happy for anyone who is spared that anxiety or consistent feeling of apprehension.

I, too, believed in explaining. I'm proud to say, Michael's environment could be understood by him; it was explained. Decisions weren't made based on a whim or on my particular mood. Decisions were made logically, considerately, respectfully and were rational. Because of those reasons I could provide details.

In a toxic environment, decisions are made arbitrarily. They lack consideration, are often self-serving and have no plausible explanation so none is given. That breeds anxiety and uncertainty. It damages the self-worth of a child and has long lasting effects.

When you make decisions with your children's' best interest in mind, details are readily available and happily shared. That said, they are not always negotiable. Non-negotiables can also be explained although may not always be understood. In the end, there may not be an agreement or an understanding; however, I believe there can be respect. I could respectfully make a final decision, explain the reasons why and end the conversation. I did not mind giving the details as to why things were happening.

Explaining is not a waste of time; it's an act of love.

Thanks for explaining, Marco and for all the love. I could feel the love and respect all the way across the wharf at the rally.

#41 Don – It's Their Life

Don is a Dad who has retired but continues to work full-time, as he closely approaches eighty years of age. His knowledge, expertise, willingness to share and collaborate inspires all who meet him.

Don, originating from the *"slums of Hamilton"* (as he put it), has enjoyed an exemplary career and a beautiful family. His children, now all in their fifties, have been a joy all his life. Don shared how he loved every aspect of parenting, all stages of development. He loved sharing a world with them and watching things unfold from their perspective.

Don attributes his successes to three key people: his Mom, his parish priest who kept him on the *"right track"* and his beloved wife of sixty years — who helped to ensure he remained on that track.

1. Do unto others what you would hope they would do unto you. This is the common moral principle for life and the best one, too.
2. Teach them to do the best they can in areas of life — activities, sports, school, community, and work.
3. Ensure they always remember the importance of family, friends and a positive social support.
4. Listen to your children and do things with them. Be a mentor and a parent.
5. Be careful in recommending life decisions for your adult children. Focus on discussing options, rather than pushing your preferences.
6. Adapt to their own life changes, in age and other respects.
7. Tell them you care and love them. Back up your words with kindness and an interest in what they are doing.
8. Don't be afraid to show them your own vulnerabilities. Remember, you are not without fears and worries but how you deal with them is important.
9. Show by example as well as words. Suggest guiding principles.
10. Life is short, so, at different stages, think about what means the most to you and is consistent with your values. Follow that path.

Don's tip to the empty-nesters, *"Be careful in recommending life decisions for your adult children. Focus on discussing options, rather than pushing your preferences. Adapt to their own life changes, in age and other respects."* In sharing his dream for his family Don said, *"I hope they maintain closeness even when distance is a factor."* This dream, and Don's fifth and sixth tips, really resonated with me as I continue to accept my role with an adult child, and an empty nest.

As Don suggests, I try to be careful with recommendations, as well as adapting my expectations to the many new obligations and interests in Michael's ever-evolving life. I appreciate he is running his life and I don't want to be a competing priority. I want to be sure Michael has the space to spread his wings and grows in a way that best suits him.

Most of my friends do not yet have adult children. Hearing from parents such as Don, who have been through this phase, has been a great help in my transition. A non-parenting parent is a different role, with different challenges.

Michael did begin preparing me early on with his steadfast perspectives and solid logic. I could quickly see his decisions were sound, even when I was in compete opposition. Acceptance was difficult, although the only option.

I realize our different opinions are healthy and positive, although, an unexpected outcome in raising a critical thinker. I didn't want to raise a mini-me, but sometimes a little agreement would be nice. I intended to raise Michael in an opposite manner from how I was raised, I sought opposite results. Given I've obtained my goal, it doesn't make sense I would struggle when our opinions are opposite, yet I do. Initially, and to this day, I never like when Michael disagrees with me. I will admit, ninety percent of the times I understand and am proud of his logic, consideration and his final decision. The remaining ten percent, well, it doesn't matter. My disagreement or agreement is irrelevant.

One of my many parenting goals was to raise a solid and sound decision maker. Goal accomplished!

I'm honoured to have Don's messages, and I'll take each tip under advisement. I also share Don's dream that no matter where we land, I share his hope we, too, will always *maintain closeness.*

Thanks Don!

#42 Jimmy – A Kid's Journal

Jimmy his heading into the teen years with his daughter and son. He loves learning and teaching, but his favourite thing is parenting which allows him to do a lot of both. Personally, professional and parentally Jimmy is deliberate about learning more, advancing his skills and sharing what he's learned.

He continues to enjoy all things parenting, from the memories to the yet-to-come. This Dad appreciates success, failures, laughter and tears. He loves to sing, dance and even just sit around with his family. Jimmy is a master at finding teachable moments and a life learner when it comes to patience.

With some great mentors in his life, he recognizes the value of those influences. Jimmy appreciates what he's learned from others and is willing, and happy, to 'pay it forward.' It's no question, with his efforts, the journey will be as wonderful as the destination.

1. Don't just say you love your wife, show your kids that love. This is something that I am not excellent at doing but am improving at.
2. Work out ways to communicate with your kids with signs and signals. I do this a lot with my son when coaching him in hockey. It allows

him to get advice and feedback without feeling like he is being singled out in front of others.

3. Every day when my kids get home from school, they have some free time to unwind. When I get home from work, I ask them how their day was. I do this every day. If they say a one-word answer like *"Good,"* I ask follow up questions like, *"What was good about it?"* and *"Who did you spend time with today?"* Sometimes I get some good updates on their day and what they are working on. Regardless of their responses, they know I care about how their day was.

4. Play backyard sports and activities with your kids. They can play the sport with made-up rules or without any. Having this time with my kids lets me get away from the everyday stresses of life, and almost always provides a good laugh for me and for them.

5. Every night at bedtime I tell my kids that I love them, every night.

6. Both my son and my daughter have small booklets that they write in at bedtime, if something is bothering them. They write in it and leave it on either side of our bed. They can write out their worries, concerns, or questions without having to ask us face to face. Whether it is embarrassing or maybe they just didn't think of it sooner, they get a chance to communicate it to us. They write out their thoughts or questions and end with *"Write me back."* This started with my wife and my daughter then spread to my son and wife, finally to me. I can't tell you how happy I was to be included in these writings. Sometimes it's just easier to write to someone than it is to say to them in person, and I feel like it provides another way for us to stay connected.

I love Jimmy's focus and attention to communication. In his tips he highlights everything from communicating love to concern. He is deliberate in providing various communications methods and does his part to check in and encourage it be ongoing.

Having grown up in a home where communication was discouraged, it warms my heart to consider a childhood where communication is taught, welcomed and even encouraged. What a great foundation this will provide for future relationships. It's great to see the step-by-step process Jimmy shares in his sixth tip. I had never considered this method in my own parenting but think it is genius.

I recall learning first about alternative communication in *100 Moms 1000 Tips 1 Million Reasons*, (*Mom #45*):

"I give my kids options for communication. If you don't feel comfortable telling me what's bothering you in words, how about an email, a text, or a journal we can write in back and forth? If you do go with the journal, that's the only place you can talk about what's in it unless you have the child's permission to speak about it outside of that. When a journal entry is

the preferred method, I've never had an instance where she hasn't come to me in the end to chat in person. I always felt like I'd rather have the information in some way, rather than to not have it because she didn't feel brave enough to come to me with it."

Jimmy and his wife have implemented a soft, respectful and effective method of communication that works well for everyone. Not only will this method provide an alternative to dealing with tough stuff or a forgotten highlight, it provides a parent time for consideration and consults before addressing matters.

There are so many levels of learning involved. The most compelling is Jimmy's mention of enhanced involvement. "*I can't tell you how happy I was to be included in these writings.*" It's inclusive, time sensitive, respectful, thoughtful, kind, caring and even more: It's beautiful.

I appreciate these parents sharing this personal outlet of their practice. I hope the idea reaches parents everywhere. It really is a win-win, unless a mean big sister finds it. I absolutely love this approach.

Thanks Jimmy. I'm so happy to be learning from you, yet again.

#43 Chris R. – Just Chat

Chris is not only a proud Dad, he's also a self-described "*Household Goofball.*" He loves the name Dad and the depth of love that comes with the title. With one young son, Chris is enjoying both the quite times and the incessant chatter.

Chris confesses that when struck by the intense responsibility of parenting, the awareness can be a bit overwhelming; however, with the guidance and support of his "*amazing wife*" he has no question he can handle the job. Laughter and learning are at the core of his parenting values.

1.   Not everything out of your mouth must be some momentous or pontificating life lesson. More can be learned and shared between both you and your child in a casual conversation.
2.   I have always found the greatest heartfelt conversations happen with my son during nature walks. Hiking, meandering, through the

outdoors always seems to provide an open cathedral for soulful discourse.

3. Shut up and listen. Just… listen (see note #1).

4. Pick your battles. There will be many. I try to ask myself: Is this worth the freak out I'm about to have? Normally not. Breathe and move on.

5. Laugh. If you can consistently make your child blow milk out their nose from laughing too hard, you're doing okay.

6. Soooo many questions. Those big LIFE questions and little ones too are plentiful. A child will make you review your own perceptions. The bigger questions give you an opportunity to reanalyze your own philosophies. Remember, your child will get most of his early start on prejudices from you. You can influence everything from their enjoyment of broccoli to their thoughts about people regarding colour, race, religion, creed or orientation. It is up to you to share with your child the awesome wonder of our diverse world. If you aren't careful, you may burden them with your own personal blinders.

7. Lead by example. They will mirror everything you do and say and make no mistake, they hear everything.

8. My son was very colicky and cried often as a baby. Earplugs can be inessential tool to have in your My-Child-is-Actually-a-Howling-Banshee-from-Hell coping arsenal.

9. Power naps rock! When baby naps, you should nap. The house does not have to be spotless. Your sleep-sated sanity is more important.

10. Parental leave should be mandatory. If you can get it, take it. I was fortunate enough to be able to take some parental leave when my son was born. When my partner was on maternity leave, I would come home every day to discover my lovely wife frazzled and bleary eyed. I would ask myself (inside voice): How is this possible? All she has to do is kick back and watch the baby. How hard can that be? Isn't she on, like, a vacation? My turn at parental leave quickly dispelled this myth. It is a 24/7 vigilance gig! It was one of the hardest but most rewarding things I have ever done in my life.

11. For the first two years of your child's life you are basically on suicide watch. All children seem to have the uncanny knack of being able to recon any room and find something to harm themselves with, from gleefully hurling themselves down flights of stairs to sticking a key you gave them into handy toddler-height electrical outlet.

Chris highlights, "*Not everything out of your mouth must be some momentous or a pontificating life lesson. More can be learned and shared between both you and your child in a casual conversation.*" This tip sure did bring me back to the early stages.

From choking hazards to nature hikes, there is so much to cover. It was interesting to reflect on his cautions regarding the intensity in parenting, accompanied by encouraging simplicity. I haven't mastered this balance, even after almost thirty years.

I appreciate his mention of casual conversation. I've come to recognize it's not something I'm generally good at. Particularly in my parenting days, I looked at my role to be primarily teaching and sustaining life. Maybe casual was not within my reach or had never been suggested. I love the suggestion.

I recall seeking teachable moments in all activities, from morning routines straight through to bedtime rituals. I was attempting to cover all topics and expose Michael to everything within my reach. I rushed to the playground to ensure I could check it off my list. I carried him to the top of a tree because I had never climbed one myself. I assigned meaning to each interaction. Everything was purposeful.

I asked Michael about his day primarily because I was seeking to teach him about daily management. I wanted to assist him with problem solving rather than celebrate the happenings.

In my case, my own childhood was bleak; I was ensuring Michael's memories would be plentiful and vibrant. I rarely sat quietly. I rarely felt calmness. I did accomplish my goal of providing Michael a rich and memorable childhood; however, in hindsight, I recognize I maybe didn't have to be constantly seeking, doing or pontificating.

Now my little boy is a grown man, with a family of his own. I must admit, I still seek to teach and still pontificate. Often time a casual conversation leaves me just wanting more, or believing Michael wanted more.

Forever learning, I will take Chris' first tip under advisement. I do believe, as he states, "*More can be learned and shared between both you and your child in a casual conversation.*" I really didn't think of things in that way. Thanks Chris. I will work more to appreciate the casual time.

#44 Darren B. – Your Friends

Darren is a friend of mine and a Dad I've come to know and admire. He's a proud Newfoundlander and a world traveller. Now enjoying his three adult children, he takes a special pride in seeing where he and his own parents have influenced their life and their personalities.

Although his children are now in their twenties, Darren continues to worry about their safety and well-being. He shares, worry is the only negative thing about parenting. Darren adds that he realizes, as a Dad, worry is completely unavoidable and also what makes you special.

If Darren had a genie's lamp his three wishes for his children would be that they are happy, honest and kind. His tips serve to advise other Dads, as well as his children, on achieving happiness and success for themselves. Darren lives all he has learned and has found the road to happiness though a deliberate attempt to follow and share his principles.

Darren's top 10:

1. Find your own happiness; never depend on others for it.
2. Find the compromise in yourself and look for it in others.
3. Choose your attitude. You have the power to decide your attitude and this will influence how you are received by others.
4. Joke and laugh at yourself with others; laughter opens many doors and breaks through walls.
5. Be honest, you'll sleep better. Most importantly, honesty will give you an iron clad position with friends and into the workplace.
6. Be yourself, then you will find friends who genuinely like you.
7. Own your mistakes, say you're sorry. Don't dwell!
8. Best friends are the best. Find a few good friends and keep them.
9. Learn every day. Learning will keep you current and help to grow your mind. If you have knowledge you can make better decisions.
10. Watch your pennies (nickels now). Bank debt is a vicious cycle.

Darren's eighth tip about best friends reminded me of a quote attributed to John Rohn, "*You are the average of the five people you spend the most time with.*" In my journey I have come to learn, peers are key. I'm happy to have found a friend such as Darren along the way.

Finding, as Darren mentions "*a few good friends*" was one of my most challenging endeavours. In my early days, days of limited coping skills, my peer group was not strong. In fact, it was damaging. In retrospect it matched my decision-making ability, and sadly my family dynamics.

In order to be the parent I wanted to be, changing my peer group was crucial. At the time many encouraged I let go of my "*friends.*" That advice seemed unfair and the task seemed impossible. I argued and resisted. I felt judged and misunderstood. It was a tough time.

My Mom, and my therapist, insisted it had to be done. I insisted they didn't understand. They understood, they understood perfectly. Of course, it had to happen. I'm so fortunate they didn't give up and am also fortunate they not only told me to, they showed me how.

The first thing I did was quit drinking. After that, letting go got a lot easier. After that, most of my "*friends*" let go of me. I definitely don't want to make that step sound easy; it wasn't. It took frequent counselling and years of it. Which brought me to the next step, healing the past.

From there, I went to school, to church and to the library. I took advantage of all available personal development opportunities, also not easy. I showed up in every way, for everything. I put myself aside and did what was right for Michael at every juncture, also not easy. I remained largely uncomfortable. I smiled when I was angry. I acted strong when I was weak. I demonstrated confidence when I was petrified. I asked for help when I wanted to be alone. I talked to others when I hated everyone. I pushed through loud and nasty voices and let go of loud and nasty people.

It took all of that and more to let go of old "*friends*." I can confidently report, it was worth the effort, the valiant effort! After a few missteps combined with years of personal development and therapeutic interventions, my past is merely a piece of my story. Those "*friends*" are long since gone and those "*friendships*" are far better understood.

The "*average*" of my top five back then does not compare to my "*average*" today. It's not that anyone is better; it is that everyone is healthier. As a result of these early yet difficult changes, I make healthier choices, my son was provided a healthier foundation and in turn he, too, makes healthier choices. This could not have happened had I remained in that peer group.

Without completely abandoning the life I once held so tightly, I could never be the woman or the Mother I am today. My son could never be the man he is. Our lives, well… I can't even imagine. Trying to do so would be wasted time and painful speculation.

My top five today are positive and progressive, people such as Darren. They are well-wishers. They are happy, content and accomplished. They love me and I love them. They add to my life, not deplete or derail it.

It is true, a strong peer group makes all the difference.

Thanks for the reminder, Darren. I'm happy all the efforts connected our worlds.

#45 Miller – Swearing

Miller is husband to Cathy (*100 Moms, Moms #45*). Together, in retirement, they enjoy every minute with their beautiful family. They have raised a soldier, a police officer and a doctor, three men now raising their own children. He was an ever-present Dad and loved showing the boys all things boyish and beyond. They played together and learned together.

Having come from a great family himself, Miller was sure to instill strong family values in his children. His wish is they continue to live a healthy and happy life enjoying all the same things with their own children.

I'm happy this team decided to share a piece of their journey. They are one of only eleven couples to do so. Now their next generation can have meaningful bookends.

1. Be honest with everyone, including yourself, in hopes those around you will do the same.
2. Fight for the elderly, stickup for them, treat them with respect and compassion, and try not to upset them with arguments.
3. When in conflict be positive. Be sure you know what you're talking about and try not to get too upset. Don't resort to name-calling or raising voices.
4. Money matters to the family but children shouldn't be involved with money issues. Finances should be private, between parents/partners. Don't burden children with adult issues.
5. Don't talk bad about someone, especially in front of children. If you can't talk positively, try to find a softer way of explaining the situation. For example, if a child wants to go for a ride with an irresponsible person, explain it in a way that doesn't talk bad about the person. Don't make excuses or false promises.
6. Be equal with your kids. Don't favour one over the other.
7. Play with kids and their friends. Show them you can enjoy other children and don't favour your own while doing so. Play fair with everyone with toys, sports or whatever you're doing.
8. Vacation together and make good times. Take time for family vacations and make happy memories so the children will always have something to share later on in life.
9. Don't swear in front of your kids and don't make a fool of yourself or your kids, in public.
10. Watch your drinking, especially when any children are in your presence. Avoid arguments and if drinking causes you to change your personality, don't drink. Be responsible.
11. Be a good role model, a hard worker and have good morals. Stay humble and kind.
12. Try to make a good life for your children without spoiling them or giving them a sense of entitlement.

Miller and his wife upheld strong family values in raising their boys. As seen in his tips, he was always careful to model respect and responsibility. From attention to elders to watching his language, children remained at the centre of his behaviour. Miller and I shared a similar level of awareness and restriction when it came to role modelling.

I'm happy to find another parent who believed swearing in front of the children was not OK. I know some people think it's a minor thing; I was not one of those people. I followed Miller's ninth tip, *"Don't swear in front of your kids and don't make a fool of yourself, or your kids, in public."*

There was so much we agreed on. I maintained a no swearing policy and think I was successful in not making a fool of myself or of Michael. In order to insist on not swearing, I had to ensure impeccable self-control. Being raised by a man who lovingly and not-so-lovingly, referred to me in a variety of colourful ways, one might (correctly) imagine I had grown to have quite a nasty tongue.

Early in my parenting I had picked up a theory that those with high self-confidence didn't need to swear; *likely a word of advice from someone trying to help.* With that awareness, combined with my governing principle (*be the type of person you hope your child will marry*), I was driven into a cleaner vocabulary. To truly apply this rule we, as parents, had to refrain from cursing. I am proud and amazed I was able to do this. It was hard.

Michael didn't hear me say a foul word until he turned eighteen. He later stated, *"Knowing her as an adult, I know how hard that must have been."* He doesn't know half of it. My cursing was never far below the surface. As soon as Michael was out of earshot it was as if a switch was flipped. I would go back to my *"Mother (Father)-tongue,"* in seconds.

Big Mike let loose a little sooner than I. He brought Michael to the construction site at an early age. He wasn't much to hold back; however, at home the bar was high.

I'm a strong believer that as parents, we don't have the luxury of *"losing our shit."* To me, cursing in front of your kid is *"losing your shit."* It's modelling low standards, poor behaviour and loss of control. (*But, maybe that's just me.*)

In Miller's case, it may not have been such a struggle, especially under the fine tutelage of his wife. I know she, too, has a high standard on appropriate language and conduct. With these role models their boys were off to a great start!

Thanks Mr. and Mrs. P, all my love to you both.

#46 Steve C. – Follow Your Dreams

Steve is a brand-new Dad to a little baby boy. He's adjusting to his lack of privacy while at the same time thrilled his life has been invaded in the sweetest of ways. Watching his son grow and learn is the greatest joy of his life.

Having been largely influenced by his own Dad, he looks forward to being and having a great and positive influence on his son. Steve is intending to ensure his little guy has everything he needs to follow even his wildest dreams. He was thrilled to share his recently learned tips and rushed to do so. I'm happy to have his fresh perspective to add to the mix.

1. Travel and make sure your kids know the earth is an amazing place.
2. Find and follow your passion so your kids will do the same. Begin by teaching them to learn something new every day. Teaching your children to dream will enrich their lives.
3. Remember to be kind. A little kindness will go a long way. Do something kind for someone and expect nothing in return.
4. Teach your children to give their all to any situation. Remind them you will only get what you put in. Nothing will come without action and effort.
5. I like to follow a phrase that I coined back in high school: "*Within life there are boundaries but within these boundaries there are no limits.*"
6. Teach your children to never be afraid to fail and to always push themselves. Model the same thing for them. Everything you want is on the other side of fear.
7. Make your own bucket list and do things that scare you.
8. Teach your children that full throttle will usually never solve your problems, but sometimes it will in motorsports.
9. Be open to different cultures, beliefs and ideas so your children will learn acceptance.
10. Spend time with and remember the good people in your life. Don't go backwards.

It's clear Steve values living full out and is encouraging Dads to model that for their children as well as support them in finding their own passions in life. I'm sure he and his son will have great fun as they explore the world and the many opportunities in it.

I also encourage finding and following dreams. Sadly, I learned that lesson by way of Michael's spinal cord injury and through his advice. On the day of his injury he stated, *"If there's anything you want to do you should do it, this could happen to anyone."*

Big Mike and I took that message very seriously. Following Michael's rehabilitation, we had some in-depth conversation into what dreams we had and how we could accomplish them. It was only then we started to find passions and capture our dreams. One of the first dreams I caught was swimming with dolphins. It was amazing to experience something I truly believed only happened in dreams, maybe to the most fortunate, but I surely didn't think it was something I would experience. I was even afraid to say it out loud. A light was ignited.

Since then there have been dozens of dreams captured and we've identified a few passions. I won't list all the details, but one of them was writing this book. I'm very thankful for Michael's inspiration; however, I wish it hadn't taken such an unfortunate situation to have learned the lesson. Regardless, at least we did learn and embrace it.

It's an added bonus that Michael has been able to see us follow our passions and realize our dreams. As Steve advises in his second tip, *"Find and follow your passion so your kids will do the same."* I can say for sure that's true.

Although it was Michael who taught us to chase our dreams, we have since showed him you can catch them as well. Steve further added, *"Teaching your children to dream will enrich their lives,"* which I can also validate. Finding our passions and following our dreams has enriched all of our lives.

Thanks for your thoughts Steve. I hope you and your son will always know when to go *"full throttle"* and when to just let things idle for a bit.

All the best!

#47 Chris E. – Hugs

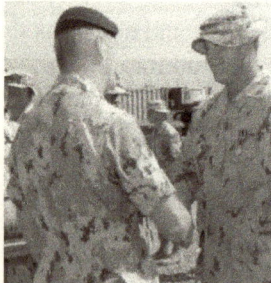

Chris is a retired member of the Canadian Armed Forces, and the husband to Jen, (*100 Moms, Mom #47*) another veteran of our Forces. This big, broad biker has had two tours in Afghanistan and takes great pride in having served and protected his country.

These days, Chris enjoys a peaceful life in a beautiful world surrounded by love and wilderness. His retirement has been well earned.

With all six children now tackling adulthood, Chris recalls parenting brought a lot of fun; however, his most recent title hits him right in the heart, "*Poppa*." Happily, Chris is lit up by a sweet little grandson. Each minute of their time together is a precious memory and not at all lost on Chris.

Chris was happy to share his wisdom:

1. Always be truthful, honest, and don't lie.
2. Take responsibility for your actions.
3. Help those in need.
4. Don't smoke.
5. Drink and indulge responsibly. Don't overdo it.
6. Call your own parents at least once a week.
7. Don't be ignorant or rude.
8. Don't swear.
9. Hug often, everyone. It will feel great and release tension.
10. If you don't do all of the above, do not expect your children will.

Chris may appear to some to be an unlikely source reminding Dads to hug but, to those lucky enough to receive one, he's the perfect hugging advocate. I'm happy he shared that hugging is also a tension reliever, loving and practical.

In the *100 Moms* edition, hugging was one of the most common tips. I was hopeful it would continue to come up with the advice from 100 Dads. Thanks Chris.

A popular tip in *100 Moms* was from Nicole, *Mom #80*, advising parents to hug when a tantrum occurs. She also felt, as Chris explained, hugging is a great tension release and a very effective parenting practice.

I thought it was worth sharing Nicole's example, her sixth tip:

"When one of my children was screaming out of control, I just wanted to scream back to try to get control. I realized very quickly this did not work so I took a different approach. What I did learn, every time I asked them if they needed a hug during this time, every one of them said yes and every time it calmed them down. We could talk out the problem. I would encourage them to figure out ways to fix it. It was a learning point for us all."

As she stated "*every time*" she asked if her children wanted a hug, they said yes. That is solid research, a tried and true method. Hugs hold a lot of meaning. In hindsight, it makes perfect sense. It is likely tantrums are a clear sign children are feeling out of control. Maybe they are hungry, tired or stressed in some way. Like grown-ups, a hug can help.

Although in hindsight it makes perfect sense, I can appreciate in practice it may be hard to identify. I was rarely in a "*hugging mood*" when Michael was unhappy. Recognizing Michael may have needed a hug, reassurance or to feel safe was not a level of awareness I had. I also didn't realize how tension reduction could have helped us both.

There are a lot of interesting facts about hugging. Hugging helps with loneliness, fear, self-esteem, tension and even blood pressure. Hugs also serve to silently say hello, welcome, goodbye, good night, good morning, I love you, I see you, you matter, I care and you're not alone. Hugs are free and accessible, although not universally enjoyed.

Sometimes I'm not much of a hugger myself, but when I see Michael it's a visceral reaction. Luckily, I have a few people in my life that activate my automatic hug reflex. I am thankful for every one I get and give. Even though Michael is an adult, we still hug hello and good-bye. Occasionally, I try to leave my lipstick kiss on his cheek. It's not so easy anymore.

I hope hugging continues for all Moms and their babies, big and small. If you're longing for a hug, giving one can feel just as good as getting one.

Thanks to Chris for his service abroad and at home. I happen to know firsthand he is a great hugger and I'll be looking forward to my next one.

#48 Tim – Do Less

Tim is Dad to two adult girls. Whenever he speaks of them, he stands a little straighter, smiles a little bigger and sparkles a little brighter. His pride and adoration for his daughters was the first thing I learned about him.

Largely influenced by his own Dad, Tim carries forth his legacy. Having great appreciation for this special bond, he describes his Dad as, "*Father, friend, teammate and role model.*" Tim works to ensure his girls find the same traits in his relationship with them.

Tim actively participates in their lives and remains closely connected. Together they've travelled, accomplished goals and celebrated many successes. Tim is a curious guy who loves exploring the world and shares the joy of adventure with his daughters as often as he can.

1. Prepare your children for life, not so much protect them from it. We all want our kids to be safe. The most important job we have as parents is to prepare children for life.
2. There will be moments of sadness. It is OK. Sadness will pass and you'll gain appreciation for the moments of happiness.
3. There will be pain, but you will heal.
4. There will be heartache. I had it too. Share with your children what helped you get through it.
5. Have integrity in everything you do and say. Do the right thing, especially when no one is watching.
6. Be fun. Have fun. People are drawn to others who are fun to talk to and be with. Have fun with the people you surround yourself.
7. Whatever it is you are doing, make a conscious decision to enjoy it, or discard it.
8. My message to my girls: I am going to do more for you by doing less for you. I will feed you. I will care for you. I will love you. I will help you with things you cannot do on your own, but I will not do for you. Independence does not evolve from dependence.
9. Don't focus on recording the moment. Or taking a pic of the moment. Be in the moment. That way, you will always remember it.

Tim shares the message to his daughters in his eighth tip, "*I am going to do more for you by doing less for you. I will feed you. I will care for you. I will love you. I will help you with things you cannot do on your own, but I will not do for you. Independence does not evolve from dependence.*" I, too, attempted to "*do less*" when parenting Michael.

I've enjoyed the conversations Tim and I have shared about our children. It's fun to hear from a Dad who is so visibly proud of his girls. It was clear to me he valued their individuality and their independence, so I'm not surprised to see those values emphasized in his tips.

I speculate Tim always knew he was raising young women, not just parenting kids. I think that is something we've shared. I also knew independence was the goal. Through my parenting, from the earliest days, I worked to support Michael where he needed it, while allowing him to do what he could, simultaneously encouraging him to reach higher than he considered.

I recall one time in particular where I launched into a lesson on independence just a bit too soon. Teaching independence was mentally challenging for me but great for Michael's overall development.

One of my first attempts was "*the milk story*." It took place when Michael was about five years old. Not unlike a couple of other instances, I was a bit too hasty and premature at rushing into a teachable moment. I vividly remember thinking this task might be a little much, but maybe not.

I sent him into the corner store to pick up a carton of milk. I coached him on where to find it, what colour to buy, how to pay, to wait for change, I covered every detail. I pulled up in front of the store and in he went; he was only five. Upon entry, I noticed the door was a little too heavy, but he made it! Then, I waited with bated breath for what seemed like hours. I remember thinking of a million horrors that could have been taking place. I considered busting in and saving him but held on tight to allow his success.

Out came my little boy. Oh my, what the clerk must have thought. Michael could barely lift that two-litre carton. Likely it was too high for him to reach and it was too heavy. Not to mention he also had to push open that heavy door. I felt like the biggest idiot. I reached for the car door to open it for him, grabbing the milk from his hand. He jumped in and he was beaming! I snicker to this day, while shamefully shaking my head. Michael knew it was a huge undertaking. What he didn't know was his Mother had ridiculous judgment.

Michael likely felt, in some subconscious or conscious way, I believed in him enough to give him this enormous task. Based on his posture, he was feeling very '*manly*.'

For me, as a Mom it was hard doing less. I did less because I knew it was best for him. Although I may have misjudged a situation or two, I did remain close by so I was on hand "*to help with things he couldn't do on his own*," as Tim further states.

Things were not always perfectly timed. I tend to think it's better to assign a larger task a little too early, although maybe not that early. Doing so will facilitate confidence within them and build their capacity. Typically, I did expect a lot from Michael, at times too much maybe.

I've heard it said if you raise the bar high, they will meet it every time. I found that to be true. I worked to create opportunities for self-mastery, some big, some small and some premature.

Another scene is etched into my mind, a unique instance from Michael's teen years following his spinal cord injury. It's a good thing I had a lot of practice as this required great strength.

Having worked very hard to support Michael with independence in the early days, when he was injured and had a significant hit to his mobility, we both had to learn the lessons all over again in our new world. Letting Michael 'stumble' and re-learn all things once mastered became a deep internal struggle for me.

Inclinations to 'help' him required much consideration. There were many things I wanted to do for him, things he could do but differently. Some things took longer or required increased effort. Time and expectations needed adjustments. Once simple tasks now were now labour intensive.

I remember, for the first time, watching Michael butter his bread with newly paralyzed fingers. Once a mindless and automatic activity was now a challenge. Watching this required my *"Meryl-Streep-Mother-Mode,"* every bit of it! I secretly watched as he handled the knife and spread the butter. I choked back my tears of torture. I remember my efforts to conceal my sadness, the fact I was watching and the fact I was breaking.

I sat on my hands, resisted the urge and mustered shards of gratitude. He was able to do the task, even though it now looked different, difficult. Upon completion, the look on Michael's face was worth my epic display of self-restraint. I could see he was proud. He looked as he did in *"the milk story."*

Michael, of course, knew buttering his bread was different. He knew better than I. It was harder, requiring concentration, patience and time. He knew it would get better, and he knew he *'owned'* that bread, that butter and knife. I remember realizing in the moment, had I taken that task away from him, he would have taken longer to realize his capability. He was now one step closer to getting better at the task. He knew he could do it, which he wouldn't have known had I jumped in.

Knowing where to help and where to wait is a delicate balance. It is vitally important we not rob our kids of self-mastery, whether they have *"special"* or *"normal"* circumstances. This practice is not for the weak of heart. It is an act of selflessness to allow our children to grow when we want to save them so we feel better.

Today Michael creates his own opportunities for self-mastery. Whether it was carrying the milk, buttering the bread or rappelling down a twenty-two-storey building, he knows when he works hard and he achieves great things. He sets his own standards and has for many years. He doesn't rely on external validation and is aware of his own worth. My restraint is his reward.

I'm excited for children raised by parents who can put their feelings and urges aside in support of the greater good. It isn't always easy to let them learn, but it is worth every painstaking minute. Maybe, that two litres of milk was the beginning of Michael's journey to self-actualization. He may have learned in that moment he could do anything!

Thanks Tim. The world is a better place when we *"do more for our children by doing less for them."*

#49 Nelson – Build Trust

Nelson is the only Dad in the entire book to be joined by two sons. Nelson, Jim and John to follow are the only trio. He is best described as both handsome and handy. He is loved by all who have been fortunate enough to have shared space with him, including my family.

Now over eighty, Nelson has three grown children each with families of their own. He has a lovely group of the most adorable and adored grandchildren and even a great-grandson. He is the quintessential Dad, big, strong, magical and unforgettable.

Nelson, a Cree descendant, comes from a large family. His Dad had thirteen siblings, his Mom ten. Strongly influenced by his Dad's talents and values, he was an exceptional tradesman and an exceptional person. He could do all things and respected all people. Nelson emanates love.

Nelson's best tips to all Dads:

1. Teach your kids to have respect for everyone regardless of age, race or ability. They should be taught to be friends and companions, not bullies.
2. Teach yourself to understand all kids have their own problems, no matter how big or small these problems may be. As a Father you should prepare them to handle whatever situations arise, and to understand and care about others.
3. Train yourself to pay attention to your kids, through the good times and the bad times. If you come home from work and you have had a bad day, you must learn to ignore the problems. Be prepared to spend time with your kids. A daily occurrence in our home: Our front entrance had a few steps going to the basement and a few to the living area. When I would walk in the door, quite often all three kids were waiting to jump into my arms from four feet above. It was up to me to catch them, sometimes all three at once. This went on for years; I eventually had to give up when they reached their twenties.
4. You must make it a point to never fight or argue with your wife in front of your children. Your family problems are not theirs. They don't understand why their parents are mad at each other. Take these problems somewhere else and try to settle them. Always remember, kids do not understand why you are fighting.
5. At an early stage, teach your children the value of good work ethics. Teach them to do household chores such as mowing the lawn, shoveling snow, cleaning their room, etc. Farm children have their duties to perform at an early stage of their life. Your children could learn some responsibilities as well.
6. Sports and other activities are important. Take the time to go with the kids to these events as much as possible. They are a great source of

entertainment and it gives you the opportunity to meet new people who may eventually become good friends or acquaintances.

7. Never be critical of their performances in any activities, whether it be for lack of effort or ability. Praise them even for small achievements.

8. Teach your children how to deal with adversity. Whether it be a breakup of a friendship or a situation where they are being shunned by the so called "*In Group*."

9. Teach your children to respect employment and their employer. They should know to give one hundred percent effort toward their work duties. Teach them that good work ethics will be the cornerstone that builds a successful career.

10. Make your home a safe place for your children. Don't have them come home and be alone with their problems. Take the time to help them to deal with the situation, no matter how big or how small. Remember, in most cases they believe you have the right way of dealing with these matters. If you sense they may be dealing with a serious problem, you should delve in and seek outside advice if necessary. You have to be aware; parents are quite often the last place children will look for help.

11. Stick by the "*wayward son*". In today's life, dealing with booze and drugs is a serious problem. Most parents do not have the ability to deal with this and they should seek outside help. In some cases, they work themselves out of this problem; in others they require professional help. There are many success stories in these situations.

12. Keep in mind, a strong and respectful family background can develop healthy caring children and will help create a happy and successful adult.

How great!

When Nelson described his children waiting for him after work, I could feel my heart swell. Oh, what a welcome he had! What a gift to his children. How life would have been different to have been received in that way by my Dad. Knowing his adult children, and the light in their eyes, I can bear witness to the long-term impact of finding time for your children even at the end of a long and tiring day.

Along similar lines, I was particularly drawn to Nelson's tenth tip advising Dads, "*Make your home a safe place for your children. Don't have them come home and be alone with their problems.*" As a little girl, I didn't feel my home was safe. It was certainly not a place to discuss my problems or any problems. Talking was not encouraged; actually, it would only elicit disdain and disapproval. I was very much alone and on my own.

Having grown up in such despair I, as Nelson did, wanted to provide a safe home, one in which Michael never felt alone. I'd like to think Michael never felt alone. I know he certainly wasn't afraid to speak!

Sometimes it is hard to know how well I really did. My only measure is my childhood home. I know I did much better, but I can never really be sure just how much better. Luckily for us Big Mike gave much love and light. We both provided Michael with a warm welcome every day, even every entrance. I think if only a warm welcome is provided, it would go a long way in building a sense of safety and security.

Nelson stated in his third tip, "*train yourself.*" I really did have to train myself to be attentive. It is up to us as parents to stay tuned in. A sad child will not always seek guidance.

At times, it may be difficult to be attentive. It was for me, as a parent.

As a child of inattentive parents, I promise if you are inattentive in your parenting it will be deeply felt by a child. It may take a lifetime for them to recover, if they ever do. Be engaged. Please do not rest on their time. It is *their* time. Be present. Please care. Stay connected. Ask questions. Love. Give. Hug. "*Train yourself.*" The return on this investment of time will be immeasurable.

Jumping into Nelson's arms was not something I experienced; but his heart and his devotion to his family, and to any child in his presence, I have had the pleasure of witnessing firsthand. His advice is tried and true.

Congratulations Nelson for always finding the time for your three little monkeys, even when you were tired and cranky. The smiles they had when they were air-born, continue on their faces to this very day.

Beautiful!

#50 Jim W. – In Sickness and in Health

Jim is half of a highly dynamic duo known as Jim & Jan. I am in awe of this team and would designate them with a PhD in Parenthood, *if I had the authority to do so.* Together they have done the unthinkable, the inconceivable and unimaginable: Jim & Jan have been successful in keeping their teenage daughters off Facebook, until graduation! I know, I know, it sounds like fiction, but it's true!

Jim is not too quick to accept full praise for his stellar outcomes. He states, "*So much of what we do as parents comes from our relationship with our own parents. I am grateful for the foundation my Mom and Dad gave to me."* Through them Jim is an amazing family leader. He's a proud *'Girl Dad."* His devotion is as great as his smile.

When I had the pleasure of spending a few days in Jim's home, my eyes were like saucers and my heart swelled. The love and respect within those walls was palpable. This family oozed togetherness, unity. It was one of the most peaceful and loving environments I have ever experienced. Jim's home was easy.

Jim & Jan poured a lot of love and consideration into their entry. In fact, they enlisted the whole family. Everyone took part. I could feel the love and energy pour out of each tip. The first four tips represent Jim's entry for 100 Dads. The remaining tips represent their collective family effort in support of Jan's entry with 100 Moms.

Given all family members contributed their time and attention, I think it's a great representation of their values which have been carefully guided by this unforgettable parental team.

Nuggets	Explanation	Example	Value
Help with their homework.	Spend time helping your kids with their homework. While it may be easy at first, the subject matter does get more difficult even to the point of testing your own ability. Learning together can be challenging but it also can be fun and if you can bring the elements into everyday life, it makes it all the more relevant for them.	If you know what your kids are learning in school you can show them real life examples, like when driving up north we would have them take note of the exposed rock face and identify the type of rock.	Practice lifelong learning. Show them that you are learning too and model being inquisitive.
Kids can't drive.	Mother's Day and other special days are not only important to the adults but they are often more eagerly anticipated and exciting for the kids. Make sure you include them in the card making /gift giving process. It empowers them and allows them to show their love too.	There is one piece of advice I give to every new father. It sounds embarrassingly obvious to me now, babies can't drive. You may be used to thinking of YOUR Mother on Mother's Day, YOU now need to think of your baby's mother too! Babies can't go get a gift on their own. (*Rookie Mistake*)	After becoming a Dad you begin to see things from a family perspective more than from the individual perspective.

Dads are not "babysitters."	Be mindful of the role you play, as interpreted by your children. They must know that you are not just filling in while Mom is out, you are just as capable and there is no such thing as *"babysitting"* your own kids. There's a lot to teach, use your time together wisely.	When you are alone with the kids, find ways to include them in things you want to do as well. I have always used sports to get the kids out, active and engaged in new things that we all enjoy doing. It can be as simple as basketball in the driveway, road hockey out front, baseball at the local diamond with a bunch of friends or teaching them to swim and skate.	Own the responsibility; it builds strong ties, independent of anyone else.
Be there "in sickness and in health."	While I am no expert in the field and I can only draw from my own personal experience, strong communication has been the key to how we have been managing our family's sudden yet ongoing health crisis.	Dealing with the ongoing stress of an unwell child is exhausting. Parents need to unite and find strength, together. Open communication, sharing raw feelings and deep concerns may take you way out of your comfort zone but will help to ensure unity on how to manage the unfamiliar in uncertain times. Regarding the unwell child, just be there and *"sit in the yuck."* Don't get stuck in the mud, gently switch gears to the positive. Encourage them to tell you how they are feeling, including their worries and expectations. Remember the other kids in the family as well. You are all affected and are 100% in this together. Seek help from supportive family, friends and engage all of the medical and alternative options that your community offers. You may be surprised at who steps up and becomes just what you need at the time. Don't think you can do it alone. It is often a	You won't always have all the answers but you will remain open, listen and do better when you know better.

		marathon, not a sprint. Communicate!	
Collective Nuggets	**Collective Explanations**	**Collective Examples**	**Family Values**
Share moments of gratitude.	Try to share moments of gratitude aloud whenever you feel them. Don't save verbalizing gratitude for the 'big' moments, do it often and for the small stuff too. It is the seemingly small things in our daily life that are to be celebrated as much as the big ones.	Be grateful (aloud) for being snuggled under a blanket watching a movie together (even if you have seen it 100 times). Highlight special moments snuggled up. Share gratitude for the kids by saying something like, *"How did we get so lucky to get the two best girls in the whole world! "*	Teaches the kids (and parents) to stop and appreciate what they have.
Seek help when you need it.	We are not subject matter experts on every issue, opportunity or circumstances that are faced along the way. Seek help when you need it, and if you are honest, you will know when the time comes for help. Help can be in the form of your doctor, teacher, trusted member of the family or friend but try to seek out someone that has a broader experience than you, for balanced advice.	Sometimes your child will be the one having issues, maybe even be the one 'causing' them. Either way we need to understand, provide some coping / problem solving techniques and give it some time to work itself out. If needed, we must engage in the most respectful way, and request help. Some things get better with time and some don't. Start with a non-judgmental attitude.	Confidence that they possess the ability to deal with their problems on their own, but they are in a safe environment and help is available if they need it.
Joke and reminisce about the past often.	We continue to quote the funnier things the kids said, or how they pronounced things when they were little in our everyday vernacular.	Sometimes when kids are small you playfully negotiate with words. We may give the food funny names or deliver via 'airplane.' In our home Soya sauce got rebranded with the name "poo-poo sauce". To this day we still say, pass the "poo-poo" please when having rice! In our house Auntie Lynne is still "AnnLynne." Have fun.	We share goofy words, phrases and traditions unique to our family. This makes us feel intentionally different, and heightens the sense of belonging with each other.
Every parent blackbird	Something, often naturally, takes over	Baby groups can be a wonderful resource to help	We already are enough just as we

thinks their baby blackbird is the blackest.	when you have children. You are certain that they are the cutest, smartest and most enchanting creature on the face of the earth. Some are much stronger in that conviction than others. Getting into a "bun fight" over whose offspring is the best at, well…anything, is not worth the emotional energy. Try to share in other's happiness (even if boastful and misguided, at times) and sit secure in the knowledge that your blackbird really is the blackest. ☺	parents to connect with others, and provide a healthy social and physical environment for children. These groups often draw from a wide range of people with a common thread (baby). With a wonderful mix of personalities the most important thing to remember is, all mama blackbirds think their baby blackbird is the blackest. At times, you just have to make some room for that.	are no need to sell it.
Help kids to learn value of money using their individual "currency" as teaching tool.	Kids have no way of really understanding the value of a dollar, unless you put it into perspective in a way that they can understand and relate to in their own world. Keep the theory of needs vs. wants top of mind when discussing the value of money over time.	Consider the "Build a Bear." They knew each bear cost about $50. Once they understand the cost, show them how that cost fits into other purchases. We used to say, "*That tank of gas cost the same as two Build a Bears,*" or "*Those groceries cost same as three Bears.*"	Things cost money. Needs and wants need to prioritized. At times, wants will be very important, but the awareness of needs and wants can be reinforced over time.
Told you so.	Many parenting books say you should never say "I told you so". I disagree. Although I don't think you should celebrate if your child fails to heed your warning and is caught in a situation. I do think that it is OK to show them you actually do know what you are talking about, a kind reminder.	Anything from wearing moccasins to school when they are calling for a snow storm, to the amount of prep time they have set aside for a test, to more important things like the choice of some friends or how to respond to certain social situations.	Enforces for the child that parents can be a helpful resource. Provide some freedom for choices, unless of course, it is a matter of safety.

The days go slow but the years go fast.	While squarely in the phase of sleep deprivation, endless feedings and diaper changes, the days can seem so long and sometimes lonely. But blink, and there are birthdays, dances, graduation and suddenly they are off to post-secondary.	The encryption on every "Welcome New Baby" card I write is, "The days go slow but the years go fast." Ask any parent whose child is celebrating a milestone, and I think that they will agree with that sentiment.	Find things to enjoy each stage, phase and age. This, too, shall pass in the large scheme of things.
Team "insert family name."	Make sure the kids know they are an invaluable member of the team, your team, "Team (_____). This team works together, plays together, laughs together and cries together. All members bring their own uniqueness, their strengths and weaknesses. All team members have to fall in line for chores, and jobs needed to keep the team/household running smoothly.	Creating a happy home can't be achieved by just one team member. It takes all members rowing in the same direction. Based on ages, assign appropriate chores (unpaid). Little kids can learn small start-up tasks (i.e. pick up toys, help clear the table, and put things away). As they grow so do their responsibilities. But don't let them get away with doing a poor job. Layout the consequences for poor performance and stick to them.	You are not alone; you are a critical part of a team…your team.
Physical touch.	Provide an overabundance of hugs and kisses. Never stop, never let it get awkward.	Kisses goodbye in the morning, kisses good night…kiss for spouse / kiss for kids and the dog too if you have one.	You are loved.
I Love You.	Say "I love you".	Never let a day go by without an "I love you."	You are loved.
Love language.	Know what each person in your family values and what makes them feel loved. For some it will be service, for some it will be gifts, others will be time spent together.	I learned more about "Love Languages" after I saw the author, Gary D Chapman, on Oprah. We all took the "Love Language Test." We discussed results and talked about practical application. One of my love languages was 'service,' which could	Show people love, in the way they need to see it. For example, if it is a friend's birthday and spending time with someone is their preference, they may not feel valued if you

119

		mean people demonstrate love by cleaning. Others prefer playing games and having, more interaction. Lesson learned: Love comes in many forms. ☺	drop a gift off at their door. Maybe drop by for tea and a chat instead.
Nobody's perfect … and that's OK.	Nobody is perfect. We all make mistakes. We all say things in the heat of the moment, when we are tired or misinformed.	Own it. Say you are sorry, you have had a chance to think about it and you could have behaved differently. You may not even reverse a decision, but you can acknowledge your delivery may not have been the most effective. This opens the door for the kids to own it when the time comes.	Nobody's perfect, but we can be imperfect together.
Parental alliance.	Mom and Dad may tease each other, joke or nitpick, but when it comes down to it the kids must know with complete clarity that their parents are on the same page. They are the co-leaders of the family.	It's not the boys against the girls, or kids against parents, even at times some temporary alliances may be formed but after the negotiation occurs, parents work it out and bring down the verdict, united.	Parents cannot be divided and conquered. They are united and have your best interest at heart in all matters.
Friends are part of the family too.	Friends are a very important part of our lives. You must know your children's friends and make them feel like part of your family, from an early age. It will help the friend feel comfortable with you and open the door for fun times shared.	Try to make friend visits special with snacks, treats and a warm welcome. Don't leave the room right away; build a relationship with them so they will feel comfortable. Some friendships will last a lifetime; you want to be a part of those memories too.	Your friend is my friend. I am interested in you and in your friends.
No question is too big or too small.	Maintaining two-way communication is key. Being open, available and someone your kids trust for the seemingly small questions helps to set you up for success with the big questions.	From *Dad, "What's your favorite colour?"* to *"Where do babies come from?"* to *life decision discussions,* be present for it all.	I am interested in you and you are worth my time.

Jim & Jan's deep dive is representative as to why their parenting techniques have been so effective. The inclusion and leadership used in collecting these tips is the same process used in their day-to-day operations. This style has guided their girls into learning and understanding all stages of their family's development.

Their efforts have produced a heart-felt, beautiful account of their best stuff. They not only provided tips, but added explanations, examples and demonstrated values. It is this type of care and attention which has resulted in their children being on side with them through the more challenging times and decisions. They are a *"team"* in every sense of the word.

Jim's comprehensive, rational and purposeful approach to parenting assured understanding within his family. They got *"buy-in!"* The girls knew exactly why things were being done and that things were being done solely for their benefit. They understood they were all on the same side. To me, this quartet encompasses all of what a family should be. Everyone mattered. Everyone was important. Everyone was special, involved and heard.

Jim's fourth tip addressed a new phase of their life, when their oldest girl became ill, *"Be there in sickness and in health."* This tip speaks to the unexpected occurrence of a significant health crisis, an experience shared by both our families. For Jim's family it was dealing with what is known as PPPD or 3PD (Persistent Postural Perceptual Dizziness). *"In sickness"* there is much to learn and many new people to meet; vocabulary changes and experts rush in. We, too, learned a great deal *"in sickness"* with our journey in the world of spinal cord injury (SCI).

Jim covered a lot of ground when expanding on this tip. He touched on stress, communication, support of others, family unity, uncertainty, feelings and finesse. It takes careful navigation and consideration in an ongoing health crisis. As Jim so profoundly noted, *"it's a marathon not a sprint."* Also mentioned is the support of the medical team, family, community, along with an ever-so-special mention of the *"other child/ren."* There is so much involved. In our case, Michael was an only child. I often thought of families with other children. I'm not sure how they did that.

Jim's mention of communication and unity are anchors that will certainly prove helpful in dealing with the most complicated matters. For us, there were two scenes, *"behind the scenes"* and *"on the scene." "Behind the scenes,"* Big Mike and I were shook. We were emotional, afraid and confused. We leaned on each other sharing our fears and our tears.

"On the scene," was different. We were unshakable! Unshakable not in a false or phony way, rather a different way. The responsibilities and requirements *"on the scene"* were different. We had to be alert, clear, strong, present and most importantly Michael-focused. We had to demonstrate positivity, strength and hope.

Our feelings came second to Michael's security and well-being. *"On the scene"* we did what was best for him, his recovery and his mental health.

"*Behind the scenes*" we did what was best for us, our recovery and our mental health. Both areas needed attention in different ways.

We worked to protect Michael's rehabilitation, surroundings and his goals. In doing so we needed to attend to all areas: Michael's well-being, the family unit and the parental unit. At times I wondered about single-parents and families with multiple children, in terms of a medical crisis. I felt so fortunate to have a partner and the ability to dedicate such focus on Michael's recovery. We had good employers and secure employment. We had resources. We had a solid inner circle of family, friends and colleagues. It took "*the village*" and "*the village*" arrived.

What is required in a health crisis could certainly be a book in itself. Priorities shift, everything shifts. Ironically, less matters while simultaneously everything matters. It was intense.

All of the questions and the answers are unique to every family, crisis and situation; however, some of the tenets identified by Jim are constant. As he states, communication, unity, consideration of others and family support are much of what is needed.

I hope that anyone managing a health crisis of their own, or with their children, will review this tip and explanation. Jim provides solid wisdom in this all too brief section on how a parent can get grounded, on what is needed and some ideas on where to find it.

Thanks to these parents and their sweet girls. This amazing work provides only a glimpse into an unforgettable family, one which I am so honoured to have met and enjoyed.

Until next time, sweet people.

#51 John W. – Accountability

John is the youngest son to Nelson, brother to Jim W. and the last of this Dad trio. He, his brother and their Dad have given their tips, and their parenting, a great deal of effort. It's been wonderful sharing space with their families over the years. I'm so proud they've joined in with their wisdom and learned lessons.

In a home bustling with teenage energy, John and his three teens work to set and accomplish goals in a meaningful way. This family is ambitious and engaged in tackling the world and their dreams.

John's dreams for his family have already been realized in their happiness and their love for travel. To date they have conquered the world of land and of sea. John has dedicated a great deal of time and resources to ensuring their lifelong vision for his family did not take a long life to achieve.

1. The most important tip I can offer is on accountability. Keeping your kids accountable for their actions, their promises and their responsibilities is key to raising responsible adults.

2. Let your kids play with knives, fire and other somewhat dangerous things. It's scary as hell to watch your kids learn to use an axe, but if they are fully aware of how dangerous it can be, and treat it with respect, they'll have another skill and another tool in their tool belt.

3. Your kids are going to have friends that are a bad influence on them. Don't get in the way. Teach your kids to make good decisions, and they will eventually gravitate to other kids that make good choices.

4. Keep your kids active. Sports are not for every kid, but physical exercise is a must. Find an activity that your kids enjoy, preferably outside, and make sure they devote time to it.

5. Tell your kids you love them every day. They already know it, but they need to hear it.

6. Take your kids out of their comfort zone from time to time. Kids need a chance to prove to themselves that they can conquer things that scare them.

7. No media during the week. We made the decision years ago that TV, iPads and technology are only made available on the weekends. This took a while to get used to, but now they don't even ask for it. I think they're proud that they don't touch the remote during the school week. It's amazing how much time kids spend outside after school. Now their challenge is finding other kids to play with.

8. Eating healthy should be a priority. This is a tough one. After years of battles our kids respect food and make good choices. It doesn't mean they are vegans, but they know that a couple of cookies are reasonable; a bag of cookies is ridiculous.

9. Give your kids chores and hold them accountable if they don't do them. Even young children, three or four years old, can clean up their room, wash a window, or feed the cat.

10. Once your kids take ownership of their chores, pay them for it. Teach them about money, and to respect it. Kids will take better care of their belongings if they have to pay for it if it gets broken.

In John's first tip he mentioned accountability. I love that topic! I feel it is one of the most important aspects of parenting. I was confident I had written about accountability at great length in the past. I quickly searched my previous work to review that material.

I did a word search for "*accountability*" in my 100 Moms document. I searched previous columns and blogs to no avail. I found the word only once, the word "*accountable*" just twice. I was in complete disbelief. I followed that search with two more and a quick scan.

Oh my! How, in well over one hundred thousand words, has this topic not been thoroughly and proudly covered? This is a mystery. Thankful, through John, I've been given another opportunity.

First, to credit two Moms before me, Linda and Mel, who both highlighted this area:

Linda, "*Don't let them think they are right when they are wrong, or that they do not have to be accountable for their own actions.*" Tip 1

Mel, "*Holding kids accountable early on makes the real world much easier to deal with, it will also help establish routine and healthy habits.*" Tip 4

Despite having overlooked accountability in my writing, I can say with certainty I didn't overlook it in my parenting. Like most parental messages, in order to expect accountability, I had to be accountable myself. I could not expect from Michael what I did not model. Michael knew where I was and where I would be at all times. He had advanced notice, lead time and fair preparation with most things. I was accountable to him and he was accountable to me.

One of the most vivid and difficult moments of accountability came when Michael and his little friend threw mud pies at a seniors' complex. I can't recall if Michael independently confessed or if I was notified by a third party, but I do recall feeling this instance would not go unnoticed or unresolved. I remember speaking to a representative at the complex and informing them I was aware and would be bringing Michael by for an apology. I did exactly that. This scene did not turn out as I had envisioned.

The adult he faced was, in my opinion, much too hard on Michael. I felt terrible. This man clearly lacked understanding in not only childhood development, but the intended moral.

An unintended outcome was a teachable moment for us both. As I processed the situation myself, I shared with Michael that not all individuals respond in a kind way to apologies. Regardless of how others react, it is his actions he must focus on.

This occurrence is our largest example of accountability; however, there were dozens more — small and large. Such as letting Michael not wear mittens and feel the natural consequences of that choice, not rushing his forgotten lunch to the school, and not adding extra money when allowance was poorly managed.

At times, most times, not running to Michael's rescue was the tough decision and also not popular with others — including my own Mom. It was my core belief that a little natural consequence now would protect him later and also add to my credibility.

Michael was responsible and accountable for chores, grades, finances and fun. I reminded him often he was a good decision maker and a responsible person. He was both of those things. Michael would quickly acknowledge when he had made a bad decision. In fact, at age five he put himself on "*time-out*" and notified me the next day as to what happened. Amazing! I knew in that moment my parenting and his life would be a bit smoother because of his internal self-discipline.

I believe if parents begin teaching accountability early, in small ways, we can help our children avoid major pitfalls and also develop strong critical thinking and decision-making abilities. It worked for us.

Thanks John, I'm all for accountability!

#52 Steve M. – Do Better

Steve is the Dad to four grown boys who are now entering the adult world. Together they share a love of football and of family. His love of the game, and the influence of his high school football coach, have helped him in the development of his sons and of his family values.

Through football Steve learned a lot about hard work and dedication. He has modelled the importance of teamwork as well as the joy of victory. Along with modelling high standards in sportsmanship, Steve also ensures a happy home environment. He hopes they will all carry his teachings with them as they continue to build their future.

Now enjoying retirement, Steve has time to appreciate the view resulting from his dedication and hard work. His dream for them is that they become positive role models for others while always remaining true to themselves. Undoubtedly, they have a solid foundation built on love and authenticity.

Steve's tips reflect his messages to his sons and his best advice for all Dads.

1. Make someone smile every day.
2. Always say I love you, always.
3. Make time for family. Your time on this earth is very short.
4. When you're wrong admit it. Do not make excuses, just admit it and grow from it. Remember: just because you say sorry does not mean all is forgiven; but sorry is a start.
5. Call your Mother often, not just on special occasions. It's great to see how she's doing and good for your children to see you do it.
6. If you're not happy in your relationship talk to your partner before it gets too late. We are wired differently than women and usually that's not a good thing. So, talk and figure each other out.
7. Do things for other people. Never expect anything in return. If you do get a return that's just a bonus.
8. It's OK to cry.
9. Don't try to fix all your children's problems. Making mistakes is a part of growing up.
10. Remember: when you know better, you do better.
11. When someone shows you who they are believe it, good or bad. You do not have to keep trying to figure it out if they already showed you who they are.

Steve and his four sons are avid football players and have been active in both leadership and coaching. Together they have achieved numerous awards and have been recognized academically and athletically. All that said, Steve's tips did not at all promote a sports-related focus. Instead, they offered a great deal of consideration to women, relationships and Mothers.

While this family has been on many teams and holds a deep respect for sportsmanship, it's clear the strongest and most successful team for everyone has been this Parenting Team! Steve highlights family time, maternal relationships, sharing emotions and, in closing, wisdom from Maya Angelou. His internal force and most predominant values come shining through in his tips yet may not be easily recognized by the outside world.

Steve's final two tips are teachings from the great Maya Angelou. I have also come to cherish and promote both her philosophies, "*When people show you who they are believe them the first time,*" and "*When you know better you do better.*" It's great to know that Steve has imparted these values to his son and is now sharing them with Dads everywhere.

According to Wikipedia, "*Maya Angelou is known as an American poet, singer, memoirist, and civil rights activist. She published seven autobiographies, three books of essays, several books of poetry, and is credited with a list of plays, movies, and television shows spanning over fifty years. She received dozens of awards and more than fifty honourary degrees.*" Although accomplished, it is her love of Oprah that first brought her to my attention.

Her message on "*when you know better you do better*," has provided me with a comfortable place to land when I'm feeling guilty about parenting or life choices. As with most parents there have been times of regret, wishes and what-ifs. Because of messages such as this I've realized I was doing my best, even if it sucked.

One of the phrases I thought I coined, but Google indicates it may not be original, "*Don't judge yesterday using today's standards*." In reflection, with education, resources, love and a sense of self, I would have certainly made different choices. In fairness, lacking education, resources, love and a sense of self I did what I thought was right.

Maya Angelou's quote reminds me that I did "*do better*," when I knew better. I sought education, resources, love and a sense of self. When I found any piece of any one of those things, I did choose better and did do better. I'm also reminded I have more to learn.

I continue to grow. I still hope to "*do better*." I learn new things and new ways of being which I will now share with my grandson. I hope to always "*do better*." Sometimes the knowing better can be hard, but the doing better is great.

Thanks Steve, to you and your special lady. Thanks for all your efforts in raising four great men. Your dream of their positive influences impacting others has already been realized.

I'm so excited for the glorious chapters that await.

#53 Dave T. – Love Your Wife

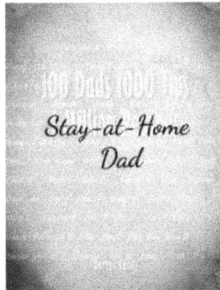

Dave is a stay-at-home Dad to a young daughter. As a part-time employee and a full-time parent, he prides himself on keeping things smooth while balancing the conflicting priorities of work and home life. There's no conflict when it comes to his top priority: his little girl.

Dave's favourite part of life is meeting his daughter at the bus stop. She comes running into his arms after a tough day at school and it is his joy to greet her. The love for his daughter has given him a deep understanding of his own Dad and of Fathers everywhere. He realizes the responsibility is great, almost as great as the reward.

Dave shares his top tips in the hopes they will someday guide his daughter in her journey and will serve to support other Dads as they move through the world of parenting.

1. Patience, this is one I wish I had more of.
2. Your time is your best currency. Kids may seem like they want everything in the toy aisle but in all reality, they just want you. If that means reading a story, sharing a break or engaging in their favourite craft, they just want your time.
3. There will be times you're exhausted, times when things are tough; stay connected, play and make time for your kids. It pays off.
4. Let them be them. It's OK to not be OK with the things they like. This can range from how they dress to the activities they choose. My daughter has an eccentric fashion sense but it's the old 'hey *at least she has clothes on.*' Same with sports, I'm a sports nut and she's not. She likes arts and crafts and I don't. Our differences are OK.
5. Love your wife! You will be their first role model and the person they look to for guidance on how to act with their spouse. If they see you love your wife and treat her with the utmost respect, then in turn they will seek that out when they start dating and looking for a mate. It may seem like they are not watching but they are.
6. Take care of you. You can't take the best care of your child if you're tired, stressed out and hungry. Make sure you get your rest, proper nutrition and take the time to deal with your everyday. Kids sense when things aren't OK and will react. This is two-fold; when you're taking good care of you they'll learn proper care as they grow.
7. Remember, being a parent is tough. It's the most difficult thing you will ever do. Know though, that no one parent is perfect. No one parenting style is the best. What works for some doesn't work for others. It's OK to feel like you're doing it all wrong; trust me, we all feel that way. Know you're doing a great job. The best thing we can do is know that if you love them, spend time with them, everything will work out.
8. Leading by example is massive. When they see you doing laundry, dishes, sweeping etc., they see what it takes to be an adult and what responsibility is. To expand on this, having them help with the chores is a great way to teach and spend some quality time.
9. Say I love you every day. To me this is huge! It's important for them to hear and know they are loved.
10. The early years go by so fast, just enjoy them. One day you will pick up and carry your child for the last time but not know that at the time. One day instead of hearing *"Dada wanna play?"* you'll hear, *"Dad where are the car keys?"* My daughter is only seven but I can already see her wanting to spend time with her friends more and more. It

won't be long before they are a bigger part of her social experience. Taking all the time I can with her is tough. At times I want to just sit alone but realize she won't be small forever.

I started thinking about Dave's tips toward the end of developing *100 Dads* and having reviewed all entries. Given that several Dads have touched on the importance of this primary relationship and of modelling respect, I'm happy to have the opportunity to expand further.

He states in his fifth tip, *"Love your wife! You will be their first role model and the person they look to for guidance on how to act with their spouse. If they see you love your wife and treat her with the utmost respect, then in turn they will seek that out when they start dating and looking for a mate. It may seem like they are not watching but they are."*

Dave does a great job in thoroughly explaining not only the relationship itself, but the modelling of partnership as well as the impact our actions will have on the choices of our children.

In my writing I have identified the parental relationship and the need to prioritize it, both in *100 Dads* and in *100 Moms*. That said, I thought I'd use this opportunity to identify the most distinct difference in Moms and Dads, and there were not many.

The most distinct difference is Dads were more likely to mention Moms than Moms to mention Dads. I feel it's worthwhile to address that difference in appreciation to the many men who have considered the value of Moms and the importance mutual respect has on our children, their future and their view of the world.

I also believe it is worthwhile to reflect on my own relationship and to ensure I am inclusive and appreciative. Maybe at times Moms, or I, can take for granted that our partners feel appreciated and valued. Maybe Moms don't feel Dads need to be told. It could be some Moms forget to acknowledge the importance of Dads; possibly some don't feel they're important at all. Moms might believe Dads already know of their value, others may minimize it or have failed to realize it.

I want to take this opportunity to emphasize the importance of Dads and to firmly state my belief in their value, their presence, their input, their teachings, their time, their love, their thoughts, their opinions, their perspective, their involvement and of course their contributions to this book, to my work and to my improved insight.

Dave's tips are a great illustration as to the value Dads add to the parenting process and their collective recognition on the value held by Moms. It's paramount we never forget, as Dave states in the second half of his message, *"If they see you love your wife and treat her with the utmost respect, then in turn they will seek that out when they start dating and looking for a mate. It may seem like they are not watching but they are."*

Witnessing love and respect in the home will ensure love and respect outside the home. A loving and respectful childhood will guarantee our children grow into loving and respectful adults. They will enjoy a world where love and respect is expected and it will be the foundation for all the generations to follow.

Thanks, Dave, for reminding all Dads to love us Moms. In reference to your first and third tips, sometimes Moms are also impatient and exhausted. I advise, love us anyway, "*it pays off.*" In addition, I promise to pay closer attention to my partner, to not take him for granted and to also not just assume he knows how much he matters.

All the best with your little girl.

#54 Jay – Snuggle

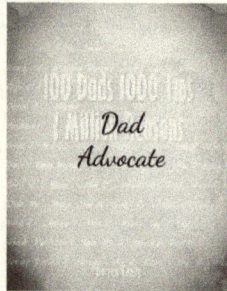

Jay is a leader in his community and among Dads. Unable to locate resources for himself after leaving an abusive relationship, he found supports for Dads and male victims were non-existent in his province. Jay became an activist.

These days, this Dad now develops programming at a local parent resource center, in the same community he lived as a young boy. A former touring musician and award-winning rapper, Jay has been using his status to reach more Fathers.

Through this work, he is the co-founder of DADS Canada, a not-for-profit group helping Dads experiencing crises. Jay is also the Nova Scotia representative for Dads Central, a network focused on promoting paternal involvement in Canada.

Currently raising three sons and a newborn daughter, Jay finds time to develop his role as an educator, a musician and remain a strong advocate. His primary focus is to be a good Father and his only concern is that his children find that to be true.

Jay's joy is watching his kids grow and develop while working to provide them with a stable environment and surround them with strong role models. He was happy to be a part of this book and quickly contributed his thoughts on parenting.

Jay's top tips are:

1. Always be patient and kind, you never know what your child is going through in their head.
2. Listen, really listen to them, and do not listen to respond.
3. Don't talk about it, be about it! They will emulate what they see more than what you tell them.
4. Affection is key. Children must feel loved along with being told.
5. If you co-parent, never speak ill of their mother in front of them.
6. Give them a *"Me - Day,"* where they pick the activity, or the food served etc., for an entire day. It helps them feel special and validated.
7. Read to your child, it helps them in so many facets of life.
8. Your children will grow up to have healthy relationships if you are in a healthy one. Lead by example.
9. Don't be afraid to act silly with your kids, or for them.
10. Cherish the stage before your infant can walk and talk, as those cuddles are the best. Once they are mobile it's a wrap!

Jay is doing a great deal for Dads and their children on a local, provincial and a federal level. It's wonderful, given all he's involved in, Jay still finds time to cuddle and to appreciate the special moments. In his final tips Jay advises all Dads, *"Cherish the stage before your infant can walk and talk, as those cuddles are the best. Once they are mobile it's a wrap!"*

I remember when Michael was a little boy, he would crawl up on the sofa with me and we would cuddle. I recall cherishing that time, in the moment. Even throughout the early years, I knew cuddles were precious and limited. I was aware cuddling would be short-lived. I attempted to be ever so present.

To my fortune and surprise, cuddles were not lost in the adolescent stage. On occasion, Michael would crawl up on the sofa with me and snuggle in. It was always such a warm and welcomed moment. I began to soak it in, deeper as the years passed. Each time I secretly wondered which snuggle would be my last. Every time I felt like the luckiest Mom in the world!

In 2008, Michael was injured in a snowboarding accident, I remember thinking my *"cuddles"* were over. I consciously reflected on those beloved moments. I was certain his physical limitations would no longer allow it, even if age was not a barrier. A transition to the sofa was now labour intensive, not to mention he was six feet in size.

I worked to accept his disability and impaired mobility would prevent those moments. I understood those days were over. I focused to appreciate having ever had cuddles. I knew, given our situation, there would be no more.

One day, as I worked to find gratitude and acceptance, to my delight, at age seventeen, Michael crawled on to the sofa with me! That scene is vivid in my mind's eye. More than ten years later I can still feel elation.

I'm glad Jay and I have cherished each and every cuddle. I will forever hold out hope that there will always be just one more. I'd encourage all parents to never give up the dream, any dream. Try to get just one more cuddle, invite it — initiate it even. Maybe your teen will surprise you, too.

You never know, it may not always be "*a wrap.*"

#55 Edson – They'll Figure It Out

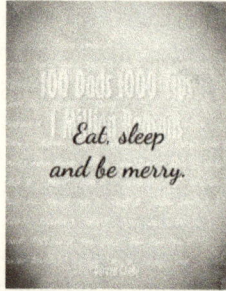

100 Dads 1000 Tips

Eat, sleep and be merry.

Edson is an excited and energetic Dad to an equally excited and energetic son. His career as a registered nurse has provided him a strong foundation in the realm of parenting and child development. Although he's not afraid of dealing with complicated medical issues, he admits sleep deprivation and mealtime almost got the best of him.

Highlighting togetherness with his "*sweet and funny son*" as his greatest joy, Edson is also quick to empathize with the challenges of the early days and the early years. He wants to remind all Dads that the times when you feel sleep will never return and mealtime will never be normal, they will pass. He confides that even though he felt those times would never end, they did.

It may not be of much comfort to know, Edson also found, those days of uncertainty are quickly replaced with new days of uncertainty. Now in the throes of the school years he's working to ensure good health, instill family values and a drive to enjoy and maintain a meaningful life.

In the meantime, this "*sweet and funny*" boy will always be the star in his home. His bright light is now dazzling the school yard and heading for a larger world. Edson is happy to share all the ways in which he hopes to keep that light beaming.

1. Food – Remember that it is your job as a parent or as part of a parental team to offer your child nutritious food, it is his or her job to eat it. Your child knows better than you how much they need.
2. Toilet training – Don't do it! Your child will figure it out between about two and three years of age no matter what you try to do to make it happen.

3. Sleep – Don't be in a rush to attain the magical goal of *"sleeping through the night"*. Your child will eventually let you sleep but on his or her schedule. The times when your sleep is interrupted will seem like a distant memory about two days after your child learns to let you sleep without interruption.
4. Reading – the more the better.
5. Sing to your child. It makes you feel good and he or she will love it.
6. If you want them to learn to ride a bike, let them on a balance bike by the time they are two or even younger. They will be riding a pedal bike the summer after they master the balance bike. Incredible!
7. Take them camping, especially with other kids. There is no better babysitter than the woods.
8. Children love the water. Get your child in the pool, the lake, the ocean as soon as you can, hours of fun.

I loved Edson's tip on toilet training. I remember I was in a big rush for some reason — likely because I couldn't afford diapers. Michael just didn't seem to get it. He obviously wasn't ready.

I called my Mom worried I was doing something wrong or something was wrong. She gave me Edson's advice, but I didn't listen. Actually, her exact words were, *"Even the dumbest people know how to use the bathroom. Don't worry, he'll learn."* He did. I must admit I do think Edson said it best, *"Your child will figure it out between about two and three years of age, no matter what you try to do to make it happen."*

Edson's advice on not rushing, and his focus on activity, also resonates with me. He provides some practical examples of loving interactions such as reading, singing, riding, camping and playing. For some parents this stuff is automatic but for those of us who had to learn the parenting tips, they are well received and, I think, manageable.

I mentioned outdoor play; play in general, was not something that came easy to me. I needed clear examples and free examples as to how I could play and what fun there was outdoors. Time spent exposing children to a healthy lifestyle and outdoor play is of such value and will give them the fondest of memories, the sweetest of childhoods.

If outdoors and healthy lifestyle is not 'your thing,' as was my case, another great benefit is the impact on bedtime. Michael slept best after outdoor play. The fresh air was always sure to provide a peaceful evening for us both.

Thanks for the reminders Edson. Although I'm no longer raising a child, I think these tips are something I still needed to hear. They serve as great advice to parents and also seniors, which is a stage I'm racing toward.

Much love on your sweet journey.

#56 David R. – Reflect with Kindness

David is a Dad to two grown and lovely young women. He's a recent Grandfather and is learning about all the love that the second generation brings. He describes this stage as "*awe-inspiring*."

I'm certain David will continue to relish in this new-found love. He not only adores this generation, but those before it as well. David identifies his Grandmother as his biggest influence and has a very honourable mention regarding his in-laws. Having lived close to his wife's parents he deeply values the support of extended family.

As a retired member of the Canadian Armed forces, a strong family network was a gift to everyone. Required to spend several months away, it was a great comfort for him to know his wife and his girls were surrounded by love.

1. Try to make good impressions with your children's friends, especially in their early teens. Welcome the chance to get to know them. A conversation, no matter how short, can sometimes end up making a lasting impression.

2. Make your home a welcoming place. Welcoming others into your home can bring a lot of joy. Invite friends. Sit with the children who visit. Getting to know them will give you good insight on the type of people to whom your children gravitate. Their friendships are like a mirror into the type of person your own child is when they are outside of your home.

3. Have home birthday parties. Parties provide a great opportunity to get to know some of the kids and their parents. Take some time to chat. You don't have to spend a lot of money on lavish parties that may not encourage personal interaction. You can learn a lot about the people in your children's lives.

4. Our children can become our teachers. Some things you say may seem insignificant to you but they have the potential to stay with kids for a lifetime. This, I fear, may be a lesson I learned too late. At my daughter's wedding reception, she referenced a compliment she witnessed I said regarding my wife: "*She still looks beautiful after all*

134

these years." My daughter told that story and repeated my words verbatim, as an example of the kind of marriage she hoped for. That moment brought a tear to my eye. As I was moved in the moment, I later reflected on less proud moments. I started wondering, if she remembered that insignificant sentence (at least to me at the time), how many other things might I have said, or done, not so flattering that may have also stuck with her. I try to use this lesson daily. I look forward to this awareness.

5. The same upbringing doesn't mean the same personalities. I had only a small "*control group*" of two children. I have found that even though we raised them the same, they grew up much differently. One daughter was quite social during her teens, and the other was more of a home body. One mixed with me like oil and water while the other was a steady personality, always quiet and sensitive. Don't expect your kids to grow up to be the same type of person.

6. Lessons can be fun, at least for you. One of my children was always reachable by phone. One night she went over to a friend's house, I couldn't reach her by phone. My co-pilot and I decided we should go and see if everything was alright. Let's just say, she wasn't as bright-eyed as she normally was. She was a bit squeamish but agreed to come home with us. I noticed a grocery bag in the back and told her she was to use that bag because I wouldn't be pulling over. She had the bag suspended over both ears reminding me of a horse's feed bag. It was all I could do to not let her hear me laughing. She went straight to bed and from that point on she was easily reachable by phone.

David was a Dad who clearly appreciated the value of a "*village*." He did a great deal to ensure love and support always surrounded his girls. From hosting parties to making friends, he saw each individual person as a member of his Family Team.

Making friends with other parents, as well as the neighbourhood children, David was sure to learn all he could about those in the lives of his daughters. He had a soft understanding of different personalities and of the various impact friends and family had in family life and development.

I have a personal appreciation for how David identified the privilege of learning from our children as he recalls the scene from his daughter's wedding, in his fourth tip. "*Our children can become our teachers. Some things you say may seem insignificant to you but they have the potential to stay with kids for a lifetime.*"

I also related to the awareness that the lasting impact of our words can be positive or negative, and the pressure that comes with this realization. It's difficult for any parent to engage in reflection and not question choices. Regardless of a valiant effort, hindsight and maturity will gift us, and burden us, with memories of the past.

I think, although at times heavy, reflection and awareness come to only the most attentive parents. It would be an unfortunate journey to lack insight and to feel you've parented perfectly, without regret. Ignorance may be bliss, but it can also be tragic.

I think Socrates said it best, "*The unexamined life is not worth living.*" That's the way I feel about parenting. Another good one from John F. Kennedy, "*Too often we enjoy the comfort of opinion without the discomfort of thought.*"

Of course I have some wonder, wishes and what-ifs. I highlight again the quote from Maya Angelou, "*Do the best you can until you know better. Then when you know better, do better.*" I think it's important to reflect; I also think it's important to be kind to ourselves. I don't want to judge myself, or anyone, on decisions I made yesterday based on the knowledge I have today. I am confident I did, do *the best I could.* I am also confident, when *I knew better I did better.*

My wish for David, myself and all parents is we will not so much judge our parenting practices, but rather reflect in a loving and kind way, giving ourselves the same love and kindness we would give our children for any misstep along the way.

Parenting is certainly not a success only journey.

Thanks David, and your "*village.*"

#57 Eric – Camping

Eric is a Dad to two grown boys. He's kind of like a "*neighbourhood Dad,*" known by all as ready-to-help in a moment's notice. A hands-on Dad and a high energy guy, Eric loves the outdoors and camping with his boys. With an old-school flare, respect was at the core of his parenting practices as well as his principles.

Although Eric admits he was not a fan of changing "*shitty*" diapers, he didn't mind doing the hard work. Much attention was given to togetherness, family values and ensuring his boys were always looked after.

1.   Teach them respect at a young age.

2. Teach them to read and write before they start school.
3. Take them camping. Show them how to cook, clean and leave wood in the camp when you leave.
4. Teach them to respect people's property.
5. Model respect for your parents and family.
6. Help with homework.
7. Try to find an answer when they ask a question. The answer is usually, "*Ask Mom.*"
8. Coach them in sports they like, don't force them.
9. Keep in touch with them when they move out.
10. Share a drink once in a while.

Eric identified great parenting themes: teach, respect, help, try, coach and model; such a beautiful collection of words and love. This Dad was able to weave all of his themes through camping experiences. Not a camper myself, I didn't realize how valuable this outdoor adventure could be.

I was never in a position to "*leave wood in the camp,*" so I've never been given that advice, as stated in Eric's third tip. As soon as I read, *"Take them camping. Show them how to cook, clean, and leave wood in the camp when you leave*". I recognized how this small piece of advice could be used literally. It was also a powerful metaphor.

Eric clearly demonstrates how camping can be a solid training ground for life skills, as well as respect for others. There were many teaching moments found. It's wonderful for a Dad to emphasize and model some of those basic life skills. It seems like it would be extra fun in a camping environment. I can imagine the scene, as if a Norman Rockwell painting — beautiful.

Michael was fortunate to enjoy Eric's camp and likely learned a few things. We didn't camp much as a family; however, I definitely saw the value of ensuring he was well equipped when it came to life skills.

When Michael was about six I told him, "*It's my goal that you be running this house by the time you're sixteen.*" He too was excited about that possibility. I wanted him to be independent and he also wanted to be independent.

We tackled this goal with vigor, as if there was a tight deadline because there was. The deadline is eighteen years, but I like to over-deliver.

"*Leaving wood*" not only teaches "*leaving wood,*" it also instills respect. This practice provides an awareness as to what's been used, what needs to be replenished and considerations for those who follow. It's important to teach our kids to leave things in a respectful manner. We should be aware that what we do and how we behave does impact others.

This seemingly small practice of "*leaving wood*" could have far reaching implications if your children learn the value of those to follow. Eric's participating in this book is "*leaving wood,*" as is the participation of all 99 Dads.

I appreciate all Eric has given to his boys, and to this work. They were so fortunate to have such special memories and a fun backdrop for important life lessons.

Thanks Eric!

#58 John F. – Make Friends Everywhere

John is a proud Dad to two teen girls. He's enjoying the journey and the depth of love and meaning his daughters have given to his life.

Although John is quick to recognize sacrifices are unavoidable in the parenting world, he acknowledges the return on investment is well worth any shift in priorities that may be required. In his family the teaching and learning goes both ways. John is full of gratitude for all he's been given by prioritizing his family. He is surrounded by love and continues to grow through their influences. In looking to the future his hopes are for more of the same: happiness, health and gratitude.

The advice John provides to Dads is the same advice he shares with his children. People of all ages and in all stages can benefit from his gentle reminders.

1. Happiness is a choice, not a destination.
2. Don't burn bridges or make enemies. You want to have no regrets.
3. Remember birthdays, everyone has one.
4. Love your family and take care of each other. If you think they have a big issue, get them the help they need.
5. Focus on making good choices. Always think long term.
6. Take vacations, often.
7. Only you can choose how you react to life.
8. Make friends wherever you go. People are interesting.
9. Always look for a win, work together. Set up an environment for collaboration rather than competition.
10. Remember where you come from. Don't get trapped by a big ego.

John's tips for parenting are also helpful as tips for general wellness. I appreciate his theme of selflessness and reminders of the long-term, and a larger picture. In each tip I could see many sub-tips to follow.

In John's eighth tip, for example, "*Make friends wherever you go. People are interesting,*" I immediately saw the far-reaching implications of that advice. Teaching children about kindness and humanity can do so much for their overall development. As parents, if we don't model respect for others our children will lack that awareness as they move through life.

Modelling an appreciation for the people we meet, regardless of their position in the world, can give our children a great foundation of understanding, and a way of being. People are interesting.

Ironically, it is Michael who has been my best teacher in this realm. Admittedly I can be swept up in the day-to-day and at times lack awareness of those around me. When spending time with Michael I am consistently impressed with his treatment of others. He has respect for everyone.

Michael learns the names of others whether it be the cab driver, a waitress, a colleague, a friend of mine or any new introduction. He is keenly aware of those crossing his path. He looks everyone in the eye, smiles always and is appreciative of the interaction he is having in any given moment. Michael is ever-present. His phone is down, and his eyes are up, at a family dinner or in a cab, he is present.

Michael has said to me, "*You should always talk to the cab driver. They are very interesting.*" I can say, Michael finds everyone he meets to be interesting. He is inquisitive. Even in brief encounters I've noticed people are drawn to him. His genuine appreciation of life, and of others, is immediately apparent to anyone in his presence. He is pleasant, mannerly, interested and kind — genuinely.

I can see much of Michael in John's tips to Dads. It is a gift to watch him interact with others. I learn from every scene.

Thanks for imparting your wisdom on parenting and on "*peopling.*" It serves as a reminder to me and to all parents that how we treat others, in large and small ways, really can make the world a better place.

#59 Paul – Have Fun!

Paul is a proud *'Girl Dad.'* He and his wife share their lives with two strong and capable young women. With both a silly and a serious side, this Dad loves all things about Fatherhood. His focus has been on building confidence and with his dedication that was sure to happen. Paul provided strong family leadership ensuring his girls felt safe and loved, always. He taught family values, encouraged high standards, grounded morals and was sure to cover goal setting.

His attention to parenting and love for his family is clearly described in each tip he shared.

1. Always be on the kids' level to show them that you understand. Remind them you were once was a kid.
2. Have fun. Fun creates affection and love which all kids are looking for. Make them laugh by acting silly.
3. Agree to disagree. Show them you are listening and there is room for improvement.
4. Kids need to learn boundaries within themselves and they should know the boundaries held by their parents. You don't always need to be in control, or *'the boss.'* Let them show you their way. Provide suggestions and model understanding.
5. Suggest, not demand. Suggestions allow kids to make decisions on their own and to create independence. Kids work better with positive direction. For example, *"You might want to try it this way."* instead of *"You should do this."* Choice allows them to consider options. *"That is a good idea. Did you conside*r..."
6. Spend quality time and one-on-one time. That time will develop trust and help them to be open about things. It's one thing to 'take them' but were you engaged when you were there? To be engaged adds quality. Kids are looking for support and for you to be present. This time will build their self-confidence. They will learn they are not alone. Even a walk around the block, find good quality time.
7. Create a trust, a friendship with your child or children. Encourage them to trust you with their concerns early in life, which helps them later in life. Open communication provides safety in sharing feelings instead of keeping them inside. Suggest talking.
8. Help them broaden their social circle. Let them choose their friends, help them do it wisely.
9. Be honest with your kids. Beating around the bush accomplishes nothing except illusions and insecurities. Honesty provides a positive energy and will result in positive values throughout life. It creates a blanket of security when kids know they can come to their parents with concerns and will not be judged. Children deserve to have an honest answer. Dishonesty will set them down the incorrect path.

10. Be involved in their lives, whether it is sports, school, music etc. This shows kids that you're helping them grow and advance their life skills and also that you're willing to grow yourself. This will further add to their self-confidence. They will strive to be a better person knowing someone is there guiding them through the process with love and support. I suggest coaching a sport and attending their events.

11. Involve your spouse in their lives and be a team. Having your spouse involved creates a different perspective and allows the kids to depend on both parents. They'll have a second point of view and even more support. Show a confident and united front.

12. Discipline with explanation. Always give an explanation when dealing with discipline. This will give the child an opportunity to know what went wrong and how to find other ways to deal with the situation. This also helps them learn from their mistakes. Allow them to know you have made mistakes as well. I suggest giving one of your examples and let them relate. Discuss the situation.

13. Be your own kind of Dad, have fun. A Dad is always special, no matter what. There is no perfect Dad. Be yourself, cherish your kids.

14. Let your kids know you have a funny side and a serious side.

What a well-balanced approach to parenting.

Paul's tips represent being firm and fair, holding the positions of both team player and coach. He shares tips on strong leadership yet was willing to let his children lead him at times. What a secure and loving environment these values would create. The mention of fun conjures up feelings of inadequacy in my own parenting, as well as a void in my childhood. I always question if I brought enough fun to my family. Given I had no foundation in fun or permission to engage in it as a child, I'm not sure how fun things were.

Play and fun is something I wish I had more experience with and was better at. Even if I did provide fun, I'm not sure I was so good at actually feeling it. For me, parenting required such deliberate attention. If fun was present I'm certain it was well-planned.

Having fun has been a stumbling block for most of my life. I did make things happy and positive, but having fun is an entirely different level. In my adult life, I've learned the importance of fun. I have made great gains and am better at it. Luckily Big Mike is an expert at fun! It's not my strong suit but it is his.

All that said and acknowledged, when I look at Michael's life it's clear he did figure out the importance of fun. He is light, happy, fun and funny. Thankfully he had solid role models, such as Paul, to pick up my slack.

Thanks Paul. Hope the fun will always continue.

I have a great appreciation for all of the Dads who were interested in contributing in this book. To me, their willingness to do so indicates their love of parenting and their interest in helping others. Although each entry has carried a unique voice, and diverse experience, the next ten men have an added layer of complexity. The Dads to follow provided these tips while incarcerated in a federal penitentiary.

Because I work in the field of Justice, I realize finding motivation within the walls of an institution requires a tremendous search. I also realize thinking about your family, and your children, can bring great pain and regret. These men participated during a time when many feel all is lost. In doing so, they convey hope, and demonstrate strength.

These Dads are working toward their education, participating in programming to rebuild themselves, and they continue to dream about the day they can reconnect with their children. They are looking forward!

I am forever thankful for their commitment to themselves, their future, and to their families. I appreciate they trusted me while living in an untrusting world. I am honoured to share their messages.

Every voice matters.

Springhill Federal Penitentiary

#60 Jamie R. – Share Bad News

Jamie is the first Dad in this series. He is 32 years-old and the Father to two school-aged children, a boy and a girl. Jamie likes everything about being a Dad and it brings him peace to know his children remain proud of him.

All he wants for his children is happiness. Jamie hopes they grow into the people they want to be, and not feel they have to live up to the expectation of others. His parenting tips are bound to help children find happiness.

Jamie provides some parenting tips bound to help children reach happiness.

1. Always support your kid's decision, even if it's not what you want.
2. Don't hide important news from them. Sit down, explain what is going on. Let them ask questions.
3. Tell them about your past, if you got in trouble. Help them to learn from your mistakes.

4. Read to them until they can read back to you.
5. Let them get their own personalities. Don't try to make them the way you want. Give them the tools to be the best person they can be.
6. Don't talk down to them. Let them know their ideas are important and they are an important part of the family.

Jamie is a Dad who believes in the truth. He states in his second tip, *"Don't hide important news from them. Sit down, explain what's going on. Let them ask questions."* As he adds in his final tip, it's also important to not "*talk down to them.*" I also believe we need to share important news with our children; it isn't easy. I think if we are honest with our children, they will come to us for answers.

I wanted Michael to know he could count on us for the truth, even when the truth was ugly. It's important to start tough conversations early.

There will be many not-so-fun experiences up ahead. It's our job to prepare our children. They need to know how to handle the tough stuff. They should expect things will not always go well, while knowing things will be OK, that *they* will be OK.

One of my key parenting principles is, "*parent truthfully.*"

When my Mom passed away, Michael was nine. At her funeral, through his tears he said, a little too loudly, "*Mom, what will I ever do if you die?*" He was so grief stricken. In that moment it dawned on him, he also could lose his Mom. My approach, instead of telling him *that* would never happen, I pulled him close and contained my grief while consoling him. Later we had a soft discussion about how he would find the strength to move on. I surrounded the conversation with comments and suggestions of comfort. It was a delicate ballet.

These conversations take time, finesse, and most of all guts. If our children can't trust us, they might rely on someone untrustworthy. I always tried to get as close to the truth as I could.

Sometimes the truth is too much, and a version of the truth will do. I think age-appropriate language and content is the key. Gentle and deliberate conversations will help them to trust us and will prepare them for the big stuff.

One promise I can make to Jamie: if we are painstaking about our honesty with our children, our adult children will come to us for consult and counsel. When that happens, warmth and a pride will fill our hearts. My "*baby*" is now in his late twenties and needs almost zero support from me these days. Michael has come to learn I will do all I can to give him the best of what I have and what I know. That's trust.

I'm confident that if Jamie follows his advice, he will be given similar gifts. All the very best with honesty. It's not for the weak.

Thanks Jamie!

#61 Pat – Imagination

Pat is a forty-five-year-old man with a French and English background. He has two young boys and deeply enjoys watching them grow. The only sadness parenting brings to Pat is the inability to lift their burdens away.

Pat is thankful for the parenting that he's received and places high importance on family values. It is his hope his boys will become successful in all their aspirations, and that they will reach every dream.

Pat's top 10 tips:

1. Always take the time to listen to your children.
2. Never discourage a child.
3. I want my kids to be successful, therefore, I don't let them quit until they have tried.
4. Always encourage your kids to try new ventures.
5. Try to make educational materials amusing and enjoyable for the kids.
6. Just be there for your kids.
7. Read to your kids.
8. Engage and be enthralled with their imagination.
9. Don't fight in front of the kids (parents or family).
10. Tell your kids you love them every day.

I love Pat's mention of imagination. Gee! Reading that tip made me wish I had considered imagination in my own journey. I encouraged Michael to play a lot, by sending him outside and letting him bring friends over. I don't think I really considered helping him to develop imagination. He had a grandmother who was great at that kind of thing. Her expanding his mind in this way added a great deal to the man he is today.

I was in so far over my head in terms of parenting and coping skills, I was just doing my best to get a day done. How fun it would have been to have some *"castle-play"* or to run and hide from dinosaurs. I hope I left him space for imagination, but I didn't really participate in it. Fun was not my strong suit. I think sometimes life gets so busy; it sweeps us away. I know it has far too often swept me away. Maybe it isn't too late to practice imagining. I think grown-ups might call it manifesting.

Using imagination can be a good tip for anyone really. Hiding from a dinosaur might give me a nice break. I'm going to tuck that little nugget away, for my next generation. Pat's tips sure do paint a picture of a wonderful home. I hope someday he and his boys find themselves in homemade castles, slaying dragons with cardboard tubes. I'm going to imagine fun forts, and many victories in all our futures!

Thanks Pat!

#62 Troy – Say It and Mean It

Troy is thirty-two years old and has one young son. It brings him great sadness to be missing out on memories with his boy and being away from him during this time.

He is hopeful he will soon be growing with him, and before long he will be at his graduation.

Troy's biggest influence was his Dad. He hopes to be that same influence for his son, as responsible support to him now and in the future.

Troy's tips:

1. Don't take your time with your children for granted.
2. Pay attention to your child's words and body language.
3. Life's short, make as many good memories with your children as possible.
4. Be there for your child no matter what the situation is, be the one your child wants to turn to.
5. Always tell your children you love them and how much they mean to you.

I practiced Troy's fifth tip on a daily basis, "*Always tell your children you love them and how much they mean to you.*" I did my best to speak often and authentically about my love for him and all he meant to me. I made sure each and every "*I love you*" had meaning behind it.

I never really felt loved as a child and I was sure that would not be the case for Michael. I told him and I showed him. I demonstrated love in all I said and all I didn't say. I did not call Michael a "*fucking idiot.*" I never told him to shut up, never. I didn't ask him *what the fuck he was thinking,* and I didn't tell him he was *stupid.* I didn't berate him. I didn't criticize him, and I didn't humiliate him or mock him in front of his friends. The things I didn't do were also very important. Michael always knew what he meant to me.

Saying "*I love you,*" to a child means absolutely nothing if your actions and words are delivering other messages. If your lip is curled while you are professing love, it will not be convincing and likely not believed.

The second half of Troy's tip, telling them "*how much they mean to you,*" is a great start in conveying your love. I told Michael and showed him he mattered and meant everything to me. I provided for him. I met his needs and sometimes even anticipated them. I didn't blame him for things beyond his control and I loved him through all his feelings. It was a privilege to love him and I treated it as such.

I hope both our boys will always feel the love we have in our hearts for them. I hope we will successfully convey our love in our words and in our actions. I'm confident Troy's little guy, and my not-so-little guy, will forever feel the depths of our love if we express all it means, and all they mean!

Thanks Troy!

#63 Casey – Education is Forever

Casey is a fifty-nine-year-old man of Persian descent, born in Iran and raised in California. Although currently incarcerated, Casey did not have any prior criminal history. The details of his incarceration were not disclosed, other than it was due to a single catastrophic event.

Casey did say, "*I just hope I will get another chance at redemption.*" Now with two grown sons and a teenage daughter, redemption is of the utmost importance. Casey is painfully aware of the anguish his imprisonment has caused his children.

Aware of their sadness, he works to focus on their positive attributes and his adoration of them. Casey describes his children as "*wonderful,*" "*law-abiding,*" "*responsible,*" "*smart,*" "*kind*" and "*caring.*" It is clear they are a great source of pride for him. His only dream for them is that they find and hold happiness.

Casey identified four key areas of focus for parents:

1. Love must be unconditional and constant.
2. Trust must be mutual.
3. Respect must be uncompromising.
4. Education is a value that must be instilled. Children should know that the knowledge gained through education can never be taken away.

I share Casey's value of education, as well as his other parenting values. I instilled the importance of education from their very beginning, inception even. As I mentioned before, I began reading to Michael as soon as I found out I was pregnant. Both myself and Big Mike attended university while we were parenting. We not only emphasized education we modelled its importance. We talked about all aspects of life and how education can impact freedom, opportunity, and as Casey said, "*it can never be taken away.*"

Proudly and fortunately, Michael was listening and watching. He attended graduations, the first was mine and he was just one. He's sat through grueling and lengthy post-secondary graduation speeches as a young child. At age eight he took notes. He was seeking wisdom and knew the value of it.

Michael completed three university degrees and now enjoys a career in law. I could never have guessed our example and messages would have had that level of impact.

I do realize school, or a lengthy educational journey, may not be everyone's path. Education can be formal and informal. Much of my most practical education came following my formal educational. Therapy and mentorship were my best teachers. Learned experience, failures, hardships and betrayal have been my most memorable lessons.

There is just no easy way through the world. Formal education has its challenges, as does the lack of formal education. Some challenges are certainly more surmountable than others.

Although Casey and I have closely aligned parenting values we live in polar opposite environments. My informal education has taught me that although we are different and in extremely different places, we are far more alike than not.

With parenting values aligned, Casey and I also share personal goals on publishing our work and leaving a legacy. With shared history in "*harsh and unpredictable*" environments we both want to educate others on victories and possibilities.

Casey remains forward-focused and continues to work on his dreams, most importantly his dream of redemption. I share Casey's vision for the future, a welcoming and warm reunion with his three children.

I hope his continued work and achievements will keep him bright and sharp for what lies ahead. The world of publishing is also "*harsh and unpredictable*," but good thing we're well trained!

Thanks Casey.

#64 Chris C. – Be There

Chris is a thirty-seven-year-old Father of two young children. Even though he is relatively new to the world of parenting, Chris has firmly established goals for his children. He's enjoying the early years as he helps them learn and grow.

Although Chris admits being responsible and settling down has its challenges, he states the biggest influence in his life has been sharing his daughter's first year. Watching her learn to crawl, walk and talk has had a large impact on him.

Chris noted three key dreams for the future of his children.

1. He hopes to give them all the things he has never had.
2. He wants to guide them to a good career.
3. He hopes they both attend university.

Along with Chris's dreams, he shared his top six parenting tips.

1. Cherish every moment you get because you never get lost time back.
2. Spend lots of time talking and teaching things to your children. They never forget anything you teach them.

147

3. If possible, be there every morning to see them wake up and each night to see them go to bed.
4. Be very patient with your children. They look up to you and take everything to heart.
5. Always put your children first and yourself second.
6. First six months are hard with a newborn, but it gets better every day.

For some unknown reason, Chris's tips reminded me a lot of my Dad, some for what I had wished he'd done and others in recognition of what he did do. Chris's entry allowed me to appreciate a little more of what my Dad did for us, some things I took for granted.

My Dad, a very damaged and unhealthy guy from an old and dark "*school of hard knocks*" located under a bridge, didn't have much to give in terms of love and tenderness; however, Chris reminded me how important it was for our family that he was ever present, even if not ever pleasant. After reading Chris's comments I immediately had some childhood flash backs. How I wish my Dad knew some of the suggestions shared by Chris. I know today, Dad did his best.

Although Dad didn't seem to "*cherish*," "*talk*," "*teach*," "*put us first*" or show "*patience*," all things Chris suggests, he did get some check marks. My Dad did come home, work hard and was there every single morning. He did bring home his pay and was a hard worker. My Dad loved our Mom and was a loyal husband. He did what he thought was right.

I think one of the most important things my Dad did, which I never before considered: he was home every morning and every night. I didn't realize the value of that as a child, as an adult I hadn't considered that even happened. Now, with this new awareness I can appreciate that him doing so provided some family stability, even in the midst of much instability.

It warms my heart that Chris highlighted that tip. In doing so he reminded me of something special my Dad brought to our family. Sometimes it's the little things, and other times it's the big things.

Thank you for your third tip, "*If possible, be there every morning to see them wake up and each night to see them go to bed.*" I hope it hits the heart of others as it has reached mine.

I agree being home for your children should be a parenting priority. It might be the one thing that makes all the difference. I hope before too long, Chris will again see his children morning and night. I'd also encourage a combination of Tip 4, adding some "*patience*," combined with Tip 3. It'd be even better if a Dad could find patience while he was home.

Thanks Chris!

#65 Jamal – Connect

Jamal is a young Dad with one son. His favourite thing about being a Dad is knowing he will always be loved. It is great sadness for him to not be present during the early years.

He dreams about his son and his future and hopes university and success will be up ahead. Jamal envisions he will be there to share in the future and the many successes to come. His focus for parenting is principles on trying and loving. He was eager to share his tips for all Dads.

1. Try to be the best Father you can be.
2. Try to remain involved in your child's life as much as possible.
3. Never give up on your child.
4. Always tell them that you love them.
5. Try to do the best you can with co-parenting.
6. Always ask them how their day was at school and how they are doing.
7. Know if there is something wrong so you can fix it.

Given Jamal is still young, I am hopeful he will hold hope in sharing in his son's future. His tips illustrate he places high value in sharing time with his little boy. I am hopeful he will have a chance to experience more of the parenting he suggests.

Jamal understands the importance of having love in your life, someone who will never give up on you. We all deserve to have someone asking about our day and hoping to help with our problems, as he also suggests.

Sadly, many of us don't find such things in our childhood. Parents don't always "*try to remain*" in their children's lives. Some Dads walk away by choice, others may not be present for a variety of reasons, some within and some outside of their control.

Those of us who do not have engaged parents as children should not give up on finding connection. We should seek to find engagement as adults, from friends and family. If we are fortunate enough to have parents who practice the tips Jamal is encouraging, we are spared much sadness and confusion. Any parental involvement is of benefit to a child. Parent engagement and effort will clear a softer path for our children, providing them confidence and comfort.

Jamal also mentions co-parenting, and provides a solid tip to separated couples. Co-parenting is a journey for the strongest and most dedicated among us. I myself have no idea how people do it, but do have great admiration for those who can.

In my case, much counselling was needed to identify what Jamal is saying. I required professional support to develop coping skills, techniques for effective parenting and for my own personal emotional regulations. It was largely advice outside of my immediate family that enabled me to provide a secure and loving home for my son. I had to learn how to give my son what I didn't have. I am forever grateful that I was able to access professional support and was open to receive it.

As teen parents, Jamal and I have to learn as we go. I can assume both of our lessons have been hard-earned and will continue to be ongoing. Although mistakes are sure to be made along the way, we have never given up on ourselves. Doing right for our kids has carried us both through the toughest of times.

My son is now grown, and I remain involved in his life, "*as much as possible.*" I believe regardless of where we are in our parenting journey, there is a role for us to play.

As Chris a fellow inmate mentioned in his tips, "*They never forget anything you teach them. They look up to you and take everything to heart.*" Never underestimate the power of a letter, a card, a hug, a kind word and the efforts made. Everything, simple and complicated, we do for our children will help them to feel loved, valued, and worthy of the future we hope for them.

Best of luck to you Jamal, and to your little boy. Thank you for your thoughts and for not giving up!

#66 Andrew – Start Early

Andrew is the Father to five girls and one son. He loves everything about parenting stating it's "*fun*" and "*grounding.*" Andrew dreams of leading a large happy family in the future. He wants his family to always grow toward health and success.

1. Always try to be honest to your kids.
2. Start discipline from a young age. Start early so you don't have to do so much disciplining when they're older.
3. Don't only be a parent, try to also be a friend if you can.
4. Talk about everything and anything with your kids. They can learn from your stories.
5. Time with your kids is worth more than any amount of money. They never forget it.
6. No matter how hard you are on your child (hopefully not too hard) they will always love you.
7. Always encourage them, even when they fail at something. Kids take failure hard sometimes.
8. Tell them they are the best and the greatest every time you get a chance. It builds them up for the future.
9. Sometimes they make mistakes, to only then see your point of view. Don't get mad at them; be there for them so they know they can trust you with other things.

Andrew advises in his second tip, "*start early*" when it comes to discipline. Starting early is a huge nugget of wisdom with discipline and with all other skill development. It's true, the sooner you start the easier it will be.

Having completed raising a child I can attest early discipline leads to less discipline later. I unscientifically (yet scientifically) believe, if you can do a solid parenting job for the first six years, you will have a smoother parenting journey in the long run. I think a parent can find a little more wiggle room if their efforts were outstanding in the early years.

We gave parenting one hundred percent and had less and less parenting to do every passing year. I too started early. Before Michael could even speak, I was introducing important words like responsibility, success, compassion. I provided him behaviour targets before he even had behaviour. Rather than correct behaviour, I installed it, developed it and evoked it. I started to tell Michael who he was before he developed the trait, understanding, or vocabulary. I introduced key words very early.

When he was three: "*You're so responsible.*" Michael may reply, "*What does that mean?*" "*Remember when you put your jacket on the hook? Doing things like that is responsible.*" "*Michael, you don't make a mess and are so 'considerate.*'" Michael, "*Considerate, what's that?*" The conversations continue.

"*Michael, you can handle anything.*"

I think as parents, we have a beautiful opportunity to develop a growing mind. We defined and discussed words such as responsibility, integrity, and loyalty. We introduced topics such as education, family, leadership, careers, and scholarships. We as parents set the targets, the standards.

Andrew mentions starting early with discipline and I agree, expanding that we should start early with everything. Discipline, building character, earning trust, teaching respect and responsibility, financial management, relationships, love, health, should all start early, as early as possible.

Sometimes, I think parents misjudge our window of opportunity. In my case, I felt it was a pin hole. I moved maybe faster than I should have or needed to. That being said, I still urge the sooner the better.

The more topics you cover, the more topics you get to cover!

Thanks Andrew! Nice to have you '*aboard.*'

#67 Ronald – Value Money

Ronald is a fifty-one-year-old who comes from a middle-class family unity. He has four grown children and his greatest joy has been watching and supporting them in reaching their goals. Ronald admits it has been difficult to allow his children to make their own mistakes, but he was confident they would learn from each of them.

In the future, he hopes for only their health and happiness. Ronald wants them to enjoy long and fulfilled lives and, with no pressure, mentioned grandchildren might be nice!

Ronald's top tips are:

1. Allow children to make mistakes and learn from them. You may have to bite your tongue. *"Grow up"* with your children. Mature in ideas together and establish *"family specific"* traditions. Some traditions may include those learned from your own upbringing.
2. Be involved in your kids' education by attending PTA meetings, after school functions, etc.
3. Establish and maintain a *"blame and question free"* list of actions. For example, calling to be picked up from a party, drinking, etc. Discussions take place afterwards.
4. Enjoy your kids, the good and the bad. What doesn't kill them only makes them stronger.
5. Ensure your kids know the value of education, money and work. Give allowances for in-home tasks (some though should be done automatically) and tasks outside the home support these values.
6. Know that there will be times that parental decisions will make your kids *"hate"* you. This will pass and they will thank you for it later. I did with my parents!
7. Let your kids have outside interests, and friends. Be supportive and when necessary be decisive. *"Yes"* is not always wrong. *"No"* is at times correct.
8. Never forget what it felt like to be your kid's age. Remember how you felt and related to parenting ideas. Use this experience to be better than your parents.
9. Enjoy your family time together and remember there will be a time when the kids will leave.
10. Finally, revenge can be achieved through grandchildren and sugar!

Ronald's fifth tip encourages teaching the value of education, money and work ethic. Those values were pillars in our parenting as well. Our focus was laser sharp. We started to talk to Michael about education, finances, and career pre-school. Having mentioned *fun* was not my strong suit; serious *business* I handled like a champ!

I remember a banker friend of mine introduced me to a financial system which we began when Michael was about six. I'm so thankful for her tips. Michael continues to organize his money in much the same way more than twenty years later. I started with three Tupperware containers (small, medium, and large), and a determined amount of money. For us, it was $5 per week. The smallest dish was labeled *"Quick Cash"* and I had a little image on the front displaying stacks of coins. This would be used for things such as trips to the store, recess at school, or when the ice-cream truck came whizzing by. In this dish Michael would deposit $1/week.

The middle dish was "*Short Term Savings*," also with a picture on it. In it he would deposit $2/week. This would be for a pre-determined item, a larger priced toy, a planned outing, something special he identified wanting to save for. The largest dish, "*Long Term Savings*" was described as something he would want as an older teen. This would be a big-ticket item. He understood it would not be touched for many, many years. He determined it would be for a motorcycle. About two years later he announced it would be his college fund.

Michael had a clear understanding as to what his money would be used for, as well as the concrete knowledge he was responsible for establishing and achieving his goals. He understood if there was a shortage of funds, he would be required to go without or to wait.

I am forever thankful to my banker friend for having introduced us to this concept. I'm also thankful I was fortunate to have had the presence of mind to organize this, as well as five dollars weekly to support the learning.

We paid careful attention to teach Michael about the value of money. As he was an only child, we had to resist the strong urge to over-indulge him. We were deliberate in implementing teachable moments and an appreciation for practical items. We were just as deliberate when it came to guiding Michael in the areas of education and work ethic. Starting early served us well.

Michael rarely asked for an advance and always paid his debt. He worked and saved for his education and has been a driven employee since his early days with his Dad on the construction site.

I'm hopeful Ronald's children have also embraced his values. It's a great comfort to witness a transfer of values in education, money management and work ethic take shape in the next generation.

Ronald mentioned in his future wishes, he's holding out hope for grandchildren and dreaming of a generation yet to come; a time where the demands are not so plentiful and the responsibilities not so intense.

I'm thrilled to report I have recently been given the privilege of meeting my grandson. I'll happily leave the '*hard stuff*' to the parents and enjoy all the fun that is promised with the next chapter.

Thanks Ronald!

#68 Abraao – Do Your Best

Abraao is approaching his seventies. He is a welder of Portuguese descent, with one grown daughter and a grandson. His favourite memories of being a Dad are of the love and affection he has felt from his "*little girl*."

Abraao hopes to model for her all that his Grandfather has modelled for him. His dream for his family is that they will always remain healthy and friendly. He believes with hard work and solid values you will be a good parent and will raise a good person.

1. What it takes to be a good parent is you have to be a good person.
2. Be friendly to your children and to everyone else.
3. Be a good listener and a good talker.
4. Be honest.
5. Be strict and soft at the same time.
6. Be patient.
7. Have a good relationship with your children.
8. Be their role model.
9. Try your best.

I appreciate Abraao's ninth tip, *"Try your best"*, as I also feel we must try our best, our very best!

Years ago, I remember doing an exercise asking participants to describe themselves in only four words. The directions advised folks to consider how they would most want to be remembered. I pondered the possibilities and narrowed it down to, *"Trying my very best."* Over the years *"my very best"* has changed drastically. In the beginning, my early years of parenting, my *"best"* was to shut my son away so I didn't hit him. I lacked in skills, knowledge, ability, supports and options. Today, I'm happy to say, *"my very best"* is much better.

Ensuring my world and Michael's world would be free from physical abuse and our home would be safe, that was at first *"my best."* My best, once a mustard seed, grew to into a glorious oak tree. My capacity expanded beyond my wildest dreams. I did give Michael safety and so, so much more.

In time, I became an impeccable role model. Sometimes it was exhausting. I attempt to live my life to the fullest, set and achieve goals and reach for new heights. I try to live the life I hope for Michael.

I can honestly say my journey through parenting and self-improvement has required me to practice all nine of Abraao's tips, and likely 999 of the tips in this book. Some, of course, were easier to apply than others; however, all have equal value. I think it is patience that has been my most elusive goal. Similar to Abraao I, too, continue to seek improvement, focus on my family and accept opportunities. I'm a work in progress.

Thanks Abraao!

#69 Chris A. – Watch Your Mouth

Chris is the final Dad in the series of incarcerated Dads. While completing his sentence he is working to advance his education. Chris has one young daughter who fills his heart with love. The love she has for him is his life's most favourite thing.

It's difficult for Chris to be away from his little girl. He has a deep sadness and he misses her every day. His dream is that his daughter will be happy and free all the days of her life. He's confident she will have a life full of success and all the good things the world has to offer.

1. Spend as much time as possible with your children.
2. Always follow through on your promises.
3. Make plans with them and be social for their benefit.
4. Set good examples for them to follow.
5. Let them know you're there for them when they need it.
6. Help them set goals.
7. Keep them active.
8. Always tell them how much you love them and will always be there for them.
9. If separated, never speak badly of the other parent.
10. Always encourage and push them to do their best.

I agree with Chris' ninth tip, "*never speak badly of the other parent.*" Upholding this suggestion is only possible for those with the most advanced levels of maturity and self-discipline. I held up, barely; not because I was so mature and advanced, but because I surrounded myself with mature and advanced people.

I think as parents we do not have the luxury of acting like a jealous, bitter, put-upon victim, if you call that a luxury. I am responsible for my reaction and as to who sees my reaction. When parenting, rather than bad-mouthing anyone, I used disappointing occurrences as teachable moments, a way to build capacity within Michael. It broadened his perspective and developed resiliency. A lot was gained as I attempted to contextualize immaturity and irresponsibility. Michael learned early in life those were unappealing qualities.

If you teach your children to observe others and to critically think, you will not have to bad-mouth anyone. The actions of others will speak louder than negative rhetoric.

In terms of a separation, things are certainly challenging. This period in time sticks forever, for everyone. It's a painful and confusing. Separation reaches our deepest most exposed nerve; maturity is a must. Maturity will minimize the damage.

A friend, a Mom who attempted to shield her children from an absent Father, shared some learned wisdom. She recommended, I did not have to explain for, lie or make excuses. She was told by her therapist, "*Don't try and make him out to be a hero. It will cause a great deal of confusion and conflict between you and your son.*" I took that advice. I didn't speak poorly, even when it was well-earned. It did take my "*Meryl-Streep-Mother-Mode.*" I didn't explain, lie, excuse or make excuses. I did not lose my cool.

I do not believe parents have the right to lose their cool. Children are the priority and *"your cool"* is second to that. Staying level is especially important when an adult is disappointing your kid. It's our job to model strength and maturity with even more diligence.

I recall my son was waiting, at about three years old. He waited peering through the screen door. I remember telling him, *"Maybe something happened, we'll do something fun for now and find out later."* Not to excuse but to extend understanding, for Michael's benefit. It's our job to teach our kids to handle disappointment. It's imperative to do it as soon as possible, before they hit any of life's major disappointments.

We assign the meaning. If we subscribe *it* has little meaning, then the children will perceive *it* has little meaning. We show the kids what matters in how we act and react. If we speak harshly, negatively, assigning blame, disgust and demonstrate poor emotional regulation, then that is exactly how disappointment will be managed by our children. These lessons start with handling our own disappointments with grace and power.

Years later, it did become necessary to explain further. I had to educate my son on dealing with liars and idiots (*not in those words*). I worked to teach him how to handle difficult and unfair situations. I taught Michael the differences between responsible people and irresponsible people (*in those words*).

So much depends how we as parents present things. Rather than demonstrate my own disgust and self-righteously rant, I would act as if it's no big deal. I would explain some people have difficult people in their world, in their family. I modelled those individuals were insignificant and redirected him to something positive.

I taught Michael how to manage and maneuver, rather than fight and excuse. As long as we stay cool, kids stay calm.

Thanks Chris! I appreciate the chance to share on this complicated topic.

Thanks fellas!
I appreciate your belief in this project and your trust in me.

#70 Dave F. – Strong Partners

Dave is a Dad who is just coming out of the woods as he bids a fond farewell to the teenager years. These days he's enjoying the shift of building adult relationships with his grown children. Realizing things are now easier than the adolescent 'daze,' this transition still requires effort and finesse.

The laughter in his home is what this Dad loves most. His favourite family moments are found when he's able to make his kids laugh. Conversely, Dave's most painful parenting moments are times when there is no laughter.

Television's "*Mr. Rogers*" was a great example for Dave as he admired an adult who could be patient, understanding and nurturing, yet imperfect. I had never considered Mr. Rogers that way, but what beautiful qualities to admire.

As we know, parenting is not all "*shits and giggles.*" Well, now that I think about it, parenting exactly is all "*shits and giggles.*" Well Dave loves the "*giggles*" and hates the "*shits.*"

The "*shits*" are generally rooted in misunderstanding. The parenting challenges arise when we as parents can't quite understand our kids, and of course our kids rarely understand us.

1. Don't be blinded by your love for your children. They will need a parent who can see things clearly.
2. Regular hugs.
3. Admit when you don't know something.
4. Read with the kids every night.
5. Don't be afraid to ask for help.
6. Don't bc bullied.
7. Don't expect perfection or anything close to it.
8. Have a strong partner.
9. Don't go to bed angry. Stay up and fight rather than end the day angry.
10. Say I love you lots.

I was happy to see I've applied all of Dave's tips in my own parenting, eventually. The thing I was lacking initially was "*a strong partner*" as Dave mentioned in his eighth tip.

I didn't always have a strong partner. Eventually I was able to find some solid resources outside the home. My Mom was my first strong partner. Because of her I was able to uphold many of Dave's tips. She helped me sharpen my senses and fine tune my radar. She hugged me, loved me and insisted I not let others bully me. I remember vividly she said (which may sound harsh), "*If you can't stand up for your son what good are you.*" – Oh my!

Sometimes it just needs to be said. Harsh or not I heard her and understood her. From that day to this I had no problem facing a bully on Michael's behalf.

In later years I found a strong "*partner*" in my therapist. She was my sounding board, at times when Mom didn't seem so 'sound.' Barb and I spent seven years together. It was because of her I was able to find my strongest partner of all – Big Mike.

I agree a strong partner is a must. Sometimes they are easier to find then others. The key is having someone you trust, and most importantly someone who will be honest with you. In the end, I share Dave's dream for his children, and for myself, "*peace and enlightenment.*" In reaching for that goal, I needed all the strong partners I could get.

Thanks Dave! I wish you more "*giggles*" than "*shits*" always and forever!

#71 Dwayne – Let Them Speak

I met Dwayne during a most exciting time in my life, on a flight to a national television appearance. He was so enthusiastic about my work, and the upcoming appearance, he quickly became a memorable piece of the entire event.

When he heard I was working on a Dad book, to compliment *100 Moms 1000 Tips 1 Million Reasons* the focus of my appearance, he immediately began scrolling through snapshots of his little girl. This "*Girl Dad*" was beaming with pride. He gushed and gushed about his daughter and the important women in his life. It was as though the flight was 10 minutes.

We laughed and chatted like long lost friends. I'm sure those around us were annoyed by our energy. I was uplifted by it!

Dwayne confided that he wants to give his daughter everything. His dream was for her to be happy with whatever she decides to do with her life. He loves all the kisses, hugs and each special moment. His pictures clearly illustrated the feeling is mutual.

Currently enjoying the life of a princess, complete with tiara and all things beautiful, the love of her Dad emanates from every image. I was so pleased Dwayne was more than willing to share his love and tips from his precious journey. He was also more than willing to share the many images of his sweet little girl. This guy is one proud Dad!

1. I am your parent not your friend. My job is not to try to win your approval but to guide you and teach you the right and wrongs in life.
2. You are entitled to an opinion, but it doesn't mean it will change the outcome of the decision.
3. You do what I say until you are old enough to make decisions for yourself.
4. Children are children and should be allowed to be children. Don't put adult expectations/responsibilities on children. Allow them to live and enjoy their childhood.
5. A parent should do everything in their power, if it doesn't commit a breach of the law, to provide for and protect their children.
6. There are many ways to discipline a child that don't include hitting, these methods should be practiced from an early age. The longer you wait the more trouble you are in.
7. Kids should not be exposed to foul language, obscene behaviour and inappropriate content. Garbage in, garbage out, so filter what goes into your children.
8. Children live what they learn. Don't do or act a certain way and then tell the child not to do the same, or punish them for following your example. Don't practice 'do as I say but not as I do' philosophy.
9. Spending time with your child is more important or valuable than any gift you can buy, so invest in that instead of monetary items.
10. Ensure you have an open communication with your child. Make sure that they know that you are always there and always on their side. Teach them nothing is too much to talk to you about.

Dwayne holds a high standard in his home and in his relationship with his daughter. It reminds me of a parent philosophy that I learned early: be the type of person you hope your child will marry. With our brief encounter, and a review of his tips, I quickly recognized how his influence will guide his little girl to a strong and respectful partner.

Dwayne seems to deliver a firm and fair approach, inviting opinion and involvement within the parameters of guidance and leadership. I can imagine a girl raised by Dwayne would be feeling safe, loved and empowered. Oh! What the future will hold.

The second tip, *"You are entitled to an opinion, but it doesn't mean it will change the outcome of the decision,"* is a good guideline. I think so much can be developed in the early years to help with the complexities of the adult world. I too informed Michael that we as parents had the final say; however, his opinion was always encouraged, and it did matter.

So much is learned through developing and articulating thoughts and opinions. It's important to remember we're training our children to become adults. If they don't value their voice it won't be heard, or valued, by others.

Sadly, it took me almost forty years to feel my voice was of value, to be honest at times I still struggle. Having been raised by a Father who had contempt for me and was easily angered by the sound of my voice, the damage was deep and long lasting, very long lasting.

I know what was involved with repairing my internal dialogue and it was intense. More than ten thousand hours of personal development and seven years of therapy have not completely healed the pain of my Father's disdain and disapproval.

My heart swells to think of Dwayne's girl as she becomes a woman, a strong confident woman with clarity of thought and direction. The world will be a different place for her. She will not need approval from lowlifes, because she's received in it the highest form. She will not have to fight for her place or silence herself. It's so exciting!

Racing toward the teen years, the love of her Dad will be an epic protective factor. She will be standing on solid ground, as if wearing a coat of armour.

Although Dwayne is bracing himself for his biggest fear — her heart break — I'm confident his love will ensure her heart will never break completely. His love will hold the best medicine for all matters of the heart. Her heart will be just fine.

Thanks for bringing love and respect to her world and mine.

#72 Terry – Friend or Parent

Terry is the husband to Debbie, (*100 Moms, Mom #72*). For that reason alone, I know he's an extra special guy. Together they make a great team and share a lot of love for their adult son.

Although empty nesters, finding time for togetherness tops their list of priorities. Weekly outings, celebrations, traditions and even random meals hold great significance in this family. All of their efforts lend not only to enhanced family values, this trio has evolved in a way that their family ties also hold all the major tenets of solid and special friendships.

Terry's best parenting tips:

1. Read to your children early and as often as possible.
2. Provide them opportunities to try new things and encourage them to think for themselves.
3. Don't expect them to have the same interests as you. Be generous with your time for their interests, these may change but your caring is a constant.
4. Encourage them to have goals. Total success may not always be achieved but a good effort counts for a lot.
5. There is a difference between being a parent and being a friend, don't get the two confused.
6. Don't be afraid to say no. They don't need everything else if they have you.
7. House rules: make them fair and firm. Some things are just not acceptable.
8. They will make mistakes. Help them to take responsibility for their actions, support them through the consequences and they will learn from these mistakes.
9. Your support now could be the pillars they build their future on.
10. Do not expect children to be perfect, they will discover soon enough that you are not, and nobody is.
11. Accept their individuality. There will be times when you find yourself learning from them. Look forward to these times.
12. If you are lucky you will get to spend lots of time with them, they grow up quickly and soon enough you will be missing them.
13. Have fun, be patient and enjoy all the experiences.

In my introduction, and in my observations, I was quick to identify qualities of a friendship in Terry's family. It was fun to see his fifth tip on the importance of knowing the "*difference*." It's a great distinction and in time, there may be room for both. I agree completely that the role of parent and friend are unique and require different approaches and considerations. In my case, I was deliberate in parenting and admittedly not so great at friendship, even in current times. The crossover was not one I feel I've been able to achieve.

In the early years and in the teen years, I think '*staying in your lane*' is key. I believe that lane is parenting. Friendships are easier to find and can be a job better suited for their cohorts. Parents on the other hand, there's only a couple of options.

In my opinion parents have the responsibility of role modelling. They must provide for, explain to and discipline. Children need parents to uphold standards, set guidelines and ensure accountability, rationales and consequences. Parents cook, clean, pay fees, buy school supplies, arrange transportation, supervision and a few other supports and services. Parents fulfill responsibilities that should not be imposed on friends or in friendships.

Friends, on the other hand, offer support of a different kind. They have age appropriate understanding and can validate in a way a parent can't. Friends have the advantage of shared experiences in real time. They hold high influence because they inherently relate to each other. Peers offer a unique perspective and have a level of credibility that is generally not granted to a parent.

Strong parenting, a progressive evolving relationship, can possess qualities from each realm. I've noticed Big Mike and Michael have been able to effectively share the world of parent and friend. It's beautiful. Big Mike continues to have the respected position of Dad and parent, while he also enjoys the trust and confidence held in a friendship. Now that Michael is an independent adult, parenting is no longer required; however, guidance and consult is appreciated by both.

The reverse is true in that Big Mike not only has a son; he also enjoys their friendship. Their joint evolution, maturity and acceptance have further enhanced the relationship on a deeper level. Their relationship has surpassed the parameters of parenting and of friendship. With a shared history and an exceptional regard for the well-being of each other, they have been able to grow and modify their interactions with great ease. I love watching them together.

I appreciate that Terry did not suggest not being a friend. His tip emphasizes "*don't get the two confused.*" I think that is a caution worthy of consideration and closely aligned to age, maturity and needs of the children involved.

I can't speak for Debbie of course, but I will anyway. I think it's fair to say, both she and I have hearts in our eyes as we watch these men learn and grow together in love and in friendship. It's a treasure in life to witness the trust a Dad and his son sustain and develop over decades.

Thanks so much for your thoughts Terry. It was great to reflect on the role of parent and friend. It's wonderful how the two have come so sweetly together for both our families.

#73 Rodger – Brag

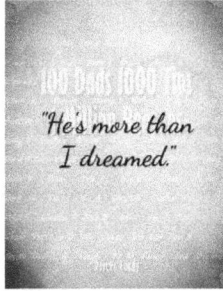

"He's more than I dreamed."

Rodger is a retired member of the Canadian Armed Forces who has raised two children, a boy and a girl, now in their twenties. Having been largely influenced by the love of his Mom, Rodger carries her legacy of hugs and encouragement. His life's joy is watching his children grow into interesting and well-balanced adults. Rodger's dream is they continue to do so while enjoying a lifetime of healthy, happy and supportive relationships. He describes it all with a quote from Pam Brown, *"Dads are most ordinary men turned by love into heroes, adventurers, story tellers and singers of song."*

Having been a member of the Forces, time spent away from home was difficult. Rodger struggled with missing activities and accomplishments through the years.

His tips demonstrate how even the little things can be meaningful. Despite departures he was able to connect on many levels and continues to do so to this day.

1. Take them outdoors. I was fortunate in that my children were not exposed to mobile devices as children. We spent as much time camping and playing outdoors as we could. As adults, my children love to be outdoors, camping hiking and generally enjoying the wilderness around us.

2. Ensure they know how to handle money. We were informal about allowances, but we did not give our children everything they wanted. If they wanted something, they worked for it. We did not tell them how to spend the small amounts they did earn. We let them make small mistakes, while providing guidance to avoid the big errors.

3. Be respectful of those around you. You don't need to swear or show disrespect; it does not make you look cool.

4. Care for animals. They will give you all the love you can handle.

5. Read to them, a lot. Instill the love of reading and you will never hear the words *"I'm bored,"* ever.

6. Never be too busy to chat with them every day, even when they don't want to.

7. Try to exercise with them as much possible.
8. Play, be silly, and use your imagination.
9. Build a fort or many forts, out of blankets, cardboard or scrap lumber. It gives a sense of accomplishment and promotes even more opportunities for play.
10. Brag about how well they are doing to everyone and anyone.

Rodger promotes a great mix of teaching and fun. I'm sure the memories of the outdoors, imaginary play and fort building will provide a lifetime of fond reflection. What beautiful scenes they must have shared.

Having had a difficult childhood myself, there was no play, fun or forts. There was also no "*bragging*" as mentioned in Rodger's tenth tip: "*Brag about how well they are doing to everyone and anyone.*"

I'm proud to say, I was counselled in some of the parenting approaches Rodger is suggesting. Michael was exposed to bragging and fun and forts, as mentioned in tip nine.

As far as "*bragging*" goes, I love it but try to refrain these days. Michael is almost thirty and feels a little weird when I gush — so I'm told. I have much to gush about, so it takes great restraint.

I'm not sure why bragging is frowned upon by some. I find that confusing. I thought I'd seek a definition to ensure I wasn't misunderstanding. Bragging is defined as, "*excessively proud and boastful talk about one's achievements or possessions.*" Maybe it's the excessive part that is off putting. I can see that. Maybe it's only when you do it about yourself, I can see that as well.

That said, when Michael was young, I did brag, excessively. I wanted him to hear what was important. I wanted to reinforce his achievements. I attempted to highlight preferred qualities, skills, abilities, outcomes and accomplishments.

I used the technique deliberately and genuinely. I meant what I said. I didn't want my praise to lose its luster, or to sound insincere and to not be valued by him. I did brag a lot and I meant it a lot. I still do.

I told Michael he was great at saving money, he wanted to save more money. I told him he was a strong decision maker and he became more aware about making decisions. Michael learned about himself through my eyes and my words. Michael only had positive messages in his world and his mind — positive in, positive out.

Bragging was effective in developing Michael's self-awareness, self-esteem and family values. I'm not sure if it was excessive or annoying to others and I don't care. I still don't care.

Michael's great! He's a smart man, a kind, loving and thoughtful partner and a connected son and grandson. He's a generous and attentive friend, an informed, caring and engaged Father and a loyal and trustworthy employee. He's a hard worker, ambitious, financially responsible and eager to learn. He makes healthy choices. He's a good decision maker, a critical thinker and is active in his community. Michael has a kind heart, a beautiful mind and a strong presence. I'm downplaying so as not to brag, of course.

He's more than I ever dreamed! There, I said it! I hope Rodger will also continue to brag. I'm sure I will.

Thanks for supporting what I always knew, bragging is OK.

#74 & 75 Archie & Greg – A Modern Family
Teach Acceptance

Archie is a fellow University of Cape Breton alumnus. He is one of only two friends I had throughout my university years. With a friend like him I didn't need many. Not only is Archie special because he helped me through university, he was also instrumental in connecting me to Big Mike. He took us both under his wing and luckily it was a match.

Archie and his husband Greg are a part of a strong, modern family. In my history, I don't know many beautifully mature co-parenting arrangements. This couple has worked to build a solid, mature and loving parent group which has surrounded their two children throughout their lives and well into their adult world.

These Dads now are finding great enjoyment as they observe their grown children reach their goals, while always carrying the values of respect and love to all humans, all the time. Watching them grow and recognizing how they've influenced their development is a great source of pride for them both.

Together, they were happy to share their parenting tips and the foundation for a successful co-parenting journey.

1. We have learned that regardless of age, your children remain just that — your children.
2. While it is instinctual to want to "*rescue*" your children from the experiences of being human, we have learned to observe and support, not always rush in to solve things.
3. As Dads we needed to grow together and respect one another's perspective in all areas.
4. Always respect and love your children and their journey, all the time.

5. Instill the importance of education and hard work. Help them to focus on enriching their lives and to be of service to others.
6. Be your children's role model.
7. Be yourself so that your children can be themselves.
8. Teach love and acceptance.
9. Mentor your children by being involved in your community.
10. Don't ever practice tough love no matter how tough a situation is.

Attributing their value system to their greatest teachers (Greg, his Dad and Archie, his sister), these Dads are honoured to carry the legacies of love and respect. This family has four unshakable values that which remain pillars in their parenting framework: Love, respect, acceptance and others.

The eighth tip, "*Teach love and acceptance,*" may sound commonsensical to some; however, at times it appears common sense is not so common. Love and acceptance is not an automatic. It need to be taught and modelled.

This duo recognizes not all families enjoy the respect and acceptance they have; they promote and practice consistently upholding and modelling respect for others. In doing so, kindness and acceptance will be firmly established in the generations to come.

Sadly, and inevitably, we will come across others who do not share our teachings as parents. I call them "*skill sharpeners.*" I have certainly *'lost my footing'* when challenged by the ignorance of others. For the most part, I reserve those stumbles and mutterings for Big Mike.

I, as these Dads, did a great job of not 'losing my shit' in front of Michael. Consultation and support are just two of the many advantages of co-parenting. Having another parent to vent frustrations to and problem solve with, made the ride smoother for us all. I always felt parenting is a job made for two.

I was briefly in the single-parent world and it was not fun. I encourage anyone on a solo journey to build a tribe, at a minimum find a confidante, a friend or even a therapist.

In my case, I needed all that and more. I could not be trusted with my own responses, thoughts or even judgments. Maturity was not easily accessible to me, internally or externally. I only knew what I was taught, and the teachings were limited, at times dark.

Seek others. It's important to uphold impeccable standards when dealing with upset. Outbursts will make children feel confused and unsafe. It can be tough to hold back I know. If you want to "*teach love and acceptance*" you can't model intolerance, not even in front of the intolerable.

This family is fortunate to have four invested, mature and loving adults who always put the best interests of the children first. They built a beautiful village on solid ground.

Please do teach love and acceptance. Doing so will add to villages everywhere.

Thanks fellas!

#76 Jamie Y. – A Little Fear

Jamie is a proud '*Girl Dad*' to three little-not-so-little girls. He's currently in the throes of adolescence and is ever-present in their daily lives. After a twenty-five year career that required him to leave the home for long periods, Jamie is especially appreciative of the sweet moments and the simplicity of the day-to-day. He loves it all and takes nothing for granted.

Jamie was one of my first Dads asked and one of the first to respond. He happily contributed his best advice:

1. Give them a little to fear. I believe it will keep them safer down the road if they have some fear.
2. Always tell them you love them. You can never say it enough. My Dad was old school and "*I love you*" was hard for him to say. I make sure I tell my girls every day, a lot.
3. Be good to others. If they see you do this, they will learn to do it as well. If we all are good to people, the world will be a better place.
4. Teach and talk about kindness.
5. I always encourage them to chase their dreams. Never discourage them from what they believe in. Guide them on the safest route to their dreams and celebrate their success.
6. Don't spend thousands on special occasions, spend time instead. They won't remember the toys you bought as much as they'll remember the fun Christmas dinners or great family vacations.
7. Keep them active. There are a lot of pitfalls in the world. If they are active it leaves less time for mischief or larger problems up ahead.
8. Always pick them up whenever they call. Be there for them no matter what. They will respect that and do the same for their children.
9. Teach them the importance of respect, especially for elders. Hold doors open for them and others. Be the person that's remembered for the good things.
10. Dance. Do silly dances around the kitchen. I love doing that.

When reviewing the tips of Dads raising daughters, I have a myriad of feelings. Initially I begin to consider what their practices would have meant for me as a little girl, a teen girl. From there I feel such happiness for the girls, having a Dad who was willing to share their tips and thoughts on this special journey.

I attempt to move quickly from my childhood memories and personal reflections to my role as a parent. At times, that journey is longer than others. Jamie's tips, having three girls and such a deep appreciation for each, resonated with me in a special way. For my Dad to have put forth such effort and level of connection without a doubt would have given me and my two sisters very different foundations.

Jamie suggests, "*Give them a little to fear. I believe it will keep them safer down the road if they have some fear.*" In my upbringing there was great fear. I was so afraid. The fear I knew has permeated my being and even decades later is still a part of me. His mentioning just a "*little*," is not such a little point. I, too, think a "*little*" fear might be a good thing. In raising Michael, I'd like to think he had a "*little*" fear. Michael was afraid primarily to disappoint us. I think that was a motivating factor in the early days.

Michael wanted to be a "*good boy*." Our many discussions highlighted we had certain expectations that were non-negotiable. We spoke about disappointment and sadness if our rules and expectations weren't upheld. Michael did not want to disappoint or sadden us.

Jamie also mentioned, "*...safer down the road.*" That was our goal as well. Sometimes fear is instilled to enforce compliance; this was not the case for us or for Jamie.

As parents we explained some of the dangers that waited, in an age-appropriate way. Our teaching advanced parallel to Michael's personal development and goal setting. Before long he was afraid of disappointing himself.

At first, we wanted Michael to fear an earache, so he would wear his hat. We wanted him to fear hunger so he would remember to bring his lunch. We wanted him to fear distrust, so he would remain honest. As things evolved, we wanted him to fear unhappiness. We wanted him to fear poverty, divorce, addiction and unhealthy people. I refer to this as "*healthy fear.*"

I didn't want Michael to fear our responses, our emotions or our home. I didn't want him to fear calling us, being honest with us, asking us for help or for truth. He didn't fear violence or have to live with the threat of it. He didn't fear starvation or homelessness. He didn't fear hate or hostility. He didn't fear losing our love.

I'm so proud of what we taught him to fear, but most proud of what he wasn't taught to fear. Breaking cycles, my life's largest and most prized accomplishment. I am thrilled for daughters to be brought up with engaged Dads, ones who also are breaking cycles with words like "*I love you*" and actions such as kitchen dance parties. What a difference a Dad can make.

Thanks Jamie! I hope you'll always keep dancing and your girls will never hold back their smiles when you do.

#77 Blaise – No Matter What

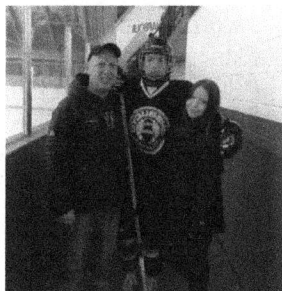

Blaise is a super fun guy and I can't help but imagine he's a super fun Dad too. In fact, I know one of his life's mantra is, *"No fools no fun."* After learning this, I began to consider this possibility. I must report, I found it to be completely true. I've also come to consider, when a place is fun, who exactly is the fool? I can also report, the fool is easily identifiable. It was enlightening to learn, sometimes I brought the fool.

He was happy to share his wisdom with me on life, fools and fun. Blaise is not afraid to be the fool or the fun. He's kind-hearted and easy to be around. Our visits are always a treat and always too short.

This Dad is very proud of his kids, even a little more extra than most. He also didn't hesitate to give some parenting messages to the world.

1. Keep them busy with sports.
2. Always tell them, "*No matter where you are, if you're not comfortable I'll be there. Anytime, anyplace, I'll be there.*"
3. Give them a hug and tell them you love them every night before bed.
4. When your kids don't live at home, make sure to get it touch.
5. Make sure your kids always know you love them.
6. Let them know that you are there for them whether times are good or bad. Do your best to lead them in the right direction in life.

I love how most of Blaise's tips emphasize ensuring your kids know you love them and have their back, *"no matter what."* He not only recommends that children know they matter, but he also tells us how to show them they matter: hug, talk, and reach out.

I remember as a child, I was looking for love, asking about it even. I was told, "*You know I love you!*" Although that was a direct order, I didn't know I was loved. It was said, but not felt. There was little hugging, less talking and even less reaching out.

When I imagine a childhood where Dad, or Mom, gave me the messages suggested by Blaise I envision it would feel safe and sound. For children to hear, and have demonstrated, full support regardless of circumstance or situation, what peace. The promise of one hundred percent support can quickly fade, despite verbal reinforcing, if great care is not taken to prove it. It's important to back up your words.

Of course, if you lose your shit over spilled milk, no one will ever call you for a drive when drunk from a party. Also keep in mind, if children hear you disrespect others, watch you behave in an aggressive manner, or if you're untrustworthy, they won't believe your words and they shouldn't.

I think if a parent promises to be a soft place to fall, they should be at least soft. Tips such as hug, talk and remind can help keep their landing place soft. Being with them in person or even by phone will serve to reinforce your love and availability.

Although I only dreamed of a Dad with these values, I did my best to incorporate them in my own parenting. Knowing the uncertainty brought by insecurity, I made sure I was going to provide security to my son. I'm not sure my actions, or temperament, instilled my desire to convey one hundred percent support. I'm not sure I would have responded appropriately had Michael called me drunk from a party. I did on one occasion incorrectly side with a teacher, when I should have one hundred percent supported Michael.

Overall, admittedly a 'hard marker' I'd give myself eighty-five percent on this topic. I'd like to think Michael would score me a little higher. Luckily, for us both, we did have Big Mike. He would have been on a late-night call, and one hundred percent on side with Michael at any Parent/Teacher meetings. He was, and still is, cool, calm and collected.

For a parent such as myself who is still growing, my message would be: have a consultant, if not a co-parent. I needed parent peers, professionals and personal development to be the best parent I could be. I needed all of that to manage and identify limitations I was not always aware of.

Blaise's tips cover the early days through to the empty nest, starting with the bedtime tuck in his third tip, to the reminder to connect even when they leave home in his fifth. He said it all. (*Even if I did have to wrestle it out of him.*)

Thanks buddy.

#78 Trucker Dad – Behave

"Trucker Dad" is an old, old friend. Once known to me as a sweet little boy, he's now all grown up, a truck driver and a heavy equipment operator. These days, his favourite title of all is the title "*Dad*."

This Dad recalls the day his little boy entered the world. He reports from that day to this he's been "*one hundred percent in.*" He was so proud on the day of delivery. Watching his son enter the world was the most moving moment of his life.

Since their first day together, being a Dad has meant everything. He loves all aspects of Fatherhood, the teaching, nurturing and guiding. Hearing that soft little voice say "*Daddy*," is his most favourite thing.

"Trucker Dad" has only one wish, to always be able to ease his son's heartache. He works to be a strong role model and hopes his son will continue to bring his aches and breaks to him. He hopes together, they will conquer even the most troubling times.

After much deliberation, his best advice to Dads on the parenting journey, to Dads working on the road, and to those sharing custody is:

1. Never bad mouth or make negative remarks about the other parent in front of, or within earshot of your children. As hard as it is for some to do, for your child, get along and be respectful to the other parent. Remember it's not their fault the both of you can be pure, hateful assholes. Do what's best for your child. Stop being selfish. Don't put more hateful fuel on the fire. The hurt your fighting will cause will never heal.
2. Interact with your kids. Ask them how their day was. If you feel they are sad or down, ask them what's wrong. You won't know unless you ask.
3. Don't ignore their words or feelings. Do what you can to boost them up when they are down.
4. Never scream at your kids, don't scare them or they will resent you.
5. Be stern, stand your ground and let them know you mean business. Always talk at their level, not standing over them.
6. Never spank or use physical discipline with your children when and if they fail.
7. Stay away from the court system and children's services at all costs. Be adults and resolve problems. Remember, the most important winner of all is your child.
8. Tell your kids daily you love them. Let them know the other parent does too. With separations, assure your kids everything will be okay.
9. Involve your kids in stuff you do as a hobby or profession. Kids love being just like their parents. Teaching them first-hand is much more exciting for them than just hearing you talk about it.

10. Ask your kids what they want to do instead of telling them or planning without their input. Let them decide on activities and how they want to spend time with you.
11. Teach them to stand up for themselves but don't encourage fighting, violence, bullying or hate.
12. Give them chores. Show them the value of a dollar and give them responsibility. When they do well, reward them.
13. I encourage every parent, together or apart, to take a parenting course or a co-parenting course. I recommend *Strongest Families*, check it out. Any available course can't hurt. Learn about parenting.

I really appreciate *"Trucker Dad's"* perspective on keeping the environment positive, despite at times feeling otherwise, particularly when it comes to co-parenting. I recognize this level of maturity and, in my experience, feel it was one of the hardest components of parenting. Co-parenting is not for the weak of heart.

In the fourth tip he advises, *"Never scream at your kids."* I have personal appreciation for that advice, and it is a tip I am happy to have learned early. Having been primarily yelled at as a child, I was prone to be a screaming parent. To add further injury, in my upbringing, screaming was accompanied by demeaning speeches and constant disapproval.

My parenting prognosis was low. In learning the source of my own pain and with the help of counselling, as *"Trucker Dad"* also advises, I kept myself on a tight leash with my tone, volume and language. Screaming at children really does have a *"negative effect."* In my case it was deep, lasting, loud, internal and relentless.

Approaching fifty and after many hours of therapy, I still feel the impact of screaming. At times, I even wait to be yelled at. It is mind-blowing to me, and to Big Mike, that after all these years the effects still linger. I am still afraid.

I believe if my parents had known better, maybe had sought out a parenting course, things would have been different. They came from a place, and a school of thought, where respecting children had not yet been developed. They were not exposed to the information that screaming was not effective and in fact was counterproductive.

My parents just didn't know. Their education, experiences and exposure to child development were highly limited. They were bogged down with their own internal wreckage and, for the most part, lacked the resources and capacity to rebuild. Sadly, my parents didn't find the maturity that is encouraged in many of these tips.

Screaming alone may not cause the extreme damage and confusion, I experienced; although, it should not be underestimated. Ironically, I've since learned of the effectiveness of whispering. Try whispering instead.

At times, in home and at work, I've practiced whispering when delivering a serious message. I can tell you it is highly effective. As an unexpected outcome, whispering not only conveyed the message, it also calmed me down when feeling the urge to scream.

I am most proud to have broken this cycle! I have every confidence the cycle has also been broken in this journey as well.

Thanks for your participation *"Trucker Dad,"* and for the hockey bag.

#79 Justin – Explain

Justin has been in the Dad role for nearly a decade. With a nine-year-old daughter and a five-year-old son, he's still in the thick of his parenting years. He loves the job and already, his children have become the most significant influences in his life.

From their birth to his worries, their well-being and happiness is everything. Justin has a lot of parenting goals. He values both the mistakes and the magic as things continue to unfold.

Justin works to teach both love and understanding. He intends to work hard ensuring his children are well-armed to grow and learn from any misstep. With his love and dedication there is no question they will be solidly prepared for the challenges up ahead.

1. When your child is acting out or having a tantrum, more often than not they are trying to communicate something to you and are having difficulty expressing their frustrations or emotions.
2. It's OK to make mistakes, forgive yourself.
3. Every child is unique, therefore, we must adapt our parenting style to meet their needs.
4. If your child discloses something and asks you not to tell your partner, take the opportunity to reinforce that there are no secrets between parents and if they need help telling the other parent that's OK, it reinforces equal partnership amongst parents, helping to promote equal trust.
5. Children are always watching and listening; even when you don't think they are paying attention the environment you create and the

energy you have —whether positive or negative — has dramatic effect on your children's wellbeing and who they become.

6. Your attitude and beliefs will likely become your children's.
7. It's OK to talk about your failures with your children and it's OK to fail from time to time.
8. It's imperative to talk to your children about how to deal with stress in positive ways.
9. When your child challenges your authority or asks why, try not to say *"because I told you so;"* often they are not challenging your authority, but they are seeking an explanation.
10. Never be afraid to have difficult conversations, it's better they receive information from you that is more in line with your belief system then getting misinformation from outside sources.

In Justin's ninth tip he advocates for explaining the 'whys' to your children. He reminds us they are likely not attempting to challenge you but are seeking understanding. I appreciate this tip and think in explaining we foster development and trust on many levels. I recognize my childhood would have been entirely different had my parents considered the possibility I was seeking and not defying or resisting.

As a child, and a teenager, I often sought an explanation or some understanding. My parents did not have the skills or insight to believe I was deserving of conversation or any rationale. As a result, it took literally decades to come to believe that I did deserve an explanation, for many things. I later came to realize my parents didn't always have an explanation themselves.

It is because of my personal challenges I have extra appreciation for Justin's ninth tip. I know how it felt not having an explanation, so I was going to guarantee one for my son. Like Justin, I felt children deserved an explanation. It was important to me that Michael knew what I was doing and why I was doing it. I even attempted to explain prior to decisions and changes whenever possible. I provided Michael as much "*lead time*" as I could. Sometimes I didn't know what I was doing or why, but together we communicated. I'd even explain that I couldn't explain. Confessing my uncertainty, but discussing my intention, was better than shutting him down completely. Communication was integral to his development.

Michael always knew he was considered, and he mattered. I've learned in explaining, discussing, listening, considering and with open communication he became skilled in each of those areas. Not only is he a skilled communicator, he feels deserving of rationales. He is able to identify bullshit because he knows what the truth looks like.

In providing a respectful environment I, in turn, raised a man who is respectful of himself and of others. He is comfortable asking questions, is willing to research issues, and can quickly identify solutions that make sense. I didn't realize the amazing outcomes that would result in a consistently respectful approach. Communication is time consuming, but I can't think of a better way to use your time.

It may seem easier to shut down a child. It's a definite option; however, I can assure you in doing so, your day might go a little smoother in that moment, but the complications of those actions will be far reaching. Navigating the world while feeling your voice doesn't matter, and you don't deserve an answer, is very painful and confusing. I wish it for no one.

Children inherently believe their parents are one hundred percent right, at least in the early years. If they don't feel valued, loved and respected by them it may take decades before they believe they are worth anything at all. Under these circumstances, only the luckiest and most resilient of them will come to realize their worth.

Thanks Justin. I'm confident your explanations will build an unbreakable foundation for your children and your family.

#80 Darcy – Patience

Darcy is the lucky man to have locked in my sweet cousin Nicole, (100 *Moms, Mom #80*). Together they are raising three of the cutest little children, the first now hitting her teenage years. With two girls and a boy, they work to give them all the great things childhood has to offer.

Darcy loves being a Dad and watching his children grow. He enjoys seeing their characters blossom and identifying how his influence is contributing to their spirits. Darcy has great fun watching them learn new things and develop in new ways.

He put together his top parenting tips:

1. All *"how to parent books,"* — burn them.
2. I know less about being a parent than I did before I had kids.
3. Young sons and daughters will always physically hit below the belt.
4. Patience, you need lots and lots of patience, especially for your wife.
5. Don't let your kids live in a bubble. Let them make mistakes and help them to learn from them.

I agree with Darcy's tips, well mostly. As far as the burning of the books goes, well maybe burn most of them but just not this one. I'm sure he didn't mean this one. He probably wasn't referring to *100 Moms 1000 Tips 1 Million Reasons* either. Burn them all except those two.

His fourth tip, encouraging patience, is always a welcome reminder. Not only does Darcy encourage patience overall but adds an extra mention for our partners as well. I appreciate whenever parents highlight the need for patience, with kids, partners, ourselves and with life in general. So much is needed on so many levels.

Patience was and continues to be a tough one for me. What a gift you can give your children if you master patience, or even work on it, if only with a slight awareness. I think it is the most fortunate of kids who do not have parents demanding urgency all day, every day.

As for Michael, he did not always have the luxury of a patient Mom. I really didn't find and apply patience until sixteen years in, and one huge spinal cord injury later. Only when urgency and haste was no longer an option was I able to develop patience. Patience became a non-negotiable. Up until Michael's injury, I truly thought it was my job to teach him to hurry. I hurried in all I did and in all I expected. I hurried to the playground and to the tree-climbing. I basically raced from one teachable moment to the next.

Come on Michael! *Move it Michael. Let's go Michael*! *Hurry up Michael*! *Get your hat*! *Mitts*! *In the car*! *Hurry and eat*! *Shower*! *Do homework*! *Grow up*! Those phrases were far too common in our home. It was unnecessary and anxiety producing for everyone. I had little patience for him and even less for myself.

I hope no parent will ever learn patience as I have come to learn patience. I wish no parent ever finds their lesson as I did: the hard-earned lesson taught to me by way of a spinal cord injury. It was only after Michael's injury did I realize the madness I created.

Following the injury my life and Michael's recovery required every fiber of my being to suppress my need to rush. I remember, within days it was evident to me; I could never use the word *"hurry"* again. I learned patience only because impatience was no longer an option.

The self-awareness was painful. I was haunted by my urge to push. I became acutely aware of constant rushing. I was even more aware — there was absolutely no need. It saddens me to know I imposed such anxiety on the simple processes of day-to-day life. I really felt all things could be done faster. It was as if life was in slow motion. I believed my incessant pushing was required to keep things in motion, to keep the world spinning. I did not have patience. If I was not rushing Michael, I was thinking about rushing him.

Today, I still don't excel in this area; however, I am much better at keeping my attitude to myself. It has taken me a long time to understand people move at their own speed, on their own time and have a schedule not reliant on my intense directives. I'm not so self-important now.

I am thrilled for Darcy's children! Having patient parents is a treasure not granted to all children. It is a virtue.

Thanks Darcy. Glad you joined in and glad we both found some patience.

#81 Jack – Coaching and Volunteering

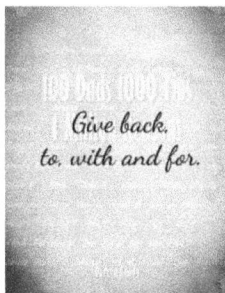

My next Dad was a recommendation from Big Mike, which Jack may not know is quite a compliment. Together they had a shared work history within the Canadian Armed Forces. I've come to learn from Jack's tips, they have many other commonalities.

Jack is still in the thick of parenting with a twelve-year-old son and an eight-year-old daughter. His favourite thing about parenting is teaching and watching them learn. He's gone from teaching them to walk to now teaching them to '*walk away*;' a lesson they'll surely need for the teen years quickly approaching.

Having been a member of the Forces, Jack has had to miss many occasions. His hope for his children is that they will enjoy careers that will afford them much more family time and togetherness for all the special days ahead.

Jack has been largely influenced by his own Dad and four uncles; he continued their legacy of family first. He reinforces to his children that education will provide them with options in life. His dream is they will be positive, educated and healthy as they head down the road of their choosing.

1. The best tool I can suggest is team sports. Involving your children in team sports will give them the skills early in life of being a team player. This experience will help them a great deal. They'll learn about leadership, managing the highs and lows of winning as well as loosing, they'll have the opportunity to learn from their mistakes and will be also learning about the importance of living a healthy lifestyle.
2. Limit "*screen time,*" on PlayStation, Netflix and YouTube. I found if kids spend too much time in front of a screen their brain does not function at one hundred percent. They seem to become too lazy which

easily leads to more screen time. We let them have ninety minutes on a school night and encourage outside activities on the weekends.

3.   We like to explore with our children. I have found an hour hike in the woods or a walk on the beach opens their mind. They ask questions about what we are doing or what we are seeing. This also keeps them fit and will improve their communication skills.

4.   Invite their friends on outings. I have found when we do things like a family day trip, explore a beach or a hike back in the woods, our kids tend to invite a friend or another family to join us. With other kids, our kids are learning how other families interact.

5.   I volunteer to be a hockey coach and a soccer coach. I think that is the easiest way for me to be a positive influence within my community and for my children. I have had lots of parents and their children thank me at the end of the season. My children see that, and they appreciate me giving my extra time to help them and other kids learn *"game skills and life skills."* My children help me plan practices for both sports and they understand what skills need to be worked on and how that impacts the respective teammates.

6.   My family spends lots of time with our extended family. We are fortunate that both my parents and my wife's parents are *"outside people"*. This easily creates different learning environments for my children. I have watched my son at ten years old haul logs out of the woods with a tractor and I have also seen my daughter when she was six (with the use of extensions) mowing the grass using a ride-on lawn tractor. I think diversity of activities is the best advice for success for future parents.

7.   Listening attentively is very important. My son is in his second year of middle school and he tells me everything from what happened in gym class to who was fighting at recess. At twelve, knows about drugs and alcohol, he knows that in moderation adults use them. He knows kids should not have them because their brain is not developed enough to use them. When he sees other children with cigarettes, vapes or drugs he removes himself from that situation. I have educated my son on drugs, alcohol and cigarettes. I've told him the risks associated with each. I believe if kids are educated early, they will make the right decisions and stay away from that stuff until they are adults and can make an educated decision. I have also not sugar coated this with my kids, I told them the truth (that I used drugs and alcohol before being an adult). In my opinion they need to know that you are being honest before they make their decisions based on the education you provide them.

I can see why Mike recommended Jack participate in this book. They share many of the same parenting philosophies and practices. Mike, too, believed in sports, coaching, outdoor play, attentive listening and in honesty. He was an involved Dad and would be quick to identify those traits in others.

Jack's values are immediately apparent in reviewing his tips. Respect for his wife, their children and their future leaps off the page. Jack appears to be a Dad who is invested and not afraid to put the effort in. Whether it is in making unpopular decisions like limiting screen time, increasing parental involvement by limiting screen time, he's in.

I think one of the most labour-intensive things a parent can do is what he's advising in his fifth tip, volunteering. I think volunteering is a commendable commitment with large payoffs. Big Mike volunteered and I was able to see the rewards first-hand.

As Jack mentions, doing so provides a *"positive influence"* not only for your children and other children, but also for the larger community. It offers a time to practice both *"game skills and life skills."* In addition, many teachable moments in conflict resolution, commitment, physical activity and leadership will frequently be presented. As a coach you're able to advance and reinforce that learning on every occasion.

Coaching a team brings things to an entirely different level as a parent, in doing *with* rather than *to*. Your children get the added bonus of increased quality time with their Dad and the pride in watching '*their Dad*' lead, support and encourage a team. What a beautiful and multi-faceted gift unique to the children of coaches.

It might be important to mention, there are other opportunities to volunteer that don't require such a high-level commitment, for those of us not so physically active. I volunteered in Michael's school breakfast program. I was given many similar rewards and opportunities. It was a fun time and I was very proud to be involved and hope Michael was proud as well.

I also volunteered to chaperone, which of course is not such a glorious or rewarding role; however, any effort to be involved in the different levels of your child's learning is time well spent. There are many ways to pitch in. Bake sales, ticket sales, chocolate or popcorn sales and the many various fundraisers throughout the years all provide an opportunity to share time and experiences with your children. Random sales all the way to the valiant efforts of team coaching will instill a sense of community and pride for the years to come. The memories will last a lifetime.

Thanks to Jack and all the coaches out there. Know you are loved and appreciated by every life you touch, especially the lives of your own little people.

Glad to have you involved!

#82 Javier – Breathe

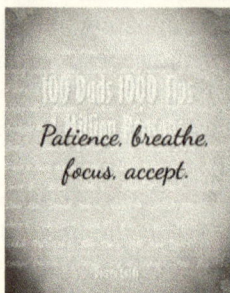

Patience, breathe, focus, accept.

Javier is the proud Dad to a baby girl. He identifies patience as his superpower. That's sure to be helpful throughout his parenting journey. Still in the early days, snuggling is his favourite thing, but sleep used to be. The only downside is also the upside — he's traded sleep for snuggles.

Like all Dads, Javier wants only the best for his girl starting with annual Disney vacations and the finest educational opportunities. He hopes to guide her into a career that she loves and finds meaningful.

Javier knows the important role he now has. With a strong and influential Dad himself, he looks forward to building on his solid foundation and his Dad's legacy.

1. Every child is different, not all tips work for every child.
2. Have a lot of patience with the baby and partner.
3. Support each other!
4. Enjoy every second, even if you get frustrated you won't get those moments back.
5. Expect the unexpected.
6. When you get frustrated, take a few deep breaths and a minute or two to gain your focus back. Do not take it out on your baby.
7. Accept any help you can get from loved ones.
8. Take care of your wife too, she is probably more tired than and as exhausted as you!
9. It is a blessing and miracle having a baby. It is the greatest joy and love you can experience.
10. Do your best to be a great role model, they are always looking at what you do and say.

I appreciate the breathing tip Javier mentions in his sixth tip. I still need reminders and am continuously surprised as to how I can forget to breathe. It is so important and readily accessible.

Many people encourage deep breathing. To many, the message becomes trite! It may sound trite, but it is also tried and true. Deep breaths, in through the nose and out through the mouth, the deeper the better, are guaranteed to help. It's known to help with pain, blood flow, energy levels, inflammation, digestion as well as rest and relaxation for the mind and body. That's a huge return on investment.

Although I didn't find literature to confirm deep breathing helps parenting, I'm going out on a limb to make that announcement. It does. Despite all the knowledge, proven success and supportive research, I still forget to breathe deeply. I'm what's known as a shallow breather. I gasp sometimes after prolonged and unnoticed breath-holding; however, that isn't the type of deep breathing recommended.

A variety of methods are recommended to ensure deep breathing is actually beneficial. One of the more common methods is:

> *Breathe in through your nose. Let your belly fill with air.*
> *Breathe out through your nose.*
> *Place one hand on your belly. ...*
> *As you breathe in, feel your belly rise. ...*
> *Take three more full, deep breaths.*

One of my favourites is 3, 6, 6. Breathe in for three seconds, hold for six seconds and breathe out for six seconds. It's worth a quick Google search to look into it and find a method that works for you.

I continue to be surprised by the power I can gain simply by capturing and controlling my breath. It is a free, available and a highly effective technique.

I can't be reminded of breathing enough.

Thanks Javier, I needed that!

#83 Randy – Smiles

Father of four, Randy loved everything about family life. From hugs and kiss to homework he was up for all aspects of being a Dad. Randy didn't miss a moment, highlighting each memory with joy: the family trips, sport events, birthdays, holidays, caroling, fishing, playgrounds, parks and bedtimes. He recalls every laughable joke and every giggle.

There is no memory too small. He even loved the cold toast on Father's Day! The sparkle in their eyes is everything to him. With so much to love, the dark side of parenting didn't escape Randy. Discipline, sickness and the teen years were, as he reports, "*nerve wracking*." Not having all of the answers, or all of the "*things*," lead to challenges.

In the end, Randy wants each of his children to find their soul mate and enjoy a love as great as he's found. He wants them to enjoy the blessings of a great career and a full, loving family life.

1. Treat people the way you want to be treated.
2. Don't go to bed mad even if you must be the one to apologize.
3. Take every opportunity to tell those you love, you love them.
4. Thank God for everything you are blessed with and pray daily.
5. Even if you feel down tell everybody you're great when asked.
6. Keep your word.
7. If you see someone is having a bad day, tell them a joke or give them a compliment.
8. Do your best at everything. You may still suck but you'll know you gave it your all.
9. Smile, it's contagious.
10. Don't be afraid to laugh at yourself because we're all a bit nuts.

Randy's tips have an overarching theme of thinking of others and staying positive. Smiling and loving seemed to be the essence of his parenting practices. I'm sure in implementing Randy's suggestions, any childhood would be full of smiles. What's not to smile about? His tips provide a backdrop of love and fun.

Smiles bring about much happiness, love and laughter. I can't help but wonder, what comes first: does happiness brings the smiles, or do smiles bring happiness?

Clarice (*100 Moms, Mom #74*) advised, "*Smile when no one is watching, you never know who is watching.*" I think it is so cute and cozy to imagine our children catching us happy.

Smiling is known to have positive health implications as well, so there are lots of benefits. Having your children catch you smiling, what could be a better reason — such a warm image. Smiling really does convey so much, to the world and to the children. Happy faces add much to a day. Smiles are not something all kids get.

Of course, with Michael as a son, smiles were plentiful. At the risk of gushing (which I'm never known to do), Michael developed my smile muscles, and the muscles of many others. I think healthy, happy, and loved babies create smiles in every room; assuming the spirits are alive.

As challenging as I found my parenting journey to be, with Michael present there was sure to be many happy breaks in my day. Even these days, his smile can make me forget all of my troubles. Hopefully mine can brighten his day also.

Keep smiling!

#84 Mike – Legacy

Having never met Mike, I already know he's great! I do know his life's partner and given that decision, how could he not be great? Together Mike and his wife have smiles that beam as bright as their personalities. They are ambitious, fun and loving – to only graze the surface. Family images clearly convey their two little boys have inherited their charm, energy and enthusiasm. This family is an adorable quartet.

Mike is a busy guy as an author, landlord and manager. Although engaged in all arenas, no activity is more preferred than the time he spends with his family. Moving happily through life, he has only one source of frustration: when the responsibilities of running a business take him away from time with his family. He works deliberately to manage and balance work requirements and family fun.

Mike loves sharing his knowledge and imparting his wisdom. The legacy of his Dad and his focus on family values has now reached the next generation. Mike works to develop imagination and possibilities in his children's young minds. With his guidance they are sure to create a life of their dreams.

Mike's top 20:

1. Let kids be kids. It is important to let kids test and push limits. Resist the temptation to tell them something is dangerous, or to slow down. One day they might believe you and stop pushing and begin to limit themselves. Never lose sight of the fact that children only get one childhood, help make it extraordinary.
2. Teach love, peace, kindness, patience and that fair is not always equal.

3.	Be firm but loving. I have one laid back child and one that is strong willed who can challenge me both mentally and physically. It's important I express love and develop an understanding of both.

4.	Having children is a privilege, they are your legacy. Make sure you know what you want your legacy to look like. Put family first. Whether your family is one parent, two parents, foster parents, regardless of the makeup, when you raise children, you are forming a family unit, a team.

5.	Raise the fuck out of your children. Give parenting your all. Don't be lazy and don't make excuses. Don't accept mediocrity, be spectacular!

6.	Build a support group around your family. It takes a village to raise a child. Your village could be friends, family, close relatives, distant relatives and even online support. We all face similar challenges. Find people who will baby sit for you, trade babysitting time. You will need to take breaks. If you make mistakes, and you will, it's OK. Pick up from that point, move forward. As long as there is air in your lungs, it is never too late.

7.	Do whatever it takes to allow your child to hang onto their imagination. Fear and lack of self-confidence are generally based on the opinions of others. The world will try to take your child's imagination away, do not let it happen. Encourage them to draw, tell stories and write.

8.	Teach them not to hang with negative people or they'll become one.

9.	Teach that thoughts become things and you become what you think about most of the time.

10.	Teach them to be patriotic. We live in the land of opportunity. It's our duty to enjoy the abundance that surrounds us.

11.	Teach them about the power of the universe and how all humans are connected. Life is a series of events based on thoughts. Relax, and let the universe do most of the work for you.

12.	Introduce them to nature. Go for walks in the woods and let them know about the connection. We are all just energy, vibrating at different frequencies.

13.	Travel, it is not about the destination, it is about the experience. Teach them how to interact with hotel clerks, bell hops, ticket agents and store clerks. Show them how to use maps, menus and manners. Remember travel is about the experience, not the place.

14.	Teach them to be patient. Life is magical. We are all spirits having a human experience. Don't take things too seriously.

15.	Be an amazing role model. Children will naturally look to you for guidance and copy what you do.

16.	See your family like a well-run business/company. The parents are the manager and CEO, the children are the employees. You bring in revenue and have expenses. You need to formulate a solid plan. Set goals and take steps to achieve them. Be a great leader, inspire. Budget, financially plan and figure out how much money you need to accomplish your goals. Every member of your family (AKA team, or company) must be aware of the direction and work together on the collective goals of the group. Work toward fulfillment. Whatever the goal, discuss the required sacrifice, be inclusive. Have team spirit.

17. Do not chase the opinions of others on topics such as money, health or quality of life. They are all important, but you need to decide what is best for you and your children.

18. Teach your children to respect themselves, others and differences. Make sure they know their mother is the queen. Model respect for her and all women.

19. Teach them about fulfillment. Whether you work in or outside of the home prioritize fulfillment. Decide how you want to structure your family to always feel fulfilled. Fulfillment comes from working towards a worthy goal.

20. Love is the key. There is no right or wrong way. Things are not always as they appear. Children want to feel love and security. It is your duty to provide it. The reality is no one has a clue, just do your best.

Mike writes about the privilege of having children through his tips, explicitly stated in his fourth tip, "*Having children is a privilege, they are your legacy. Make sure you know what you want your legacy to look like. Put family first. Whether your family is one parent, two parents, foster parents, regardless of the make-up, when you raise children, you are forming a family unit, a team.*" It's clear he's dedicated a lot of time and consideration to the needs of his family and to his life goal in leading them to happiness. He is playing the "*long game.*"

Mike highlights the need for planning and conscientious leadership. He is astutely aware that he is raising young men, partners, employees and leaders. His value for respect and fulfillment is not only clearly articulated it is a way of being.

I very much related to Mike's reference of legacy, as stated in his fourth tip, "*Make sure you know what you want your legacy to look like.*" I also advise parents to consider what they want their legacy to look like. Mike recognizes the impact of his Dad's legacy. He has used those teachings as a foundation, a launching pad, in the further development of himself as well as in the development of his boys.

The topic of legacy always hits an emotional chord with me. For almost three decades I have consistently considered legacy. I have considered previous generations and the impact of their legacy. More importantly, I spend a lot of time reflecting how I might influence a legacy going forward.

It is a great power and a great privilege.

My books are both about legacy. My life has been all about legacy. My parenting, my conduct and my accomplishments are all about legacy. Watching my son build his life has given me such pride and joy. I have seen first-hand how my attention to legacy has influenced him and will continue to impact generations to come.

My rewards in this regard have surpassed my deepest dreams. My son has become one of the greatest men I have ever known. He embodies all I have worked for, hoped for and more than I've never even considered. Michael has made every day, every doubt and all efforts worthwhile. His accomplishments are jaw-dropping. His ability to love is beautiful. His resilience is unmatched. His happiness fills my heart. Through him I have learned all things wonderful. The meaning and fullness of my life is a result of his love. He is my legacy.

I am happy to guarantee this Dad a magnificent view. I've enjoyed the results of this level of devotion. I'm so excited for him. As his young family continues to flourish, so too will the enormous pride and the joy — some he has already realized. How exciting! The best is yet to come.

Thanks to this dynamic duo for lighting up the world and for working to build two fine young men, that will surely continue to do the same.

PS: If you're interested in hearing more of Mike's wisdom, on an unrelated topic, check out his book on Amazon: Landlord by Design – Complete Guide to Residential Property Management.

#85 Wayne F. – Show Them

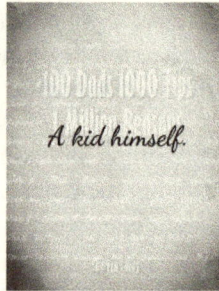

Wayne is Dad to two young girls. He loves being a kid himself and enjoys watching his girls grow and learn all about life. His biggest influence is his Mom. I'm sure his love for his Mother will bring a great deal to how he raises his daughters. His dream for them is that they will be healthy, happy and will always try their best in all they do.

Wayne's best advice is:

1. Don't tell your kids what to do, show them what to do and hope they choose the right way.
2. If you yell at your kids for doing something wrong, don't then do it yourself. They'll do what they are shown and not what they are told.
3. No matter how mad you get, you have to forgive and forget so you do not do anything you will regret.
4. Do not teach from what you did, teach from what you learned out of what you've done.
5. Show them how to live. When you just tell them how they won't listen. People tend to do what they are shown, not told.
6. Be there for them no matter what they do or say. In the end they are all that matter in this world.
7. Keep them as busy. Make sure they are doing what they want to do so they are happy and not getting into trouble.
8. Get them a pet to take care of so they will have a sense of responsibility in life.

Throughout Wayne's tips it was clear how important he values role modelling. Having never met Wayne it seems as if he's a show-me-don't-tell-me kind of guy. The strongest example I can think of is that of smoking.

My parents warned, begged, pleaded, dreamed, and harped that I never smoke, as they puffed and puffed and puffed. I remember as a young child just being curious as to what must be in these cigarettes that could cause such fear. I was eager to experience what all the excitement was about. Then, they got me! Cigarettes took hold of me. Their words and warnings meant nothing.

I wanted different for Michael. I wanted to be an impeccable role model for him. My standards were exhausting, although the cigarettes had me for far too many years, I did excel in some areas. It is a great deal of pressure to hold high standards, particularly when you were raised with a lower set yourself. Increasing standards is worth the effort.

I told myself I would behave perfectly for fifteen years. I secretly made this commitment to Michael. I'm not sure why I decided on fifteen years, but that's what I decided. I speculated if I could set a solid example, hold my shit together, for fifteen years, Michael would have a concrete foundation.

I had little fun as I worked toward my best attempt at a flawless example. I did not curse, scream, gossip, gamble, drink, do drugs, slam doors, or even shake salt on my food – a very tall order – the opposite of who I was! I modelled the future I wanted for Michael, despite what I wanted at the time.

It was a climb, and I don't regret a step! As a result of living for him, we were both given a wonderful life. (*I'm far less perfect these days!*)

I think Wayne would approve of my efforts; the pay-off was absolutely grand!

Thanks Wayne!

#86 Ben – Decision Making

Ben is an adoring and tuned-in Dad, one who loved parenting so much he took on two rounds. With four children, his oldest is thirty-four and his youngest eleven. He is happy to hold their hands or heal their hearts, whatever it is they need.

This Dad loves to be actively involved in both play and in their development. He loves to listen to their concerns as much as he loves to snuggle. There is no parenting duty he won't tackle.

Strong male role models such as his Granddad Branford, Dad Elbert and Uncle Myles have showed him everything he needed to know in life and in parenting. His dream for his family is healthy and strong relationships. He hopes all his children will find happiness and a career they love.

Ben's top tips:

1. Girls are sensitive. If you're saying something that you think is a joke or think it will hurt their feelings, refrain from saying it.
2. Always be involved with their life, friends, school, activities, etc. They will let you know when you're digging too deep and at what point to back off.
3. Don't go too hard when it comes to meeting their boyfriends/girlfriends. They know you're trying to protect them and keep them from getting hurt. Let it be known if they are hurt you will react and leave it at that.
4. Just because you overachieved or excelled in something does not mean they can, will or want to. Guide them and help them but don't push things on them.
5. Try to introduce them to music, sports, poetry, mechanics, science, you get the idea. Make it vast and include things you don't really like because they are not you. They are their own person and they might like different things. You might even discover something new for yourself that you have missed out on.

6. If your child asks you to do something silly, swallow your pride and do it. Making memories will last a lifetime and give them a fun story to tell. Be in the pictures! Many of us don't like having our pictures taken but when you are gone, they won't care if you didn't like that picture of yourself, they will just be happy to have it.

7. This is a big one: listen! I don't mean just hear what they say but actually listen to what's being said. Often times what you're hearing isn't what they are trying to let you know. Ask questions. Personally, I find people only listen to respond, they often miss the chance to understand what is being said.

8. Girls and hair, for god sake, don't touch their hair! Don't say anything about it! Unless you're giving a compliment, not a suggestion. Their hair is their most treasured possession.

9. You're a parent not a child's best friend. Know the line and when to walk it. Showing tough love is difficult but is very important. When they ask for too much or more then is deserved, it is important to understand that "*no*" is an acceptable answer.

10. Here is a really hard one, let them fail. Guidance is important, but if they have made up their mind to do something all you can do is support them, regardless of the expected outcome. Let them stand up for themselves. Some of life's best lessons are taught this way. Of course, you do not intentionally let them fail, but you will not win against a determined spirit. You can try to help them learn from your mistakes, but they will need to make some of their own too.

11. Always forgive and do it quickly and meaningfully.

12. Involve them in the home and external events. Even from a young age they should be involved in decisions. This will give them a sense of inclusion and will teach them how to be responsible. Their bedroom is a great start. If it's a mess, and they can't find the toy they want or their favourite piece of clothing is dirty, they need to know that actions or a lack of action will have results.

13. If something is their fault, don't let them pass the buck and blame a parent or another sibling.

14. When planning a trip show them what is on the route, and what events that can be worked into the plan and let them help choose. This will help with a lot of skill development and will instill a sense of belong and an appreciation for teamwork.

15. Sooner than you know your child will want to stay behind with their friends instead of coming with you, accept it. Know you have given them the tools they need to do the right thing. For me, the planning for this should start at young age. Have them know household rules and expectations. They will be responsible enough to respect them, and even make sure their friends respect them as well. I'm not going to scold another person's child, but I will let my child know that bad

decisions will result in that child being sent home and their parents will get all the details.

16. Involve them in helping others and doing it for the right reasons. Volunteer to visit ailing friends. Support your own friends by being with them. Be kind and your kids will also be kind. After you help someone, if a reward is offered respectfully decline it, which is helping for the right reason.

17. Always share in the games, the fun, and the goofy times but also in the hardships and the tears.

18. Make sure they know you are proud of them. This is spoken with words but can better be shown with actions. Be involved, show support and emotion. Show joy, smiles and share sadness. Be with them in all ways, during success and failures.

I'm so glad Ben has had the chance to raise four children. I'm happy to know there are adults out in the world with this foundation.

Ben is a military man, a burly biker, with a very bushy, manly moustache. The thought of him being "*goofy*" and learning all he did about the importance of a girl's hair, I can't help but smile. I can imagine the cozy cuddles and the comfort he gave to each of his babies.

He and I share many parenting practices. As Ben expanded on in his twelfth tip, we also provided a lot of opportunity for involvement in decision making. Building the skill of decision making is one of our most important jobs. We started in the early years, the formative years, as soon as Michael could talk, as soon as he could point. I knew the importance of decision making. I started right away.

If kids get a choice in the more benign decisions when the big ones come, they will be well prepared, "*Which sweater, vegetable, hat, book, or outing?*" Making fun and easy decisions serve as the first stage. Each decision will help to build a strong foundation for what lies ahead.

The isolation and comfort of home, and cozy cuddles are short lived. In our case, Michael was heading to day care at just eighteen months. He would be making decisions there. I was painfully aware my decisions for him would be happening in a very small, ever-shrinking, window of time. I knew, even at age two, he would be making decisions. My first plan of attack was convincing him he was already good at it. "*Michael, you make such great decisions.*"

Every time he picked blue instead of green, "*Great decision buddy.*" When he picked green instead of blue, "*Nice choice.*" He selected this shirt instead of the other, "*Great Michael, good decision!*" He '*decided*' to wear mittens, "*I knew you'd make the right decision.*" I said it at every turn. I reinforced every decision. I was alert and on deck. I quickly convinced Michael he was the best decision maker ever! By the time Michael entered elementary school he could tell you himself he was a strong decision maker.

Repeating to kids they have the ability to make solid decisions is a gold-star technique. This skill is tied for importance second only to reading (in my humble opinion). I'm hoping solid decisions will be up ahead for all our children. Ben and I can sit back and enjoy the view as their precious lives unfold.

Thanks Ben! You not only provided the country a great service with your career but also with your parenting.

#87 David Y. – Teach Observation

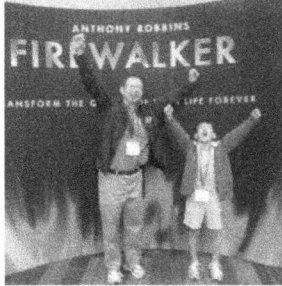

David is the first of four Firewalkers featured in this book. He and the three men to follow have attended a Tony Robbins event, making a significant investment of both time and money for the benefit of personal and/or professional developments. I know because I did it also.

I met David in 2015 at a conference, *Unleash the Power Within*. We spent four days with seventy-five hundred highly charged, positive and motivated people known as Firewalkers. My life was never the same.

I met a few wonderful folks who impacted my life in unforgettable ways. David was one of the most unforgettable. I'm so happy we met. I was thrilled when he agreed to participate in 100 Dads. I was eager to learn more about him and his parenting practice.

From our time together at the conference, I only knew he was fabulous, friendly and inspiring. Through his contribution to 100 Dad's I later learned David is also a semi-retired nuclear physician, an investment systems designer, investment advisor and of course, most importantly a loving and adoring Dad to a teenage boy.

With all of that going on, David found time to put together some of his best advice for Dads.

1. Spend time with your child, lots of it! Loving and raising children is an exercise of prioritization. One reason I semi-retired from medicine was because, as a physician, my career mandated me being on call on nights and weekends. I was burning out. Life is too short to burn out on any one facet of the Wheel of Life.* When you actively look for

more time to spend with family, you must automatically say 'no' to less priority distractions in life.

2. Spending time with your child means not just more bonding/guidance time, it also means your children do not waste their time or damage their brain on watching mindless TV or playing video games.

3. Reading tip: Mind-numbing time spent on reading the same favourite books over and over again with your two or three-year-old teaches them to read at an incredibly young age.

4. Find teaching moments, whenever you can. An example, when I was reading with my three-year-old, sometimes I'd follow my fingertip under the word, then occasionally stop and see if he could 'read' the next word. He'd often get the word right; whether because he just memorized the words or was actually reading, he associated spoken words to written words on the page.

5. Teach observation. As a toddler my child might point out something he'd be interested in while we're shopping. I'd ask how old he'd have to be to get that, then point out the label identifying the age recommendation. Then I'd ask how much it was, and that may lead into a discussion about where the price tag is, what money is, etc. When he made an observation, such as when we play with a science kit or visit a children's museum, I would explain how things work in bite-size toddler-specific pieces and help guide them to find further observations.

6. Try audio books. Ever since he was seven, car time was audio book time. We've listened to classic children's books such as Gulliver's Travels, as well as self-help books such as Tony Robbins' CDs. Proud to say, he prefers self-help books. For his tenth birthday I took him to see Tony Robbins live. That was full of huge, magical moments.

7. Find magic moments, whenever you can. It's true they grow up so fast. I knew since my child was a baby that whatever I was doing with him wouldn't last. Every baby bottle I prepared, every diaper I changed, might seem like a pain at the moment, but I knew that I'd look back fondly at these times. Every laugh, every cry, every moment of pure bonding, they will all pass. Treasure them. Don't wait until after they're grown and left the nest as you think back nostalgically. Treasure them now.

8. Lead by example. Kids are more observant than you think. If you tell them to exercise or read and you don't do it yourself, what do you think they learn to do? For example, I signed him up for kung fu class. I took the class with him. He got a kick out of his Dad being in the same class with him. Did being the only grown-up in the class make me self-conscious? Of course not, this is son bonding/guidance time, and from class, we'd get common reference points to relate to and work on outside of class. Bonus: In the beginning, he felt frustrated he

couldn't do much of the stuff I could do. In a couple of years, he was doing things I could never hope to do. This helped set in him both an internal and external example of the power of diligent practice, comparing himself to how he improved compared to me, as well as compared to how he used to be.

9. Share emotions authentically. I grew up in a family culture where emotional stoicism was valued. Grit and do it, never let them see you cry, etc. With my son, I encourage discussion about his feelings. When we're at a tournament together, for instance, and he expresses how nervous he is, I relate that I'm nervous, too, and that this nervousness before a tournament never goes away. I explain it's normal to be nervous, and that instead of fighting the nervousness, realize nervousness gives us energy to perform at our best.

10. Be in touch with your own emotional state. Be aware of where you want to model and lead from. This skill has helped me relate more empathetically with people in general. Another bonus: My son has been open to sharing poignant trouble spots in his life. I have no doubt that when the terrible emotional torrents start developing in his teen years, he'll have ingrained emotional tools to deal with them, as well as no doubt he'd trust me to talk out his emotions. Teen angst, teen rebellion, teen drug use, teen pregnancy, teen online predation, teen problems in general have a much harder time growing in an environment where the teen has a respected, non-judgmental role model he feels safe to share and relate to.

11. Praise effort, not accomplishment or trait. When my son does well on a homework assignment, or test, or tournament, or his own project, I express how proud I am at how much work he did or how hard he studied, not that he is smart or talented. Studies have shown that praising a child for being smart only makes them reluctant to tackle difficult tasks, because failure would mean they were not smart, whereas praising a child for working hard would encourage a child to tackle difficult tasks knowing that success or failure, he played full out and learned something.

12. Use questions instead of commands. Questions help focus attention and encourage thinking; questions show you respect their opinion. Instead of commanding my son it's bedtime, time to go to sleep, I ask him *"What time would you like to go to sleep?"* and then hold him to it. If he states an answer that I wasn't expecting, such as a time later than I expected, I'd follow up with, *"How did you come up with that time?"* or *"What are your thoughts, that you need that much time?"* Since he knows that I seldom judge him, he tends to openly answer my questions, and oftentimes, I learn a little bit more about him.

13. Respect them. If it's cold outside, and I see he's going out in shorts, instead of saying *"Wear long sleeves and a jacket, it's cold outside,"* I

ask, *"What temperature is it outside?"* and he'd look it up; if he decides to go out in shorts anyway, I might bring an extra jacket, or not. If later on he exclaims, *"Wow, it's cold!"* I'd agree; I wouldn't rub it in that I was wearing a jacket, he'd feel like he was being judged. If he reluctantly asks for a jacket, that blow to the ego to ask is 'punishment' enough. A lesson learned through natural consequences sticks and ingrains much more completely than constant nagging. Their self-esteem comes from being problem solvers. They would rather make their own decisions and live with the consequences; a question such as "H*ow cold is it outside?"* only focuses their attention to another fact upon which to make their decision. I see other parents commanding their sons *"You're not going outside like that, wear a coat."* and then I see their eyes rolling, waiting for their chance to rebel. As for the protective parents who would rather make their child wear a coat than for them to get sick, well, two things: 1) Nothing teaches like experience. If he gets sick, he'll be miserable for a couple of days, but he'll survive, and remember this lesson more than if we just said, *"Wear a coat or you'll get sick,"* and 2) If he really is going to do something dangerous or potentially harmful (such as cutting open a box with a box cutter, cooking, etc.), I might point out safety points and demonstrate a cut or two (always point the blade away from yourself and others, make sure handles are turned in on the stove so you don't accidentally bump one and spill hot soup over yourself and the stove, etc.) but then let him finish the task. He'll quickly figure out what kind of decisions he's capable of doing, and which ones he'll feel more comfortable deferring to you. Now, there are misconceptions that *"boys will be boys,"* but as a Dad, we can model what being a boy is.

14. Help them become adventurous and take risks. Be in the moment and be with them. Disrespectful actions reflect an unspoken insecurity that's worth exploring with non-judgmental questions and sharing of personal experiences.

15. Respect their unique traits and their unique goals in life. I grew up with five generations of doctors and professors. Did I feel pressure to become a doctor? Maybe, at some subconscious level, I may have felt an unspoken desire from my Dad for me to pursue medicine. Sons love to make their Dads proud of them. That's why it was such an excruciating decision to do something different, after all these years of dedication and sacrifice as a doctor, to reach out beyond my comfort zone and identity to do something different. Am I going to 'force' or even suggest my son go into medicine or any other profession? No way. I'm much happier now breaking away from medicine and pursuing my dream, and I wish I had the emotional fortitude to have done this earlier.

16. Find and develop strengths and interests, find what he loves to do, then step up and do it, even if there is no label for what he wants to do. In life, even in the most secure job, we can get fired or downsized. Might as well fail at something you love to do; doing something you love to do gives you that extra emotional energy and drive to succeed and thrive. It would be so easy for my son to just follow a role model such as his Dad. There are many Dads out there who hate their jobs, hate their lives, and complain a lot. Probably the most difficult decision in life is knowing what you really want, then deciding which path to take.

17. Finances, the unspoken bugaboo. I was able to semi-retire at the age of 45 because, at the age of twenty-seven, I was a broke intern fresh out of medical school and quickly learned that I didn't know how to deal with money. My parents, with the best of intentions, insulated me from the terrors and drudgery of managing money and debt while I was growing up. Great intention, beautiful intention, but with the unintended consequence of my financial crash and burn. The good news is I reached rock bottom, where I knew I had to change, learn, and get this area of my life handled. I studied personal financial skills, investing skills, until I became financially comfortable enough that I could take control of my life in other ways. Eighteen years later and I'm semi-retired. People started asking me how I managed to do this; I thus wrote my book on how I invest and opened up my own registered investment advisory service. I can now teach my son to have little, and yet still enjoy and appreciate life and be happy and resourceful. The reality is, finances are by far the most neglected and poorly appreciated wedge in the Wheel of Life.* Money may not necessarily buy happiness or magic moments, but without it, we're in big trouble. Attitudes start with the parents. The attitude, *"It's because of your kids that we cannot become rich,"* is much less empowering than, *"It's because of your kids that we MUST become rich."* Financial topics can be a voodoo, forbidden topic, or financial topics can be a common dinner table topic. It's up to the parents to step up and be a role model and guide even here.

Wheel of Life is a concept referring to a life balance tool of examining the areas of your life where you feel most strong and where you feel most weak. This is often used in life planning, goal setting and personal development. A quick Google search brings up many examples, often ranging from six to eight spokes of the Wheel. This Wheel of Life should not be confused with the Buddhist Wheel of Life, which is concerned more about your awareness of your mental state.

David and I may have sat together by chance but it's clear, since the day we met our babies, we parented by choice. As in my life, David's personal development and victory over hardship enhanced his teachings and informed his parenting.

On the surface we are very different, yet deeply similar. The love we share for our little boys and our devotion to their development led us to live parallel lives in many ways. The value of David's journey now serves as a gift to his son. What a joy to witness our influence take shape. I also worked to provide consistent guidance, while preparing Michael for natural consequences. It's a delicate balance for sure. I really appreciate David's examples in this regard. I found them to be enlightening and practical.

David gives a great example in his thirteenth tip, *"If it's cold outside, instead of saying "Wear long sleeves and a jacket, it's cold outside," I ask, "What temperature is it outside?"*

In my experience, I was sometimes a "*Wear your coat!*" or an "*I told-you-so*" kind of parent. I can tell you that approach may have seemed to work in the moment but it was counterproductive. Sure, it saved time but did nothing in the area of building self-esteem and independence which were my ultimate goals.

That said, in the rush of day-to-day sometimes my goal was just to get out the door. I wasn't always looking at the long run. Now out of the woods, with the advantage of hindsight, I can see that tone only undermines a child and does nothing to teach independence and reinforce their own abilities.

As Maya Angelou famously said, "*When you know better, do better.*" David's tips help with *knowing*. To teach children to observe and ask questions is my favourite take away. David's writing and examples provide clear guidance for any parent who is interested in trying this approach. I'm confident that any parent willing to try these suggestions will instantly see the benefit.

It will take a little bit more time on the front end to develop these skills; however, I guarantee in the long run, they will result in less hassle, time saved and skill development for both parent and child. Having used these approaches periodically in my own parenting, I can confirm these methods will make your parenting load a little lighter, establish solid ground for the decisions up ahead and will also provide safety for your child as they venture off into the world without you. It is a win for you and most importantly a win for them.

Once your children learn to observe and question independently, they will begin working through challenges with acute discernment. You will have far less 'heavy lifting' to do. My greatest joy was watching Michael discover the world using his own abilities. A gentle nudge goes so much farther than a hard, demanding push.

Another similarity between David and I was our paternal influence. As David states, "*Every life is an example, or a warning; I'm thankful my*

relationship with my Dad was rich in both examples as well as warnings."
Same here.

Thanks David, for the richness you bring to the world, and have brought to my life during our all-too-brief encounter.

#88 Jay B. – Tenderness

Jay is a virtual friend of mine and the second Firewalker in the group. He shares my love for Tony Robbins, and of fire walking. It is immediately clear at the introduction, Jay has intense zest for life, achievement and family. He is ambitious and accomplished.

This Father of three is a self-described performing artist, curious thinker, educator, board member and solution finder. Jay states the most important foundation of his parenting is his goal to *"break the cycle of generational brokenness."* We have something in common there as well.

Jay confides that men in his life have abandoned their responsibilities, on both sides of his family tree. With such a history, he's felt insecure as to exactly how to be a Dad. He appreciates the opportunity to establish a new meaning of family, a loving legacy of paternal leadership.

He shared feelings of inadequacy, impatience, high expectations and lack of a tender approach. Having made tremendous progress, Jay values the importance of sharing fears, process and outcomes.

Jay's top tips:

1. Take great care of your wife and keep her first on your list. There is no greater (or easier) way to build up or destroy your family unit. Your wife loves your children in ways that complement your own love. She'll be there when you cannot, and she will make sense of you to them when you don't make any sense at all.
2. If your ultimate goal is to see your children happy, thriving, and eager to blossom in their various adventures, being able to witness and enjoy having parents who are devoted to each other and express their love regularly is the best way to accomplish this.

3. Use your faith in God (or get some faith in God). Show your children that miracles are possible. A sense of awe and wonder are healthy and vital to a child's perception of the world around them.
4. Be tender.
5. Be fearless.
6. Set ambitious goals, for you and for them. No kid wants to have the worst story during show-and-tell. No child wants to have a boring Dad. Nobody wants to hear about their friend's awesome weekend while they were stuck watching Dad watch football on Sunday.
7. Get out, do something bold, make a statement with your parenting that raises the stakes, rent an RV, help your kids train for a marathon, make memories.
8. Be home for bedtime more often than not, and tuck your kids in. Having (and making) dinner for your family is equally important. Learn a few recipes. Give your wife the night off unexpectedly and teach your kids that Dads are superheroes.
9. Write a poem to your daughter, buy her flowers, and take her dancing – even if you have to dance in the backyard with nobody around. She'll remember it forever.
10. Take your son camping for the weekend. Make that time a priority and make it awesome. Pick up some jerky on your way, bring fishing poles, and go scouting for Bigfoot!
11. Watch movies with your family that inspires them. Sure, watch the standard fare, but make sure the larger balance of your media time goes toward opening channels of discovery and soul satisfaction.
12. Be a guardian. The world is going to attack you and your family. The failures of your past will cause you to doubt, others will throw stones, and your time is going to slip through your hands. Protect your family, defend the purity of your children, and always be looking a mile down the road – be prepared. Regret is a debt that is never paid in full. Apologize when necessary, cancel your work event if things at home are not going well, and have a vision for your family.
13. You've got this!

For some of us, the world is not such a "*tender*" place. Seeing Jay suggest tenderness in his fourth tip makes my heart skip a beat. The thought of being raised by a Dad who valued tenderness, well, I can't imagine. I can't imagine but I've tried.

It is wonderful that this man is raising three children. What a future they will have with a foundation of tenderness. Having grown up in the absence of tenderness, I can't help but ponder what comfort tenderness would have been. A tender Dad would have unquestionably been a welcomed and life changing experience. The world would have been completely different; today would have been completely different.

This tip also made me question if I, as a Mom, demonstrated tenderness. I can't honestly say I was tender. I was loving, busy, hardworking, well-meaning; frantic, but tender, I'm not sure.

I'm confident, tenderness would be a quality appreciated at any age. I will aspire to be more mindful of it. I will do what I can to incorporate a tender approach as I continue to reach higher with my next generation.

Thanks Jay, for each of your points and to your dedication to family and personal growth.

#89 Michael M. – Student or Teacher

Michael is a poet and the facilitator of 'Smiles through PocketM8,' which is an international family of people who donate key rings to inspire others globally. Michael believes in giving and loving everyone, everywhere, and has dedicated his life to doing exactly that. He, too, is a Firewalker.

Currently raising three young children ages two to six years old, Michael enjoys the pure, unconditional and unquestionable love of his children. Although the responsibilities of family security and protection have become a fresh priority, their love makes all the pressure bearable.

Focused on making a difference in the world, Michael hopes the same for his children. His dream is they will find fulfillment in doing whatever their hearts desire and will value the rewards in creating an environment of kindness.

1. Always look at your child as the teacher. They are a gift given to you to teach you. You affect their personal growth but also, they are teaching compassion, understanding and so much more.
2. Appreciate your child's questions, especially the hard ones. Question are how we learn. As we get older, we often stop asking questions. We either perceive we already know or that we may be a fool for asking. A child asks to learn and learn some more. Let them ask, especially the hard questions. It's the hard answers that give quality to the future in all areas of life. Maybe we can be more like our children, ask to learn.

3. Find your own inner child and just play. Be silly. Nobody else really cares. Play and have fun. You might just find that those moments embellish your child's memories and give them a smile. Or maybe that's the reflection of you and the smile you have even right now thinking this through. There's love in play and there's play in love.

4. Listen, really listen. You are the walking almanac, encyclopedia and dictionary to them. That doesn't mean that every question or comment needs advice. Listen and absorb their real worries and wants. Often a nod in understanding and a hug is needed as much as the education.

5. Give a little less than you want to. Yes, they're our future and dreams and we want to give them the world. You don't want them to come to expect a gift after sweets after gift after holiday after chocolate after meals out...you get my point. They sometimes need to know that you love giving them things and yet that the greatest gift is, in fact, your love and their love in this moment. That gift is greater than anything.

6. Adventure with your children, get down and dirty. Take a walk. Find some mud. Enjoy the grime in life. Take time to get grimy and dirty in the time you have together. These moments are all too rare, yet they are the memories that last. You can use the simple cleaning of a bike, getting stuck in mud or playing with stones as tools to teach so many things about life. Walk through nature and embrace the dirt.

7. How are you doing? Ask it twice. To fully understand emotions and help children understand them is an art. Asking and giving time to respond allows them to give their thoughts time and to give understanding to their answer. This does not mean you'll understand too, by the way! Inquire to what might help them continue with this good feeling or what might help them get rid of this bad feeling. Work with them and hold their hand. Shoulder to shoulder they can take on anything with Dad.

8. Don't punish bad behaviour. Praise it! Yes, totally bonkers! But think about it. We all rebelled in life against the system or else the system broke us along the way. Take time to relax and allow them to do the same. Highlight the pain created or what could have happened by asking them how things could have gone and what could have happened. Then follow things through with questioning how they can flip this and make people happy and support others in opposition of the negative actions. You've just praised them for being good and solving their negative actions. Well done.

9. You're being watched, act accordingly. Yep, you told him not to pick his nose or bite his fingernails yet you're sitting on the sofa doing what you said not to! 'Do as I say not as I do' does not work. You are the example of life and expectation. Monitor yourself and be the example of life you want them to have.

10. Breathe daily and enjoy your gift. Every moment of this life is a moment to treasure. These beautiful angels that are our children are the ultimate gift. We are here as their guardian angels for as long as we are here. Stop. Breathe. Embrace how lucky you are and how loved you are. Now give that energy to them every day and watch it grow.

"Always look at your child as the teacher." I've had no better teacher. As Michael further states in his first tip, *"They are a gift given to you to teach you. You affect their personal growth but also they are also teaching compassion, understanding and so much more."*

My son, Michael, has gifted me personal growth, compassion, understanding and yes, so much more. I am everything I am either because of him or on behalf of him. Becoming his Mom gave me a will to live, a desire to succeed, the awareness that education would matter, and employment was possible. I truly am all I am because of his love.

Before becoming a Mom, I did not have any self-worth. I did not see a future for myself. I allowed people to mistreat me, abuse me and even assault me. I didn't even know it was wrong that they did. I thought they were my friends, my family or my partner. I didn't feel worthy of love and I didn't expect respect. Those were dark times.

When I found out I was going to have a child, all of that changed. I found purpose. I found love. My son began teaching me the moment that 'stick turned blue.' I mattered. I instinctively knew my baby had value. He had worth and was worthy of love, respect and a Mother. I became *"Michael's Mom."* I was somebody and I had purpose.

On that day, over twenty-eight years ago, I became his student. I was his guide, his life manager; but he was my teacher. He taught me how to love, how to be responsible how to care about myself. Through his eyes I gained an understanding that I was worth it, his Mom deserved better and so did he. I returned to school, dropped the darkness and looked for light in everything I did. I turned my life around to honour him. I wanted to make him proud and to do the right thing. He taught me to care.

Now, twenty-eight years later I continue to learn from that not-so-little boy of mine. With each encounter I want to be a better person. I continue to grow and to seek development so he will continue to be proud of me. I want to uphold engaging conversation. I still have much to learn. All I have and all I've learned is a direct result of what was needed to be *"Michael's Mom."* I did it all so I could do that well. He taught me to be a respectable person, a reliable and loving Mom and now a responsible adult. Michael's actions continue to challenge me in more ways than he will likely ever know. He has become the type of person I hope to someday be.

He is confident, happy, healthy and makes deliberate choices. He finds time for family, friends and for fun. He is fully engaged in all he does.

Michael is an example to me. He is still my teacher, the best teacher I've ever had.

Thanks Michael M., and Little Michael, you have both contributed to my learning and legacy.

#90 John P. – Forgive Your Parents

Ann Marie and John
(My {Doreen Coady} Parents)

John P. the founder of *charitables.com* (a marketplace for charities), has four children ranging in age from two to nineteen years old. John enjoys the wide variety of ages and the specialness in every stage.

The experience of childhood wonderment combined with the navigation required for the transition of his oldest daughter to the adult world fills his days and his heart. He loves watching life through the eyes of his children and hopes they will all work to create a life they love and one that will fill their hearts with happiness.

1. Frame the questions to your kids around "*how did this make you feel?*" The more open they are about expressing their emotions the more peace they will live with.
2. Your kids only need to know they are heard, seen, and loved. If they are misbehaving, it's because of a deficiency in one of those. Trying to reprimand the behaviour without addressing the cause is like playing whack a mole. Address what they're missing and watch the behaviour transform.
3. Tell your kids how easy it is to make money. Even if you don't believe it, they will believe you and their beliefs will shape their lives.
4. Your kids are here to teach you as much as you are here to teach them. Don't ignore the lessons. That's why they chose you, that's the beauty of life.
5. Forgive your parents for the shit they caused you. They were only playing their role in making you the person you are. Even if they deserve an Oscar for their role, let the resentment go, find the lesson,

and break the cycle. Hope for the same compassion when your kids remember the shit you caused them.

6. Most of your relationship with your kids will be spent as adults. The years you have with them as little kids can be filled with stress and frustration or it can be filled with hide and seek and tea parties. Make time to play before the time is gone.

7. Tell your kids you're grateful you get to be their parent.

8. Record them singing when they're little. It'll melt their hearts when they grow up.

9. Don't stop your kids from scraping their knees. If they don't get a chance to fail, they don't get a chance to grow. If you try to protect them from everything they'll feel like you don't trust them.

10. Encourage your kids to make friends with the new kid in class.

11. Don't steal your kids' chance to feel pride of accomplishment by making it easy for them. Let them work hard in a shit job making shit money to buy something they really want. They'll piss and moan in the short term and thank you in the long run.

12. Play in bare feet outside with your kids. Introduce them to the beauty of nature.

13. Ask your kids what they're grateful for every day. You're showing them that you're interested in their happiness while wiring their brains to be happy.

14. Don't go on your phone (other than to do something immediately necessary) in front of your kids. Don't teach them the digital world is more important than the present moment. My oldest saw her mother and I go on our phones often, now she's an adult and rarely looks up.

15. Tell your kids that phones, iPads and apps are designed to be addictive. Assist with their usage.

16. You are always showing your son how to be a partner and showing your daughter how she should expect to be treated. Your behaviour is the foundation for all their future relationships. Be the man your daughter deserves.

17. Tell Dad jokes.

18. Whether you or your kids see it or not, they will likely work tirelessly your whole life subconsciously to make you proud. Don't tell them you're proud of their achievements. This will put them on a never-ending path to achieve. These achievements will bring very short-lived bursts of happiness before they will feel empty and compelled to try again. Tell them you love them for just being them. Tell them you're proud no matter what they do. Ask them if their achievement made them happy, and then tell them you're proud of them for making themselves happy. This will free them to uncover their purpose, not what they think will make you happy. Many people mourn the death

of a parent and then immediately feel a huge sense of relief that they can now do whatever they want. Don't let this be your legacy.

John is the final Firewalker in this foursome. He provides a perfect transition, into my most personal Dads which are to follow, as I move into concluding this amazing endeavour. His fifth tip gives me the opportunity to discuss one of the greatest gifts, the gift of forgiveness. I've not only given this gift to myself but have also been gifted it by Michael. My life went full circle as I was granted precious relief and understanding.

I absolutely love John's fifth tip encouraging forgiveness. "*Forgive your parents for the shit they caused you. They were only playing their role in making you the person you are. Even if they deserve an Oscar for their role, let the resentment go, find the lesson, and break the cycle. Hope for the same compassion when your kids remember the shit you caused them.*" John attributes "*The Hoffman Process*" as having been a key factor in finding forgiveness. He encourages others to look into it if they too are seeking understanding and acceptance.

Happily, both Michael and I have forgiven our parents. On a day I questioned my parenting and the negative impact some of my choices might have made on Michael, I sent him a message stating the same. I will forever cherish the moment I received this reply from Michael, "*At the end of the day I love my life and who I am as a person. You should take comfort in that any perceived deficiencies or screw ups of yours may have been an important part of getting me to where I am today.*" I was completely fulfilled, in awe.

I understand the significance of not only having and taking the opportunity to disclose my fear to him, but also the significance in receiving his acceptance and even his appreciation of my imperfections. Acceptance and forgiveness did not come so easy. For me, it required many years of therapy, countless hours of personal development to consider, understand, accept and eventually forgive the "*shit they caused.*" That said, it was worth every minute. Forgiving my parents was one of the best gifts I gave to myself and one of my longest journeys.

There were a number of concepts that helped me to reach a place of forgiveness, with the help of professionals. The first concept was realizing my parents couldn't give me what they didn't have. I now know more about what exactly they didn't have.

Another concept was recognizing they were living with unresolved trauma. Both of my parents lived in abusive, violent and alcoholic homes. That is a lot to contend with. They had an extremely limited view of the world and little to no insight as to their own childhood trauma.

A third concept was, they did the best they could, which some might argue. I might argue. Although I might argue, I do believe they were doing the best with what they had. They had limited understanding, significant substance abuse issues, no solid adult role models, and a weak social network, minimum education overall and even less education on childhood development. Considering all that, they did an amazing job and clearly tried their best.

Although I was raised in a challenging environment, and did not escape my own childhood trauma, I recognize the successes. I was not raised in a violent home. I am so thankful to have not witnessed violence. I was not physically abused. I think that is a paramount factor in my ability to rebuild my life.

My parents were both employed in their respective careers. Our basic needs were met, and I did not have to worry about hunger, also another protective factor. My parents remained together for the first sixteen years of my life. They were literally present, if not always figuratively present. I knew where they were or when they would be home. I had a bed, a pillow and the necessities. Both of my parents gave me more than they had. I think that is a great standard for all parents to reach for. It is the standard I reached for.

It's unfortunate that children expect their parents to know it all, to have it all and to be right. Those things are not always true; are rarely true. As adults we are misunderstood. Sometimes we're just old teenagers with money and cars. Sometimes we don't know anything. Sometimes we have the mind of a six-year-old; yet we are in charge of raising others and responsible for their needs and development.

As it's said, there's no certification or manual. We are all just '*winging it.*' I proudly say, they did what they knew how to do and did far better than their parents before them, who likely did better than their parents before them. We can never really measure our performance in the parenting realm.

I suggest the best measure of our performance is the life satisfaction of our children. I believe their happiness and ability to manage the world is a direct reflection of our efforts.

The greatest gifts I've ever received, the very peak of my iceberg, are two messages given to me by my son:

"At the end of the day I love my life and who I am as a person. You should take comfort in that any perceived deficiencies or screw ups of yours may have been an important part of getting me where to where I am today."

and

"You have single-handedly broken the cycle of multi-generational trauma."

I wish every parent the same understanding and a similar success. In the end, as my Mom advised, "*If you put Michael's best interest first you won't go wrong.*"

The next collection of Dads is a group very dear to me, in the most sentimental ways. Ethan and Mitchell are currently in the early stage of parenting. Their stories brought me back to my beginning, one of great uncertainty and the humblest of times. Talking to them reminded me of intense struggles, seemingly insurmountable fears and a time when all I had on my side was the love in my heart for my little boy.

I appreciate their honesty and the vulnerabilities they shared. I hope they will continue to find the strength and courage to always put their babies first. I wish their sweet families the very best.

Three Dads following, Aaron, Darryl and Brian, all represent much loved people in my past. Their involvement has allowed me to carry the memories and lives of Gloria, Shaun and Jason in this piece of my journey. I've been given the opportunity to memorialize all they have meant to me and to ensure their names are recorded in my life in a meaningful way. I honour these Dads for giving me this great gift.

My favourite cousin, brother-in-law and cherished friend follow, Kenny, Joe Moose and Mike S. Their contributions have allowed me to give them a special place in this book, and to also let them know how much I love and value their influence in my life.

Finally, the grand finale, my everything and my every reason, Big Mike and Little Michael. My conclusion, I'm sure, will speak for itself.

I am humbled and privileged to share with the world some of my most favourite Dads, and the great love they have given to me, the world and their children.

#91 Ethan – Get Help

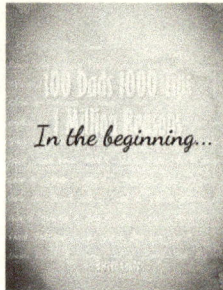

Ethan is the youngest Dad in this book, the only teen Dad. At age nineteen he's enjoying his world with a three-month old little boy who has become the light of his life. Ethan is still learning all about parenting and was happy to share his tips as a new Dad.

We had a great conversation, having both entered the parenting world at an early age. We had a lot in common. Ethan and I shared similar values, beliefs and experiences. I was reflecting a great deal about my early years as he was sharing a piece of his world with me.

Like Ethan, I felt largely influenced by my parents. He and I also wanted the same outcomes for our sons: a good education, good job and a deep hope that they would stay out of trouble. We were both willing to seek help, to look at ourselves and to do what was in the best interest of our boys.

Although still in the early days, the days of sleep deprivation, Ethan had some solid insight into what things are important to consider for new parents, and for anyone planning on becoming a parent.

1. Stay calm, don't be angry. You need to have patience.
2. If you're getting worked up don't let it show or your baby will pick up on it and won't be able to settle down.
3. Keep a level head in every situation. You don't want to go to jail.
4. Wait until you're ready to have a baby. It isn't easy, it's long and you need a lot of patience.
5. Don't fight in front of your kids; it will fuck them up. They will do what they see their parents do.
6. Cherish every moment. Don't do stupid shit when you have a kid.
7. If you need help, accept it. Don't deny it. You might end up on a path you don't want to be on. If you get help you might have an easier time. I wish I asked for help when I needed it the most.
8. In your relationship, try not to take everything so seriously. Don't take everything to heart.
9. Help out as much as you can, especially if your girlfriend has post-partum. It isn't easy but get up in the night, feed the baby, change them, help to make bottles, do whatever you can.
10. Try to make your baby smile and let them see you in a good mood. They can change your bad mood with a smile.

Ethan is putting a lot of effort into parenting. Being a good Dad is very important to him. He's right; it takes a lot of patience and hard work. Given parenting requires a great deal, it's great Ethan shared his thoughts on seeking support. His seventh tip states, "*If you need help, accept it. Don't deny it. You might end up on a path you don't want to be on. If you get help you might have an easier time. I wish I asked for help when I needed it the most.*"

In my own journey, I realize how hard it is to get help at times. I am always happy with a reminder that parents can't handle everything and don't have all the answers. Sadly, when we become parents, people think we have all the answers; our children think we have all the answers. We don't. I didn't. I still don't.

In our conversation I explained to Ethan, I think my willingness to get help was the largest contributing factor in becoming a strong parent. I got help from everywhere. Everything I learned about parenting and all of my practices are a combination of beautiful people, skilled professionals and an abundance of great love. I had to be willing to share with others, seek out professional help and accept advice as well as love. My abilities came from the efforts of, *"all the king's horses and all the king's men and women."* Truly, I've received resources from everywhere.

I've been to food banks, resource centres, libraries, playgrounds, and churches. I've used government programs such as day-care subsidy, clinical therapy, income assistance, an opportunity to return to school, and an employability project. I've attended parenting groups and made new friends. All available resources were used.

I hope Ethan's advice will continue to serve him and to remind Dads help is available. As he says, "*If you get help you might have an easier time.*" He and I both acknowledge, it's hard to reach out but we've come to learn it's worth it.

It does take a village. Fortunately, Ethan has a village and has a lot of love in his life already. His tip highlights the importance of finding and building a village. We all need a village of our own.

Best of luck Ethan. Wishing you, your family and your village much success.

#92 Mitchell – A Baby's Smile

I recently had a most meaningful conversation with one of my very favourite little boys, who is not so little and now a Father of two. Mitchell was a blond haired, blue-eyed bundle of fun with the biggest cheeks and the widest smile. I loved this little boy and even still carry his picture in my wallet. Hearing his voice reminded me of just how special he is to my heart. Learning about his sadness will be with me forever.

Mitchell is one of four Dads who have referenced parental alienation. It is the cause of enormous heartbreak for many parents and their children. He explained his deepest sadness is being excluded from his little boy's life.

While raising his young daughter, he is working to manage the paradox of appreciating waking up in her world while simultaneously feeling the loss of not enjoying the world of his son. I could feel his shift from heartache and to happiness like a grinding clutch in the background, as he spoke of each child. His gratitude and heartbreak coexist.

Mitchell loves being a Dad and conversely hates the absence of his son in his life. In his daughter's eyes he is reminded of all he has in sharing her life, and also all that he is missing in sharing the same togetherness with his son.

Mitchell is committed to moving forward and is hopeful he will someday have the chance to explain things to his little boy. He works to find the fun in his life despite the pain. He values his special time and the opportunity to make memories with his little girl every day.

Mitchell gives his advice from a broken yet joy-filled heart.

1. Be careful who you have a kid with. Make sure you're both ready to put the child first.
2. Don't stay in a relationship if you're unhappy but do make sure you are respectful, so you don't lose touch with your kids.
3. Play with your kids. Have fun and do what they want to do.
4. Get outdoors, it's fun and tires them out.
5. Tell kids the truth.
6. Remember there are some things you won't be able to control in this life. Hold yourself together for your kids.
7. Extended family is important. Make sure your kids see their grandparents and relatives.
8. Be there as much as you can, for the important things and for the everyday things.
9. Parenting is a struggle for sure, but their smiles can make you really happy.
10. Always pay child support, even if that's the only thing you can do for your kid.
11. Encourage them to stay in school.

I deeply appreciate Mitchell getting in touch. Together we talked about the highs and lows of parenting. He's in the early years; however, he's experienced a lifetime of feelings. I know for myself, and from hundreds of other parents, coming up with parenting tips isn't easy. They're hard to identify and articulate. It wasn't easy for me to come up with my tips for *100 Moms* and I was the one writing the book.

The brightest spot in our conversation was when Mitchell talked about his little girl's smile. He said, "*Seeing her smile every morning can really make me smile. She's the best thing to wake up to. I love seeing her.*" As Mitchell mentioned in his ninth tip, "*Parenting is a struggle, but their smiles can make you really happy.*"

I remember when I was a young parent; I had similar uncertainty and profound sadness. I was single, without an education and on welfare. I didn't feel I was a good Mom and I didn't know what to do next. I was sad, afraid and not feeling at all confident about my future.

As I explained to Mitchell, it took a lot to turn myself and my mess around. I began to live for Michael and to always put his interest above my desires. It was a complete overhaul, literally from the inside out. It was "*a struggle*," at times a terrifying and lonely struggle.

Mitchell looks forward to explaining things to his son and is hoping he'll come to understand that some things were out of his control. In his sadness he focuses on the smile he does see, although he never forgets the smile he's missing.

It's so important in life to focus on what we have, while working toward achieving even more. With his family, and his extended family, Mitchell dreams both his children will find happiness. He wants to them to stay in school and stay out of trouble. He's going to continue to play, to go for walks and to find the sweetness in the smiles whenever he can.

I will forever cherish our chat. I could almost see that little boy from twenty-eight years ago in hearing his voice. His call will forever be one of the special gifts I've received from writing this book. I hope we talk again, maybe even in a happier time about an easier topic.

I look forward to another chat.

Little Michael & Little Mitchell, 1996.

#93 Aaron – Teach Them Everything
Written loving memory of Gloria Mae Rogers
(May 23, 1945 – February 21, 2020)

Published in loving memory of Aaron Todd, Jolene Lori and their beautiful, much loved little girl Emily Mae, all tragically lost April 18th, 2020.

Aaron is the adored and only son to a special mentor and beloved friend of mine, *Gloria Mae;* he was the apple of her eye. I know she would have been completely elated about us working together in this way. *I hope there's a heaven.*

In her memory, Aaron agreed to share a piece of his life as both a son and as a Dad. He's equally proud of each role and is honoured to contribute all he's learned in growing with his own family.

Dad to one teenage daughter, Aaron's parenting focused largely on independence and respect. He was committed to ensuring his '*little girl*' would not need to rely on anyone for anything. He also wanted her to know that. Aaron said he was dedicated to raising a strong woman both physically and mentally. He exclaimed, "*She's ready!*"

Having been largely influenced by his Stepdad, Angus, Aaron learned the meaning of the word "*Father.*" He said, "*Angus was the best man I ever met, the best man in the world.*" Aaron told a moving story of his release from jail stating, "*When I got 'out,' Angus put a wrench in my hand. That changed everything. Together we worked on a Mustang. He gave me what I needed; he rearranged my world. Angus was the Father I always wanted. He taught me what a man should be. He taught me to cut the grass and fix the mower. He later put me in a small engine repair course. He was the biggest influence in my life.*"

I had the privilege of spending time with and have also enjoyed the influence of, both Aaron's Mom and his Dad, Angus. They were beautiful people who lived in meaningful ways. Angus was a sweet, loving and gentle man. Aaron's Mom was a giving and compassionate woman. She provided me

211

with a love and understanding strong enough to be the foundation on which I began rebuilding my own life.

It is an honour to carry their names in this book and to share Aaron's parenting wisdom.

1. Teach independence. Make sure your children value their worth and know they can handle anything.
2. Teach them how to live off the land. She can build a cabin or a composting toilet. She can chop wood and run a chainsaw. She appreciates the land and can survive in the wilderness.
3. Make sure they value themselves. I respect my daughter and treat her Mother the way a man should treat a woman, the way I want my daughter to be treated. I put my wife on a pedestal, and I want the same for my '*little girl.*' I want her to know she should always be respected and hope she will never accept anything less than the utmost respect from anyone.
4. Expose them to music. Coming from the East Coast, I introduced my daughter to fiddle music. She loved it and wanted to play. She learned very quickly and found she had a unique talent. She could play anything she touched. In no time she learned both harmonica and clarinet and even developed an ability to read music.
5. Show and talk about affection. Start and end each day with "*I love you.*" I remember I always wanted to hear that from my Dad, but he never said it. I wanted to make sure my daughter heard it from me every day. I always hug her.
6. Be truthful. I never lied to my daughter, even if she didn't like the truth or when the truth was hard. When her fish died, I had to tell her. I think we have to teach about life and death.
7. Don't take life seriously. Have fun. We do a lot of fun things together. I love when we go off-roading together.
8. Teach them what you know. She loves learning about the trades and customizing things. We've been working on a '77 Pinto since she was three. She loved using a wrench as a toddler. She still loves learning about carpentry and welding. I love teaching her and enjoying how great she is.
9. Deal with your child differently at every stage. They are always learning, changing and growing. Your approach should also be learning and changing and growing. Sometimes they need to learn things from their Dad and sometimes they need to learn things from their Mom.
10. I try to be the Dad I always wanted to have. Angus came into my life as a teenager. He taught me how to be a Dad. I try to be like him.

Aaron's closing note, "*I try to be the Dad I always wanted to have,*" really hit me in the heart. That was exactly my approach.

Both Aaron and I came from difficult backgrounds. We knew what we didn't want in a parent and worked to be all the things we'd hoped for. In some ways, his Mom gave to me a bit of what Angus gave to him. We both have much gratitude resting permanently in our hearts. The love of this couple reached our spirits and we've carried pieces of them and their teachings into our next generation.

We have decided to do things differently. We've taken the positive lessons and the positive people out of experiences and with that we parented, in all the ways we knew how.

Aaron realized love, hugs and time together are what make a great Dad and he works to ensure those things are present every day. He teaches everything he knows and gives her access to what she's interested in, whether it be dirt bikes or instruments; together they'll find a way.

The dream he holds for his daughter is that she will never forget she can handle anything. Aaron hopes she finds a fun and fulfilling career and can achieve a work-life balance. He wants her to be independent and move out but to also never leave.

As his baby will be soon graduating high school, the paradox of finally getting the empty nest while hating the silence of the empty next, is already starting to hit him. *I know that conundrum, it's weird.*

I'm sure she has all she needs and as Aaron says, "*She's ready!*" I'm hoping they'll always find time for the Pinto, some wood chopping and a lot of giggles along the way.

Thanks, my friend! Your parents and your story will remain in my heart forever.

Gloria, Aaron's Mom, with the '77 Pinto.

#94 Darryl – Consistency
In loving memory of Shaun Michael Bickerton (*July 27, 1970 – July 3, 1988*)

I was thrilled when Darryl agreed to share his parenting tips. Darryl is the big brother to a sweet young man, so sweet I named my son after him, *Michael*. I knew with Darryl's participation I would be able to weave the story of Shaun Michael into this book. I want his memory and his impact on my life to be left for the ages.

Even though he was in this world for all too short a time, Shaun was a large and loving force. I felt it fitting that my son be named after someone with a strong character, someone who was kind. In my world the choice was clear. My son would be named after Darryl's little brother, Shaun Michael, a boy who respected me in a world of disrespect. At the time, I didn't feel worthy enough to use his first name, *"Shaun."* I selected Michael so as not to offend anyone.

In short, Shaun was super cute, funny (really, really funny) and popular. He could play the drums, knew lots about cars and was loved by all. I, on the other hand, was a fuzzy-haired girl with glasses, asthma and did not feel loved by anyone.

In high school, I asked four guys to take me to the winter carnival. Four guys said yes. Four guys backed out. In the final hour I mustered the courage of a lion and, in complete desperation with little hope, I asked my neighbourhood friend Shaun. He agreed. He, too, had the courage of lion.

Shaun gave no concern to his popularity and social status. He obviously didn't know what bringing a girl like me to winter carnival might do to his reputation. He also had no concern that he didn't have any dress shoes to wear. Long story short, Shaun agreed to be my date, he found shoes and even a corsage. Off we went.

Now, this section is really about Darryl and Fatherhood; although, I've said a lot about Shaun. I'm confident Darryl didn't mind sharing this space with his little brother, not a bit. See, Shaun was Darryl and Darryl was Shaun. What you now know about Shaun, the same can be said of Darryl. Shaun could be all he was because he had the love and support of his big brother. They were a beautiful pair.

214

`Time to give Darryl a turn. Without further ado, here are Darryl's best tips:

1. Keep them active in sports.
2. Teach them hard work will always payoff in the end.
3. Give high praise for their accomplishments.
4. Model respect and encourage they treat others as they want to be treated.
5. Teach your children they can always come to you no matter.
6. Show love, respect and kindness every day because life is too short.
7. Be consistent with expectations and punishments.
8. Include them on defining consequences. At times I let them tell me what the punishment should be.
9. Help them learn by their mistakes and to understand how they would do it next time.
10. I'm a strong believer in positive behaviour rewarding.

Darryl is the Dad to three young adults, bursting into independence. There's no question his connection to his children, and his parenting practices, have given them all a solid foundation to begin building their lives. His suggestion on consistency and allowing children to self-determine consequences are both concepts we, too, incorporated in discipline. The consistency was a requirement and the self-determination was highly effective and, to my surprise, extra punitive.

I felt strongly about being consistent in all areas, expectations and punishments. Allowing Michael to contribute to or determine his own punishment was a great exercise for many reasons. It was inclusive, required critical thinking and removed blame and responsibility on our end. It gave him ownership of his behaviour and some control over his world. It was the beginning of independence and self-regulation.

Consistency was certainly present in my parenting and in our lives. There were two things Michael knew for sure: One, dinner was at 5:30 PM. Two, bedtime reading would happen. Those were two daily deliverables. I believe if any parent did only those two things right, they could do a lot wrong.

Michael also had some other constants, maybe not present in all homes. He knew who was in his home. He knew he would have food. He knew what was expected of him. He knew he was safe. He knew his needs would be met. Michael could find a fork, a towel, a pillow, and could count on us for '*milk money*.' He didn't have to think about these things, they just were.

Michael also knew discipline was consistent, although not often required. Consequences may have been different but addressing issues was an absolute. We consistently addressed behaviours, concerns, goals, standards, dreams and all things family and future. Having stability and love gave his little mind a lot of room to grow. He wasn't confused, tired, hungry, or afraid. He didn't have to worry about what was waiting for him at the end of the day. His parents were one hundred percent consistently there for him.

Without consistency every day is different and parental moods are unpredictable. In those homes, confusion is so overpowering, how can a child be expected to learn and develop? It's kind of like putting a seed in a dish and hoping for a plant. Things like mealtimes, bedtime routines, story times, morning kisses, and evening check-ins provide security. Consistency doesn't require money or a lot of time. The little things make a big difference. I know this for sure!

In a predictable environment a child will learn trust and will have more room to grow. Their little brains will make so many connections, their faces will smile, and they will learn to love in a healthy way. Consistency is our gift to them.

Thanks Darryl, for all you've given to my life by way of your little brother Shaun. Thanks for your involvement as a Dad and for your participation in this book.

Know that Shaun Michael's story, and his memory, rests forever in our family and in my heart. I'm proud to say the name "*Michael*" now sits in my next generation with my grandson, "*Seth Michael.*" I'm confident he will continue Shaun's legacy of kindness and love.

Shaun Michael my special prom date, 1987.

Side note: Darryl organizes an annual fundraiser in Shaun's memory. Details can be found on Facebook by searching Shaun Bickerton. Check it out and see how you can contribute to his cherished memory.

#95 Brian – They're Watching

With loving memory of our mutual friend Jason, gone but never forgotten.

Brian and I go back more than 30 years, having grown up in the same neighbourhood. Although I wasn't aware at the time, we had a mutual love for an adorable blond, bright-eyed and continuously bouncy young teen named Jason. Although I was a little older than Jason and Brian was a lot older, our young friend reached the heart of us both. I like to think Brian was a kind of big brother, and I was a big sister, although I'm sure Jason would have seen us all as simply just friends.

Jason and I were somewhat outcasts, well not really '*somewhat.*' We didn't quite fit in at school, in the neighbourhood or in our own homes. We found commonalities and love in and with each other. I remember how fondly Jason spoke of Brian. Any friend of Jason was sure to be a friend of mine.

Rolling the clock ahead twenty years, Brian and I crossed paths through our careers. Our memories of Jason quickly led us to shared reflection and immediate heart swells in Jason's loving memory. His boyish charm was unforgettable. We sadly reminisced, as Jason had since passed away, how he was loved by us both.

I was very happy to have Brian's participation in the book. I knew his involvement would not only provide tips from a strong and engaged Father, but it would also give me an opportunity to capture Jason's memory and in some small way include him in this chapter of my life. I'm confident if Brian parented in the manner he treated us misfits, he will have raised two great men. Oh, to have had such a Dad.

Not surprisingly, Brian absolutely loves being a Dad. He expressed how great it was to have the title. He loves the sound of the word and the meaning behind it.

1. Patience.
2. No, your children are not the same. Adjust your parenting to adapt to their unique personality.
3. Be firm but fair.

4. Keep them involved, but not over involved, in sports, organizations and clubs.
5. Maintain regular bedtimes even at their older age; my boys still keep the same schedule mostly.
6. Allow them to give an opinion in a respectful way, however, remind them you are the decision maker.
7. Love them unconditionally.
8. Talk about everything. Create an environment where they feel they can speak about any topic and yes, that includes sex.
9. Be a good role model. They are watching you all of the time and learning the good, the bad and the ugly from you.
10. Teach them respect for others, and in my case having two sons, I wanted to also ensure I taught them respect for women.

Respect is something Brian certainly had a handle on. Meeting him when I was sixteen and homeless, his respect was palpable. I appreciate that most about him. He respected two kids who weren't respected by many.

In his tips, Brian identifies the importance of being a good role model. *"Be a good role model. They are watching you all the time and learning the good, the bad and the ugly from you."* They are watching. We were watching.

I too worked to set a good example. I took the job very seriously, albeit too seriously at times. I remember learning, your kids will do what they see, not what you say. That was a scary concept to me. I was a smoker until Michael was age ten. I was terrified he would smoke, given the example I provided. That was just the beginning of my fear. Example is everything. We do teach them what is *"normal"* by the example we set. Our example establishes their normal, as in the case with door slamming, as in the case with everything.

If I exploded, Michael would grow to believe exploding was normal, appropriate and even acceptable. Our example is their base-line.

I actually thought all Dads were passed out on the living room floor? I was not ashamed. My friends and I just stepped over him and went to my room. I completely thought that was normal. From the simple things to the not-so-simple things, what we show them becomes a part of who they are.

Take, for example, a towel. If I had a home with only hand towels, my son would dry himself with hand towels. He would never even look for a bath towel. Michael would not know of, or come to expect, anything other than hand towels. If my standards were low in the home, he would likely settle for the same as an adult.

Likely there would come a day when Michael would uncover a large, plush bath towel; he might think it too elaborate, unnecessary. He might inquire as to what it was used for. He may even think those who use them to be ridiculous.

It is a great deal of pressure to hold high standards, particularly when you were raised with a lower set yourself. As a child, we had a few "*nice towels*," (they weren't even that nice). I wasn't allowed to use them. In fact, only within the last few years have I felt worthy of using the "*nice towels*" in my own home.

Increasing standards and setting a strong example is worth the effort. Even if you can't afford fancy linen, at a minimum tell your kids they are available. Even if you behave poorly, you can apologize, re-adjust and correct.

Teach them about the big, fluffy towels. Encourage them to work hard and to someday own their own bigger, fluffier towels. If you can't access the finer things, make sure your kids know they are out there. What I wanted for Michael's future I modelled in our home.

Thanks Brian! As we say in the field, "*If I only reach one*." In your case, I know at least two. I'm so happy to have met you on both sides of my journey.

Jason welcoming Little Michael on his first day home.

#96 Kenny– Be Yourself

Kenny ("*Little Kenny*" to me) is a favourite cousin and a pseudo big brother. We share a common history, and like all big brothers I just don't get to see him enough. He's funny, smart, hardworking and handsome too. He was a welcome addition to our family tree.

Kenny worked deliberately at his life. He built a beautiful family complete with all the things he'd wished for. We have a lot in common in that respect.

Kenny informs me he is an accountant and a poet, a surprising combination which I intend on learning more about. Aside from that he's quite a comedian and a jokester, which I don't want to know more about. I've been fooled by his trickery in the past.

Now a loving and engaged Dad, he's dedicated to ensuring his kids grow into "*awesome and respectable citizens.*" Having spent time with his teen daughter and adult son I can say he's achieved both.

Kenny has provided a healthy environment, a home of happiness and a strong sense of family values — all things he's hoping his children will carry into their adult lives. Under his guidance it's certain they will.

1. Talk love. Do not let a day pass without telling them that you love them – in person, on the phone, text, or email.
2. Be there. Let them know that their events are important. If you have to go to work early or stay late to attend a school concert or sporting event, then do it. The memories are priceless and let them know their accomplishments are important to you.
3. Be yourself. You don't need to follow a rule book as to how to behave. Nurture them, instill right and wrong and love them lots.
4. Share experiences. It could be chores such as raking, hammering, cleaning or fun things like vacations and travel. The more kids are exposed to in life the more developed and adaptable they will be.
5. Plan time. I try to plan time with kids together and individually. Maybe a movie with my son or shopping and dining with my daughter. Do what they like, give them your undivided attention.
6. Punishment and rewards. It is important to recognize when kids do something good like working hard in school or other achievements. It is also equally important to let them know there are consequences when they do something wrong or misbehave. Being fair but firm is what we practice in our household.
7. Cherish the moments. It seemed like yesterday we were changing our son's diaper, now he's away at university. While we are excited for his new experiences, at times we find ourselves teary-eyed with his absence. Time flies by very quickly. Enjoy each moment with them.
8. Pick your battles. Don't waste precious time arguing over small issues. If you yell and argue over everything the kids won't necessarily know what's important.
9. Instill self-confidence and build self-esteem. Let your kids know that you are their greatest supporters and are always there for them. If you are not their biggest cheerleader than you are not parenting. If you don't have anything positive to say, then say nothing.
10. Honesty is our policy. We raise our kids in an open environment in which they are comfortable to tell the truth regardless of the outcome.

They know that it is healthier to tell the truth than to be dishonest and harbour the guilt.

Having only known Kenny as a bit of a jokester, it was touching to learn more about his home life and his parenting philosophies. I'm honoured that he's participating in this book as I am aware he likes to "*hold his cards close to his chest.*"

In his third tip Kenny advises, "*Be yourself.*" I've heard that from other parents as well, but I must admit it's something I have been unable to do. It sounds beautiful. I wish I could. I did, however, do as he later added, "*nurture them, instill right and wrong, and love them lots.*" I did need a rule book, of sorts. '*Myself*' is generally something too dark to "*be.*" Surprising to most, I'm repressing a self that is best left repressed. I have attempted to "*be myself*" and most often it's been met with disapproval or disbelief.

With the help of education, therapy, self-development and 'all the king's horses and king's men and women,' I've learned positive and progressive ways to parent and to live. I combat a negative internal dialogue and a tendency for self-destruction daily. I'm not sure if it's DNA, PTSD or maybe it could be resolved with some added professional support. I am sure that keeping my true self under control is best for everyone. Being myself is not a good plan.

What I have done is ensured the implementation of best practices. I have learned from great leaders, the best. I sought guidance often. I've invested a loose calculation of more than ten thousand hours. I learned some basic principles in parenting, conducted solid research and developed a preferred way of being — preferred not only by others but by myself.

I had to learn how to behave and how to think. I wanted those things so I could be a strong parent. I am eternally grateful to all who shared time with me and to those who used their lives in hopes of showing others, like me, a better way of being. I learned kids will do what they see and not what you say. I learned security and love would provide a foundation for confidence and trust. I was certain time spent highlighting the positive would ensure Michael had a positive perspective. I vowed I would not call him names or demean him — ever.

I knew drugs and alcohol would impact my ability to deliver the above, so I removed them. I realized the people in my life would negatively influence us both, so I removed them. I trusted an education would elevate our lives, so I achieved it.

In the end I have developed a self that I am proud of, one I even like. I sought and listened to those who came before me. I trusted those who had what I wanted and applied their knowledge. This method seemed to work.

As a caveat to Kenny's point, make sure the self you're being is in order if you're responsible for the lives of others. I would also add if you can "*be yourself,*" please don't take that for granted. I would guess there were some special people who added to the great self you share, or a lot of work was done on your part.

Thanks Kenny! I love the self you are.

#97 Joe Moose – Culture

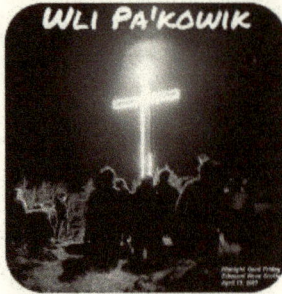

"*Being a Dad is the best thing in the world,*" my brother-in-law, Joe Moose. I know he means it; his girls see evidence of his love every day. Even though Joe's now parenting two teens, he still hasn't lost his love of Fatherhood, not even a little. He is full of fun, smiles and fancy dance moves. Joe loves all things about being a Dad.

Joe's dream for his girls is they will have good health and a solid education. He wants them to learn and honour Mi'kmaq traditions and heritage. He does what he can to teach them about the early beginnings of the culture and to instill Mi'kmaq teachings in their lives.

Joe's tips serve as kind reminders for Dads and also can serve as clear guidelines to his girls as they grow into young women.

1. Don't listen to anyone that tries to pressure you. Get help from people who love you and who want the best for you.
2. Be nice to others if you want your children to be kind.
3. Be yourself and walk away from negative people.
4. Enjoy good times with family and never be afraid to dance with people you love.
5. Always be willing to listen to both sides of the story.
6. Learn skills like fishing and hunting. Do things outdoors with your kids and explain the world to them.
7. Keep your culture alive by sharing traditions and the language.
8. Teach them what you know. When we're in nature, I like to point out plants and roots used in medicine.
9. Talk to them about getting a good education and a good job.
10. Show respect for your parents and for elders and your children will do the same.

11. Be silly and strong. My kids say I'm a *"great dancer and a good person to talk to."* That's a good combo.

I loved reading Joe's tips and learning more about his family values and the importance culture plays in his parenting. Joe not only shares his advice, he lives it. He is the perfect combo of silly and strong. Joe's appreciation for the Mi'kmaq culture is a great addition to his family and to ours. He is strong in tradition and ensures his girls are aware of their history and customs. They have a lot of fun together, while Joe's teachings continue to emphasize their aboriginal heritage.

There is a strong representation of the Mi'kmaq culture in Joe's home and in his parenting practices. A few highlights can be found in the areas such as living off the land, religion and in celebration. This family has spent a lot of time enjoying and learning about the outdoors. They love camping, hiking, hunting and fishing, even ice fishing. Further examples of Joe's teachings can also be found in religious traditions and in community celebrations.

Historically, Mi'kmaq men have taken great pride in their abilities to live off of the land, providing food for their families and villages. Joe possesses generations of these abilities and has strong skills in both hunting and fishing. As he states in his eighth tip, *"Teach them what you know. When we're in nature, I like to point out plants and roots used in medicine."*

I've heard Joe's girls talk about their trips through nature. They're very proud of their Dad's knowledge about the land, plants and wildlife. He's quick to identify healing qualities found in the wild and can easily recognize the plants and roots best known for those qualities.

Along with a respect for the land, Christianity is another protected and practiced value in this family. Joe has done many pilgrimages over the years and he and his girls have taken the journey through the *"Stations of the Cross."*

"The Stations of the Cross" takes place on Good Friday and is meant to be a memorable and peaceful experience. Families climb a mountain to pray and give thanks before an illuminated cross (*as seen in the image above*). This tradition holds multi-layered importance for not only the family and the community, it also serves to connect with Christianity on a deeper level reaching a spiritual realm.

Celebration is another area where the Mi'kmaq culture shines through. Joe's children have participated in Pow Wows, singing, drumming and dancing all associated with the traditions and customs. A Pow Wow is a social gathering which may be private or public. They are fun, displaying colourful regalia and are full of tradition. They range in length and offer activities and rituals in honour of the Mi'kmaq culture.

The Mi'kmaq medicine wheel is a circle that contains the powers of the four directions known to organize everything that exists. It's been recognized that the four areas of the wheel must be balanced in order to achieve health. There is some variation in how the categories of the wheel are described.

Some sites reference the quadrants as mind, body, spirit and emotions; others refer to birth, child, adult, and death; water, air, fire and wind are described as well. Still more commonly understood categories are the four seasons, summer, winter, spring and fall or the four directions: north, south, east or west. Regardless of how the quadrants are identified the goal remains the same — balance.

It seems as if Joe not only successfully balances silly and strong, his tips also reflect a balance of the medicine wheel. Joe has done all he can to bring forward the knowledge of his ancestors and the legacy of his heritage into the lives of his little girls.

I've been fortunate to have shared in Joe's cultural teachings and I have enjoyed learning more about him as a Dad. It's a privilege to celebrate and learn the Mi'kmaq heritage with Joe and his family.

They are each as sweet as the grass they've gifted to me.

Wela'lin Jiknam.

#98 Mike S. – Parental Alienation
Your Voice Matters

Mike is a true friend of mine from our early twenties. A little like a cousin, although not related, we've had special experiences, memorable moments in time. We've grown up and drifted apart, yet are connected by unique and deep-rooted bonds.

We met at a time we were both seeking to become better people and to live better lives. We struggled to find the right way, the best way to conduct ourselves and to live well.

We spent some time leaning on each other and other times standing strong. We rebuilt ourselves, sought education, focused on family and had some success healing old wounds. Together we had fun, met great people and enjoyed a lot of laughs.

I'm happy to report, we have both lived to see the next generation, although the journey has not always been smooth. Mike now has two great kids and is a proud Poppa to one little girl.

Sadly, in his case, the parenting journey hasn't been all he had hoped it would be. Mike has been a victim of parental alienation and it has left an irreparable break in his heart.

For those who know about parental alienation no explanation is needed; for those who don't know of it, none will do. It is dreadful. Parental alienation is considered by many to be child abuse; still much work is needed on the long-term impact. This is a complicated issue which is further impacted by complicated systems.

I don't know of any other Dad who has worked so hard to gain access to his child. I'm sure there are others; however, Mike is the hardest working one I know personally. He went through all the "*hoops*" and systems required.

I asked Mike on several occasions to participate in this book. His experience in single parenting his first child, combined with his battles through family court and with parental alienation pertaining to his second child would offer a unique perspective to all Dads. Not unlike many Dads approached with the invitation, he had great hesitation about becoming involved.

Some Dads felt they weren't qualified, others felt they completely failed and had nothing to offer. Mike, on the other hand, felt as if his parental voice had been stolen from him.

Over the years his voice was loud and strong. As time moved on his voice was diminished and eventually silenced. He felt as if his voice didn't matter. Mike fought a valiant effort to no avail.

Mike's section represents a place for those many, many Dads who have also felt unable to contribute for whatever their reason. I want to leave a space for the voice that did not get heard, did not feel value or has not yet been captured.

I want every Dad to have a place to document their tips, in their way, in their time and for their own audience. It's not too late; it's never too late. The hesitation, self-doubt or saddened soul should not exclude any voice. For some, "*the page is still unwritten.*"

Today is where your book begins...

1._____

2._____

3._____

4._____

5._____

6._____

7._____

8._____

9._____

10._____

_____

Before I charge into closing with my two main men, I'd like to take a moment to leave a heartfelt thank you to the ninety-eight Dads above. Your trust in me has helped me to realize a dream. I hope my sincere gratitude reaches each of your hearts.

I know it isn't easy sharing parenting tips.

I have the deepest appreciation for every name that stands and every tip that has been provided. Thank you all!

From the first pages, outlining my acknowledgements and the special men in my life, to the final pages of mixed emotions and lost loves, I hope it is clear to all Dads, everywhere, it is always possible to reach the heart of a child.

Whether you are a Dad late to the game, a severe alcoholic, a man incarcerated, an alienated Father, an uncle dying with cancer, or a Grandfather who is only around for a few years, never underestimate the power of your influence.

You just can't predict when your kindness will be the example that a child carries throughout their life. It may just be the very thing that helps them see they are loved and valued.

It's never too late and it's never too little.

#99 Big Mike – My Everything!

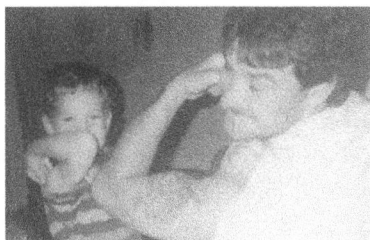

I just don't know how I will convey all this guy is and has been to my life, to our lives. I'm not sure I should even try. We are everything we are because of his love. He completed us.

I'm not sure what his tips will say, I haven't even read them yet. I do know what his actions have said. I'm fairly confident, regardless of what he's written, he could never convey all he is and all he has been.

I don't want to gush; I struggle not to. Mike's life and the life our family enjoys have been the result of a quarter century of dedication and three hearts full of love. His actions and devotion have given us happiness. Through him and his leadership we have spent our lives feeling secure and loved.

He is my everything. Together we broke a multigenerational cycle of trauma.

Big Mike's tips:

1. Show don't tell. Be an example of what you want your kid to become. I wasn't always great at this. When I veered off, I always got a nudge from his Mom.
2. Teach them to pick up for themselves both verbally and physically. When the words stop helping, the hands usually can. Remember when training your kids, watch for those random low blows. Five-year olds have a terrible reach and they punch hard.
3. Teach them basic skills and tasks even though they don't see the value in them. Changing oil, hammering a nail, the maintenance of things. When we had our heads under the hood Michael said, "*I don't need to know this, you will always be doing this for me anyway.*"
4. Be consistent in your praise and your punishment. Always try to be calm when administering a punishment. It's not always easy to keep your cool, or hide a smile, when punishing a kid. Luckily, I didn't have too many occasions to do this.
5. Punctuality is extremely important. If you are not five minutes early for a meeting, work, etc., you are late! He learned this early. Michael was rarely late. If he was running behind, he was sure to call with a valid and forgivable reason.

6. Let them see you out of parenting mode occasionally. Show them the side of you that only your closest friends get to see normally. I think it teaches them there is a time for fun and silliness and a time for seriousness.

7. Teach them what a hard day's work looks and feels like. Show them what some people need to do to earn a paycheque. I used to take Michael to the jobsite every Saturday so he could clean up construction debris. He would work hard with the crew, then get paid and go out to a late lunch with the guys. We had work hard and play hard lessons.

8. Get down to their level, playing on the floor or in the dirt is so much FUN!

9. Show them that you go for your dreams so that they will know it is OK to go for theirs. He is so proud to see his parents dream together and I only hope he and his wife will do the same.

10. Get interested in their interests. Get them interested in yours. It will lead to spending a lot of fun times together. We had a lot of common interests and we spent a lot of time enjoying them together. This is also where he got to experience my sixth tip.

Oh, my heart! I just love this guy. I so love their love and everything they've shared. I can't even decide who of the three of us were the most fortunate. All three of us have been thrilled about each other ever since we've met. On April 26th, 1997, I declared Mike my best man when I married him; then on August 22nd, 2015 he was declared Michael's best man on *his* wedding day.

When Michael told me he would be asking Mike to be his *Best Man* I said, "*Oh Michael, that's a great choice.*" He replied, "*Mike's always been my best man.*"

Mike has given three generations of unconditional and unmatched love.

Best Man, Best Son and Best Baby!

I loved reading Mike's tips. I had no idea he was working so hard. He always looked so smooth and natural. Actually, I don't even know if he did find parenting hard. He was good at it and incorporated so much fun. I couldn't be prouder!

Funny thing, in working on the last pages of the book I got to thinking, *shit*, no one mentioned punctuality. That's a big one and I didn't even get to write about it in here. See what I mean? Mike completed us!

I loved and smiled seeing Mike's fifth tip was all about punctuality. In 100 Moms, it happened to be my ninth. Here's what I wrote:

"To me, punctuality is a hill worth dying on. To this day, if Michael is late, he will call on, or before, expected arrival. I think punctuality encompasses respect, responsibility, ethics, consideration, standards, expectations, relationships, trust and maybe even more! It's a measurable. It's a transferable skill. It's a teachable moment. It is important personally, academically, and professionally. Time matters, yours and mine. If we highlight and enforce punctuality, we will be presented with hundreds of teachable moments. We can demonstrate appreciation when time is kept, disappointment when it isn't. We can reward our children with extended times, and consequence them with reductions when time is not respected. Of course, in order to expect it, we must follow it!"

I told you I had a lot to say on the topic.

Mike and I had extremely different parenting styles. It was fascinating for me to see how similar our tips were. I'm starting to wonder who was teaching whom. In the end, it's not as important as to who was teaching whom, what is important is that all three of us were eager to learn. We didn't want to disappoint each other, and we valued the opinion of one another. We lived a beautiful life of mutual love, respect and adoration. We likely took turns leading and following. It was an amazing and love-filled journey, and still is!

Much love my sweet man, my everything.

#100 Little Michael – My Reason!

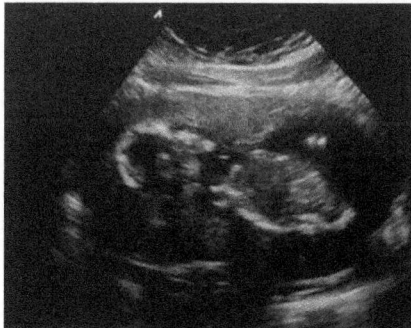

Our sweet baby Seth!

Well, here it is, here he is, my grand finale, my gift to the world, my legacy and life's work — our little boy Michael. Again, I am lost for worlds. How could I ever succinctly describe my reason for living? I just can't. I've attempted to do so in writing two books, using over two hundred thousand words and dedicating over twenty-eight years of complete devotion; yet still I come up short. I will never completely express my pride and joy.

My attempt to give him the last word is my gift to him, *well my attempt*. I, of course have to deliver a conclusion but I will let him have the last say on tips so that's got to count for something.

Watching my "*little*" boy become a Dad is one of my life's greatest gifts. Seeing him activate teachings from myself and Big Mike has filled my heart beyond measure. He is the best of us. Michael has grown and accomplished beyond our wildest dreams. He is happiness. He is hard work and grit. He is loving and tenderness. He is kind and thoughtful. He is educated and healthy. He is "*happy with his life and who he is*." He is all 1000 tips for 1 million reasons. His is our legacy and our love.

We are excited for him, for his future and for his family. He is our world.

Michael exemplifies what can happen when parents put the best interests of their child first, always and in all things. He embodies a lifetime of love and devotion from two adults who respected, valued and prioritized him. He was surrounded by love. He had a village.

Michael is the reason I wanted to provide "*a village*" to everyone in the development of "*100 Moms*" and "*100 Dads*." He's evidence of what "*a village*" can do. He is evidence a person can be an effective parent without the advantage of effective parents. I believe if we as parents ask, seek and apply we can raise strong, resilient and above all happy human beings. *It* can be done.

The tips below were shared by Michael prior to him officially becoming an official parent; although, I propose the minute we find out our baby is coming we become official parents.

Michael and his wife Chelsea were expecting their first baby. He had launched into parenting mode the moment he heard, as did I over twenty-eight years ago.

I think as soon as we find out our baby is arriving, we begin living for that child; *I hope*. All priorities shift and selfishness starts to dissipate. Life has a new focus, thinking is transformed and our legacy begins.

Michael is one of two Dads to write his tips pre-baby. He's spent three years as a parenting-coach so he's had a bit of time to reflect, not to take away from his careful consideration, attention to detail and the valuable time spent on putting together his tips and great effort it must have taken to narrow down his selection.

Michael's best stuff:

1. Make time to notice the good things. I think it is important to peek in on children when they are occupying themselves or playing quietly to tell them that you love them, and they are doing a good job playing nicely. Noticing quiet time encourages positive behaviours and prevents children from perceiving that they only get attention when they are loud or act out.
2. Use change warnings to ease transitions. Tell children that in a set period of time their activity will be changing. This could be leaving a friend's home or turning off video games. Even as adults it sucks when you have to change a fun activity without warning.
3. Follow through! I think that consistently following through on what you say is really important for a child's development. There was a study that showed that the ability to delay gratification was one of the highest indicators of future success. What teaches children to delay gratification is consistency and follow through because they are confident that the promised result will follow. I want my children to know that when I tell them there will be consequences if their behaviour continues, there actually will be. I also want them to believe that when I say good behaviour will be rewarded it will be. If I don't follow through with what I say I lose credibility and I want my children to not only listen, but to trust my advice as they become older.
4. Don't talk about things they can't control in front of them or blame them for things beyond their control. I think that talking about adult problems in front of children makes children concerned and upset with no outlet. For example, talking about not having any money in front of children makes them feel less secure. They have no ability to make money and there is no benefit to having them worry about these concerns too. They should be using their mental energy to explore the world not worrying about adult concerns.
5. Have realistic expectations when children are young. Look up what behaviours are appropriate for a child at that age and what you can reasonably expect them to understand and remember. I think that having unrealistic expectations leads to unnecessary frustration for parents and children.
6. Praise their effort and hard work, not their intelligence. Studies show that children who believe their success is attributable to their intelligence worry more about failure and avoid challenging tasks for fear of failure. Children can't change their natural ability or talent but can change how hard they work. Learning that working harder is what leads to success puts children in control and promotes motivation and self-esteem.

7. Be consistent. I believe that being consistent prevents a lot of headaches. People tend to be less consistent when they are stressed or tired or in a rush. But then children learn that when their parents are not at their best, they can get away with more. This makes these challenging times even harder. I want to try my best to be consistent even when it is the hardest. I think that developing consistent routines also gives children stability and makes them feel more secure.

8. I once read that there tends to be two types of parents: Carpenters and Gardeners. The Carpenter thinks that a child can be molded and if they just do the right things, they can shape their child into a particular kind of adult. The Gardener instead provides a protected space to explore and tries to create a rich, nurturing environment for the child to grow with little thought to the end product. I think both of these philosophies have merit and that it could be helpful when parenting to try to balance them. I feel there is also value in being conscious about whether you are being a Carpenter or Gardener in a given parenting moment.

9. Encourage them to read. The internet contains almost all human knowledge. Strong reading comprehension is essential to be able to use the internet to its full ability and really opens the world to children.

10. Listen to them and enjoy them. Not every moment needs to be a parenting moment. Think about why a child is telling you what they are telling you. If they are trying to share something with you, correcting their behaviour may lead them to be less forthcoming in the future.

Above represents the beginning of Michael's legacy, his hopes and dreams for parenting. His parenting began when he decided on his baby's first book, *Harry Potter*, which he started to read while little Seth was still in Chelsea's belly. From that day until the end of time, he will work to share all he has and give everything he's got to his little boy. It will be my joy to see even one more day of this exchange.

Michael is clear about his parenting goals, beliefs and values. Now that his son Seth has arrived it is his actions that will, in the end, determine his legacy and Seth's future. I'm so excited for them!

I'd love to close with a profound piece of wisdom and end this journey with a quote for the ages; I have nothing. As far as parenting goes, I've done it all, I've asked it all, I've said it all, I've shared it all and I've given it my all. This journey has been more than I could have ever dreamed. I want for nothing.

I will continue to enjoy the view of my love-filled family which has expanded and given me the most incredible girl and the sweetest baby boy.

I'm not sure what is to come but I am sure together we will handle it. We will find laughter and we will never know a day without love, as long as we live — *my wish for you.*

Michael's law school graduation.

In the words of R. W. Service
(January 16, 1874 – September 11, 1958)
Author, Poet, Canadian Great North Adventurer
and Father of two daughters,

Carry on! Carry on!
Fight the good fight and true;
Believe in your mission, greet life with a cheer;
There's big work to do, and that's why you are here.

Carry on! Carry on!
Let the world be the better for you;
And at last when you die, let this be your cry:
Carry on, my soul! Carry on!